Peddling Panaceas

Gary Dean Best

Peddling Panaceas

Popular Economists in the New Deal Era

Transaction Publishers
New Brunswick (U.S.A.) and London (U.K.)

Library of Congress Catalog Number: 2005043701
ISBN: 0-7658-0288-0
Printed in the United States of America

Library of Congress Cataloging-in-Publication Data

Best, Gary Dean.
  Peddling panaceas : popular economics in the New Deal era / Gary Dean
  Best.
      p. cm.
  Includes bibliographical references and index.
  ISBN 0-7658-0288-0 (alk. paper)
    1. Economists—United States—History—20th century. 2. New Deal,
  1933-1939. 3. United States—Economic policy—20th century. 4. Economics—United States—20th century. 5. United States—Economic
  conditions—1918-1945. I. Title: Economists in the New Deal era. II.
  Title.

HC102.5.A2B47   2005
338.973'009'043—dc22   2005043701

To Sergeant Christina Clark, My Hero

Contents

Preface

The 1930s was a fascinating decade that deserves more attention from historians who, for too long, have been preoccupied with events in Washington during the New Deal years. Shocked and bewildered, the American people were buffeted by events and actions and ideas that were too often beyond their comprehension. Many of these related to economic matters, where the field was occupied by a range of ideas that extended from the thoughtful analyses and proposals of trained economists to the wild ideas of quacks and demagogues like Dr. Francis Townsend and Upton Sinclair. Judging from their popularity, these latter carried more weight with many Americans than the former.

Historians have studied both of these extremes, but have largely ignored a significant group that lay midway between them. It was an age when one did not have to be trained as economist before claiming that mantle, and some were taken seriously. This middle group was probably more influential in the New Deal and with public opinion than either of the other two. This book deals with three of the best-known and most influential of their number: Dr. Edward A. Rumely, and the organization he created—the Committee for the Nation for Rebuilding Purchasing Power and Prices; Stuart Chase, and David Cushman Coyle. It describes their panaceas for the Depression, their proposals for permanent economic reforms, and assesses their influence on the New Deal.

Some of the research and writing for this book was done during the summer of 2000, as a result of the support of the Social Philosophy and Policy Center in Bowling Green State University (Ohio). It was completed during a return visit to the Center in the summer of 2003. For their financial and intellectual support, I am greatly indebted to everyone at the Center, from the director, Fred Miller, Jr.; through the deputy and associate directors, Ellen and Jeffrey Paul;

the assistant director, Travis Cook; staff members Mary Dilsaver, Teresa Donovan, Tammi Sharp, and Terrie Weaver; and two outstanding research assistants, Mahesh Ananth and Nicolas Maloberti; as well as those who furnish financial support for the Center. I am also grateful to the Lilly Library at Indiana University for a Helm Fellowship that made possible my research in the Edward A. Rumely Papers there, and to the staffs of the Lilly Library, especially Director Breon Mitchell for his warm hospitality; the Hoover Presidential Library; the Roosevelt Presidential Library, as well as to Danelle Moon of the Yale University Library, for their assistance in helping me to assemble the pieces of this jigsaw puzzle.

Gary Dean Best
Hilo, Hawaii

Introduction

In the 1920s, particularly in the later years of the decade, all eyes were on Wall Street, as millions of Americans sought their fortunes in the stock market. The financial sections of the newspapers burgeoned as their readers sought out the latest rise (and rare fall) in the value of their investments. Bankers and businessmen attained the status of American heroes; magazines were filled with articles describing their success. Speculators had, by the time of the crash in October 1929, run up a debt of $9 billion in brokers' loans, and untold billions from other sources, to buy stocks on credit.

And then came the crash, and the Depression that followed soon thereafter. Bankers first, then businessmen, were disgraced, the objects of derision, scorn, and the butts of sarcastic humor. The attention of Americans shifted from Wall Street to Washington, from bankers and businessmen to government officials and politicians. Nothing that government could do to punish and discipline the bankers and businessmen was too much in this hostile mood. As New Dealer Thomas Corcoran later recalled, the American people blamed the depression on Wall Street "bogeymen," and were "chanting for their blood."[1]

Into discard with the bankers and businessmen went the "orthodox" economists who had failed to give warning of the impending disaster and who seemed unable to provide solutions for the calamity that had followed. Rightly or wrongly, the bankers, businessmen, and orthodox economists were perceived as content to allow the deflation to hit bottom so that the business cycle could begin its upward curve as in the past. President Roosevelt, accordingly, ignored bankers and businessmen in choosing his advisors, and surrounded himself with economists and lawyers whose ideas were anathema to orthodox economists. These included, in the original brain trust, Rexford Tugwell, Adolf Berle, Frank Taussig, and

Raymond Moley. This group advocated central planning of the economy as a method for producing recovery from the depression, and, in Tugwell's case, at least, as a permanent reform of the American economy.

But Roosevelt was not totally captive to the proposals of his brain trust. He also relied heavily on advice from Harvard law professor Felix Frankfurter, who filled every level of the New Deal with protégés like Thomas Corcoran and Benjamin Cohen, to name only two. They brought to the New Deal the perspective of Supreme Court Associate Justice Louis Brandeis, a perspective that was fundamentally at conflict with that of the planners. While the planners brought to the New Deal considerable knowledge of the modern economy, the Brandeisians, who were almost entirely lawyers, brought mainly prejudices—against a powerful federal government, against big business, and against Wall Street's manipulation of "other people's money." The conflict between the views of the planners and the Brandeisians would account for much that was contradictory, even conflicting, in the early New Deal.

Into this mix, particularly during the first year of the New Deal, was added the influence of the group usually referred to as the inflationists. For them the solution to the Depression was obvious. The Depression was the result of a major deflation and it could be easily cured by an equivalent amount of inflation, the effect of which would be to raise commodity prices, increase consumer purchasing power, and make easier the repayment of debts. It was the only one of the three schemes that contemplated no major alterations in the economic system, nor any expanded powers by the federal government. In this sense, it was the most conservative of the three, although for those whose memories of the runaway German inflation of the 1920s were still vivid it represented a radical and potentially dangerous approach.

During the Depression years the public was avid for anything that would help it to understand the causes of the Depression and the possible solutions. A *New York Times* reporter noted that this was a period when the news from Washington made the transformation from 90 percent political and 10 percent economic, to 90 percent economic and 10 percent political.[2] Panaceas abounded in the popular magazines, almost always the products of amateur economists. The three factions within the New Deal each had such a publicist proposing solutions similar to its own. For the planners, it was Stuart Chase, an engineer-turned-account-turned-amateur economist. For the Brandeisians it was David Cushman Coyle, an engineer-turned-amateur economist. And for the inflationists it was the Committee for the Nation, largely the creation of Edward A. Rumely, an educator-turned-businessman-turned newspaper publisher-turned amateur economist, who had originally trained to be a physician. These three exerted various degrees of influence on the New Deal, but were even more important for their value in educating the public concerning the economic issues of the 1930s, and in explaining the actions of the New Deal to readers anxious for an understanding of what was happening.

It could be argued that their influence during the New Deal years was of greater import than the largely sterile debates that were going on between professional economists during the same period. Scarcely a month went by during the 1930s without an article by Chase or Coyle, or a press release from the Committee for the Nation, in at least one popular magazine. And Chase and Coyle supplemented these with books and booklets, while the Committee for the Nation was represented by several books written by supportive economists like George Warren and Irving Fisher.

It is with the panaceas and efforts of Chase, Coyle, and the Committee for the Nation that this book deals.

1

The Committee for the Nation

Their influence having been relatively brief, and too minor to rival the drama of the "war" between the planners and the Brandeisians, the reflationists have received little attention from historians of the New Deal, being usually dismissed as inflationists, although they were actually ardent foes of inflation. Viewed in the context of the larger ideological debate of the 1930s, however, the reflationists, who put their emphasis on recovery from the Depression through restoration of pre-Depression price levels, deserve more attention. The ranks of traditional progressives/liberals were largely made up of reflationists, although some were inflationists, and it was the failure of the New Deal to emphasize their strategy for producing recovery that caused so many of them to experience the early disenchantment with FDR and the New Deal that Otis Graham has described in *An Encore for Reform* (New York, 1967).

In an even larger context, Roosevelt's failure to embrace the reflationary solution of the traditional progressives, and to simultaneously straddle the contrary programs of the planners and Brandeisians, instead, led the New Deal up a series of anti-business blind alleys and dead end streets that not only delayed recovery, but also prevented the adoption of the comprehensive program of genuinely liberal reform that they sought, leaving the nation with a "liberal" legacy based on arbitrary rule and siphons from the public treasury.

The reflationists supported what was variously called a "commodity dollar" or "managed dollar" or "stable dollar" or by various other terms. This was a dollar the value of which would be pegged to an index of commodity prices, thereby providing for price sta-

1

bility. Some advocated doing this by altering the quantity of money in circulation as prices rose or fell—decreasing it when prices rose, increasing it when they fell. Others felt the same result could be achieved by adjusting the "quality" of money—by increasing or decreasing the value of gold. These latter viewed reflation as a goal to be attained through abandoning the gold standard, devaluing the dollar, and perhaps monetizing silver. Unlike the pure inflationists, who sought an inflationary solution to the depression by reducing the burden of debt through cheapening of the dollar, the commodity-based dollar advocates had in mind a permanent reform of the nation's monetary system, one that would permit debtors always to repay in dollars of the same value as those they had borrowed. To attain either goal, however, required going off the gold standard, and increasing executive control over the value of the dollar, and thus both groups could be found cooperating in the Committee for the Nation to Rebuild Prices and Purchasing Power, generally known as the Committee for the Nation, which was the principal group lobbying in behalf of those actions and beyond.

While there were many prominent figures associated with the Committee, perhaps the most important was Dr. Edward A. Rumely, who served as its executive secretary. Rumely was an interesting figure. Born and raised in Indiana, he was educated in Europe, receiving an M.D. degree from Freiburg University in Germany, and also a degree in sociology in 1906. After his return to the United States, Rumely established a private school for boys and worked in his family's agricultural machinery business until he resigned and moved to New York City. In 1915, he became editor-in-chief and publisher of the *New York Evening Mail*, of which he was part owner. In the witch-hunt atmosphere of the World War I years, Rumely, a German-American who had spent years in Germany, was accused of using the *Evening Mail* to propagandize in behalf of the German government, was tried and sentenced to a year plus one day in prison, but was eventually granted a full pardon by President Coolidge. The case, however, would come back to haunt him in later years when he became prominent in political affairs.

Thereafter, Rumely remained in New York City, throwing himself into the promotions and wheeling and dealing that were characteristic of the 1920s. He was especially involved in exploiting the growing popularity of vitamins during that decade, as well as continuing his interest in agricultural businesses and financing. The depressed situation in agriculture through the 1920s, and then the onset of the Great Depression of the 1930s, convinced Rumely of the need to restore the purchasing power of farmers, both for their own benefit and that of the country as a whole. By the early 1930s, he was mobilizing farm organizations and agricultural businesses behind a movement to "reflate" the value of the dollar by taking it off the gold standard and stabilizing its purchasing power by tying it to the prices of commodities.

One of the most prominent figures in furnishing scholarly support for such an action was George F. Warren, a professor of agricultural economics and farm management at Cornell University, one of whose students had been Henry Morgenthau, who would become secretary of the treasury early in the Roosevelt administration. In 1931, Warren collaborated with a colleague at Cornell, Professor F. A. Pearson, in publishing an article, "Prices and Gold," in the *Farm Journal*. In that article they argued that the present depression was not part of the downward curve of a business cycle, but was due rather to a collapse in commodity prices. That collapse they traced to a shortage of the world's gold supply, which had caused the value of gold to rise and commodity prices to fall. Clearly, then, the way to restore commodity prices to their proper level was to make gold cheaper.[1]

Stuart Chase supported inflation, believing that a wise policy of inflation via either deficit spending or devaluation of the dollar "could in a few months' time break the back of the deflation." Those calling "for what they term a 'managed currency,'" he wrote, advocated "the end of the metal standard as such, the end of laissez-faire in the whole structure of money and credit, the end of alien and 'natural' causes generally, and the deliberate control of the money supply in line with the volume of production, invention, and the requirements of purchasing power." Clearly Chase was not familiar with, or perhaps was unsympathetic with, the use of "quality" rather than "quantity" in managing the currency.[2]

Beginning in the summer of 1932. Rumely found some prominent businessmen sympathetic to the creation of a Committee for Rebuilding Purchasing Power and Prices to educate and agitate in behalf of reflation, including Vincent Bendix, of Bendix Aviation, and James Rand, of Remington Rand. With the election of Franklin

Delano Roosevelt as president in November 1932, Rumely set out to convert the president-elect as well. Rumely had forged a close relationship with Theodore Roosevelt after he left the presidency, allowing the former president to use the *Daily Mail* to popularize his views. Late in November he wrote to FDR of his cousin TR's support for the cooperative movement among farmers as a device for organizing farmers and preserving the existence of the small farmer in America. Rumely had laid the program before Harding in the 1920 campaign, but except for a brief mention of it in one campaign speech, Harding had ignored it because of the fundamental conflict between such a movement and the "interests and viewpoints" of corporate America.[3]

A day later, Rumely wrote again, this time adding the monetary problem to his proposed program for the new president:

> At the present time the farmer's situation is complicated by a new factor arising from the enhancement in the value of the gold dollar. The farmer has many fixed charges, such as freight inbound on all materials that he purchases, freight charges that are deducted from everything he sells; he has about Nine Billions of Dollars of mortgage loan obligations upon which interest and principal payments must be met in a fixed number of dollars; his taxes call annually for a fixed number of dollars.
>
> With the enhancement of the purchasing power of our gold dollar, these fixed charges against his operations have swollen so greatly as to diminish and, in some cases, wipe out his underlying equity receipts that go to make up the net farm income.

The result, Rumely warned, would be "widespread political demand" from farmers "for a devaluation of the dollar to its former purchasing power in order to bring about a corresponding restoration of farm prices to former levels." To that demand from the agricultural sector would be added that from some business leaders who likewise felt "that a reduction in the purchasing power of the dollar is of fundamental importance to a restoration of prices and consumer purchasing power."

Rumely told Roosevelt that at the instance of Vincent Bendix a committee was discussing the farm situation. He concluded:

> If, by the action of such a committee...the identity of interest of the farmer, of the industrial concern seeking purchasing power to consume its production, and the domestic and foreign debtor could be established, a solution

along the lines of devaluing the dollar in order to restore prices to their former levels might be far more easily accomplished; or, if it is possible, some equivalent banking procedure inaugurated to accomplish the same result by controlled but effective credit expansion.[4]

By the end of November, the proposed Committee for Rebuilding Purchasing Power and Prices had begun to attract prominent members, including veteran banker Frank Vanderlip, as well as Robert E. Wood and Lessing Rosenwald of Sears, Roebuck.[5] Early in December, Rumely wrote Roosevelt again, enclosing articles by prominent Americans and Europeans in support of devaluation of the dollar. "Public opinion," he told Roosevelt, "is not sufficiently ripe at the present time to grapple with this problem in a constructive way," but it could easily be mobilized.

Henry Wallace, editor of *Wallace's Farmer*, had informed Rumely, he told Roosevelt, that three of the strongest farm organizations, had "decided unanimously to demand a devaluation of the dollar at the coming session of Congress." Moreover, the radio broadcasts on the subject by Father Charles Coughlin had evoked a considerable response from his listeners. Rumely added: "It is my thought that the political actions that your administration will be called upon to take in connection with agriculture, war debts, and restoration of business activity, all must be affected by the decisions with reference to this problem," in which decisions the work of the Committee for Rebuilding Purchasing Power and Prices could help to lay the groundwork with public opinion. Rumely advised the president-elect to "discuss this problem with Frank A. Vanderlip and Vincent Bendix and such others as you might desire, as for example: General R. E. Wood of Sears, Roebuck & Co., Ex-Governor Frank O. Lowden, Henry Wallace."[6]

In response to his letters to Roosevelt, Rumely received one from Columbia University brain truster Rexford Tugwell who wrote that Rumely's letters had been forwarded to him "as the economist of the Roosevelt group," but he added: "We have thousands of plans stacked up and many more arriving every day. You may be sure that we are making many independent studies of these questions and that the point of view you represent will have every consideration." It was unlikely, he added, for any meeting with Bendix or the others to take place because of "the pressure of work under which we are working."[7] Rumely responded with news of the formation of the Committee and wrote that the "Bendix Plan" might "bring about an organization of producers and manufacturers whose primary interest lies in working together to support such measures as may increase consumer purchasing power."[8]

A few days later, Rumely wrote to David Cushman Coyle to order copies of *The Irrepressible Conflict* for himself and nine others, including Bendix, Wood, Vanderlip, and Lowden. He told Coyle of the formation of the committee, and queried Coyle on what, if any response, he had received from the circulation of his pamphlet, since it dealt with matters of concern for the committee, as well.[9]

In mid-December the committee was taking shape. Rumely wrote Bendix that he had been extremely busy with it while Bendix was in Europe, meeting with Vanderlip and "a small but selected and qualified group of leaders throughout the country," that included Wood, Rosenwald, farm machinery executives, Lowden, former secretary of war, Newton Baker, and newspaper editor Roy Howard," as well as "many economists." He sent along a copy of Coyle's *The Irrepressible Conflict—Business vs. Finance*, saying that Bendix would find it interesting, and that their committee "would be the nucleus through which business can express itself."

He had also received a letter expressing interest in the committee from James Rand, of Remington Rand.

Rumely told Bendix:

> Up to the present time I have used the name, "Committee for Rebuilding Purchasing Power and Prices." I believe that a more suitable name would be
>
> COMMITTEE FOR THE NATION
>
> For Rebuilding Purchasing Power and Prices As I see it, if this Committee functions properly on questions of money and purchasing power, it will create for itself such a platform as will give it enduring value. The words "COMMITTEE FOR THE NATION" are different from any committee that I have ever heard of and they suggest the basic thought....What we need is a group that will throw themselves in, regardless of their temporary personal and private interest, to carry through the things that are necessary in the public and general interest. The COMMITTEE FOR THE NATION might well develop into a permanent body of business men working together and putting the best thought of the entire country to a focus upon

one problem after the other, using existing instrumentalities. It may do the work that David Cushman Coyle, in his booklet "The Irrepressible Conflict," foreshadows as indispensable if business is to save itself from chaos or a Russian regimentation imposed by a disgusted and disgruntled electorate to which business men have failed to give the leadership that such a Committee as yours might help supply.

Here was an early expression of the belief that the alternative to monetary action might well be regimentation of business by government. Yet in the same letter, Rumely conceded to Bendix that the anti-trust laws must be eliminated since they checked "the indispensable development that must take place before we can have any kind of rational planning of production to meet market needs." But Rumely insisted that the first priority for the Committee must be "debts - money - purchasing power."[10]

A few days later Rumely asked Bendix to allow the use of his name as "the pivotal person" on the committee. As members of the executive committee he recommended Bendix, Vanderlip, Rand, Wood or Rosenwald, and Lowden or Henry Wallace, plus a number of other possibilities that included Newton Baker, Roy Howard, Edsel or Henry Ford, and E. L. Cord. Rumely also suggested an initial budget of $15,000 drawn equally from six sources, with the objective of eventually aiming at a fund of $250,000 for the Committee's work. Rumely added:

> The question of the weight of our dollar and the absorption of purchasing power by taxes, interest, and debt payment, is of fundamental importance; but the real work of the Committee has far larger scope. It relates to the matter of a totally new method of approach to the distribution problem. Our traditional attitudes toward wage payments, spending, methods of dealing with the business cycle, are all based upon a viewpoint that was rooted in a time when there was a scarcity of goods and tools. Today the virtues of that period and some of the principles lodged firmly in our financial thinking are no longer applicable to an economy based upon mass production and having the problem of distributing the wealth of materials which we are able to produce.

This sudden (and temporary) aberration from the limited monetary goals of the Committee perhaps came as a result of Rumely reading David Cushman Coyle's article, "New Aspects of the Distribution Problem," in the January 1933 issue of the *Annals of the American Academy of Political and Social Science.*[11]

To another correspondent, to whom he had sent Coyle's *The Ir-repressible Conflict*, Rumely wrote that the "whole question of consumer purchasing power must be solved before industry, based upon quantity production, can get back into its stride." Until that time, nothing much could "be accomplished so far as regaining former earnings is concerned." It followed, then, that "this whole question of rebuilding purchasing power is really fundamental" and should have priority over everything else. The time, he wrote, was "now here to act."[12] To Coyle, himself, Rumely wrote thanking him for "the very interesting reprint containing a restatement of your position. Your logic is compelling." Rumely described the formation of the new Committee and wrote that he hoped "to have an opportunity of meeting you personally when next in New York." He also ordered more copies of the *Annals* reprint so that he could "place them with key men interested in this problem."[13]

Coyle responded that he preferred people read *The Irrepressible Conflict*, since it cost only a little more than the *Annals* reprint and it stated his position much more comprehensively. However, he asked Rumely to write *Reader's Digest* to encourage them to re-print the *Annals* article in order that it might get wider dissemination. Coyle added:

> Your paper on the farm problem interests me very much, and I can see that for anyone interested in selling anything to farmers the problem comes pretty close home. There is of course still a lot of resistance in this part of the country to inflation of any kind, and some of us feel that we still have a long fight on our hands before that resistance will be broken down. All the pressure you folks can exert is to the good. Ultimately, I guess we all agree, the farmer's problem can only be solved as an incident to a broad general rise in the standard of living that will draw enough farmers into other occupations to leave the others in a good position to make a living.[14]

Thus, while Coyle and Rumely agreed on the necessity for in-creased buying power, they clearly disagreed on the methods for achieving that goal. The Committee's program distinctly did not call for reducing the number of farmers.

When Democratic Senator Elmer Thomas of Oklahoma made the *New York Times* with his argument that "the shortage of real money in actual circulation" was "directly responsible for the ma-jor part of the present depression," and called for "cheapening the dollar," he suggested either an increase in the amount of money in circulation or a reduction in the gold content of the dollar. Rumely quickly opened relations between the Committee and the senator, sending him a letter outlining the views of the Committee.[15] Thomas, who would author the inflationary Thomas Amendment to the Agricultural Adjustment Act during the first 100 Days of the New Deal, replied that it seemed Rumely and Bendix had "a correct and comprehensive viewpoint relative to what may be done to help the farmer." No legislation, he wrote, could be helpful to the farmers "until the money question is solved," for farmers could "not possibly exist" so long as they could not "raise enough produce to sell for enough money to pay their taxes or their interest, or to maintain themselves and their families....The dollar must be reduced in buying power which automatically has the effect of increasing the value of commodities."[16]

Thomas having quoted Professor George Warren with regard to the effect of the increased value of the gold dollar on the nation's debt structure, Rumely wrote to the professor for "a complete statement of your viewpoint."[17] Warren responded that he had no "final statement of our research work on prices, as almost everything is out of print." He did, however, send Rumely a copy of a talk he had given at the American Farm Bureau meeting, and told him that a book on prices would be available in about a month.[18] Rumely asked for additional copies of the Farm Bureau talk to be mailed to Bendix and Vanderlip. It was amazing, Rumely wrote, "how firmly the 'illusion of money' grips people's minds."[19]

When Senator William Borah, too, expressed support for revaluation of the dollar, Robert E. Wood, of Sears-Roebuck, soon to be a member of the board of the Committee for the Nation, wrote the Idahoan that he agreed with him, although "this course would have been considered dangerously radical a year ago." It was, he had concluded, "the only way that will strike at the root of the matter." He explained:

If we inflate our currency through bond issues, through a veterans' bonus or some such way, we will do more harm than good, but if we strike at the root and reduce the gold content of the dollar by one-third or one-half, we will be in better shape to go ahead, and the tide of the depression will be turned. It is only in the practical method of accomplishing this   e n d that we have to be extremely careful.[20]

This was advocacy of inflation, but not yet of the Committee's goal of a commodity-based dollar.

On December 19, Rumely wrote Bendix a revealing letter that began:

> The eleventh hour has struck, and zero hour is near. Six months ago you were the one business leader who responded to my suggestion for action. I shall never forget that inspiring Sunday morning talk in your chambers.
>
> We discussed not abstract ideas. In invention, design and production you have mastered the forces of industrial progress as few leaders of our age....
>
> In your chambers in the Bendix Galleries that Sunday morning, you outlined with vision and clearness, the fundamentals that are indispensable to carrying this thought into action. Never has a nation needed a group of men who would do what the group that surrounded Theodore Roosevelt did under his leadership; or Mussolini, or Bismarck. Each one of these men was the sponsor of a group of men acting in concert bound together by a common viewpoint. You invested of your thought and fifteen hundreds of expense money. I have invested my best energies over a six months period, during which time I have talked to forty or fifty nationally outstanding men; I believe I can say, as representative a group of key men for the consideration of this question as could possibly be brought together.
>
> A sufficient number is ready to act. The time for action is here. In fact, two or three months that should have been spent constructively have already been lost....
>
> If such a Committee succeeds in adjusting our money ills and in releasing an increasing purchasing power, the benefits to your business, to other businesses of friends who will recognize what you have done, will far outweigh what you might accomplish by devoting those few hours to within your own business. In your letter to me you have so well said that the time has come when the business man must put 5 or 10% of his thought upon the general problems of purchasing power in the market....Hence, lack of time is no excuse. It only means that you are spending too much of your time inside to have the requisite small amount available outside on general purchasing power problems where your time could do you the most good....Will you put aside two hours a week and one full day each month for this cause?

The program, he wrote, was ready. It needed "only the crystallizing word from you that will start organization and action. Will you give it?"[21]

Matters began to move rapidly. After several telephone conversations with James Rand, a meeting was arranged between him and

Bendix and Rumely for mid-January. Rumely wrote Bendix that he had also gotten Vanderlip "to get his mind working on the definite problems which must be considered and on which decisions must be made this week as the basis for organizing the Committee." He also intended to get in touch with Virgil Jordan, head of the National Industrial Conference Board, and with newspaper publisher Roy Howard before the meeting.[22] He was also able to report that after spending time with Bendix and then with Rumely, Henry Wallace had said that he was "ready to cooperate with the proposed committee, if it is formed." Meanwhile, the *Chicago Tribune* had "pledged itself editorially behind a campaign for devaluing gold or reflating commodity prices by whatever measure is best."[23]

Addressing rumors that the Roosevelt administration was considering some form of domestic allotment plan as the solution to the farm problem, Rumely wrote to brain truster Rex Tugwell:

> It might be very valuable to you to see, under the surface, the trends of opinion. Here in Chicago are centered large industries, such as implement manufacturers, meat packing houses, mail order houses, banks, railroads, etc.—all dependent in one way or another upon the farmer's prosperity. During the past three years business men formerly unsympathetic with the farmer's cause have changed their viewpoint and have come to recognize that unless farm prosperity can be restored there can be no recovery for the many important industries of this district. The report of the National Industrial Conference Board, made some three years ago, probably marked the turning point.
>
> There will be very great administrative difficulties in connection with the allotment plan. I doubt whether, with the lack of established, closely knit, cooperative organizations, such as exist, for example, in Denmark, it is going to be possible to carry the allotment plan through. This much is certain, in any event: That even among business concerns vitally interested in having the farmer's prosperity restored, you are going to find very strong opposition to the allotment plan.
>
> On the other hand, opinion here in Chicago is rapidly turning to support action for restoring prices by a devaluation of money.

Rumely enclosed a copy of "Professor Warren's discussion of this problem," and expressed an interest in meeting with Tugwell the next time he was in New York.[24]

To Professor Warren, Rumely wrote asking for additional copies of "Stabilization of the Measure of Value," many of which he had already distributed to "leading business men and publishers." He told Warren:

It seems to me that the only political action that will deal
simultaneously with -
(a) The War debt problem,
(b) The agricultural problem,
(c) The burden of domestic debt,
is a reduction in the gold content of the dollar. Reducing this
by 40% would handle the situation in three directions at once. The
domestic debt problem is pressing. There are enough in these three
groups to make an overwhelmingly effective political majority.

It was "very important" he told Warren, for his view to be "brought
forcibly to the attention of President-Elect Roosevelt and his economic advisers."[25]

A few days later Rand, who had been elected chairman of the
board, wrote to Virgil Jordan of the National Industrial Conference
Board (NICB) that the Committee, of which the executive committee was composed of Rosenwald, Bendix, Vanderlip, Rand, and
Henry A. Wallace, was desirous of using the NICB's "economic
and statistical research facilities" for a study "of the various monetary and fiscal remedies that are being pressed with a view of securing the most expert judgment that can be brought to bear upon
these problems." Rand asked if the NICB would be able to make its
facilities "available for investigations and analysis of the problems
with which the Committee will have to deal along these lines?" If
so, the Committee would be willing to "underwrite all necessary
expenses incurred by you and such charges as you may make for
these services."[26]

Jordan responded that the NICB was "greatly interested" in
the Committee's proposal "because of the great public importance
of the problem with which your Committee is planning to deal."
The NICB would, he wrote, furnish three kinds of material:

First, data showing the extent and nature of the contraction of monetary
purchasing power in this country in recent years, and the causes of such
contraction. Second, data reflecting the effects of the contraction of purchasing power upon the various group and economic interests in the United
States, with special reference to the relations of debt and other fixed charges
to the income, debt-paying capacity, and resources of the various
groups....Third, the Board's staff would undertake to assemble, analyze,
and evaluate all of the important proposals that have been made for the
alternative procedure of raising the price level and restoring purchasing
power through controlled expansion of the monetary media of exchange.

For these services, the Committee would furnish the NICB with $5,000 for its immediate use, and an additional $10,000 as it performed the research.[27]

In late January, the Committee brought Professor Warren to Chicago for a talk at the Union League club, and broadcast invitations to businessmen and bankers throughout the Midwest.[28] Warren would, however, be only one of several speakers on the program advocating a variety of programs, and officially the Committee was endorsing none until the NICB had completed its study and furnished the results to the Committee.[29]

By now four of the five largest farm organizations had affiliated with the Committee.[30] Rumely's attention now turned to financing the Committee, and he solicited a letter from Bendix that would convince businessmen their money was well spent on the Committee. Rumely wanted to raise $100,000 to get the Committee going.[31] Bendix suggested to Rand that if "twenty to fifty concerns took $5,000.00 each - which would represent but a small fraction of their sales budget, possibly 1% - and pooled it in the hands of the Committee for the Nation, the Committee's work would be financed." This investment of 1 percent was likely, he wrote, to bring a greater return than the expenditure of the other 99 percent.[32]

A prodigious letter writer in pursuit of monetary reform, Rumely even wrote to Eleanor Roosevelt on January 9, enclosing information. Six weeks later, Mrs. Roosevelt responded that she had forwarded his letter and enclosures on to her husband's advisor, Louis McHenry Howe.[33]

While most of Rumely's correspondents agreed on the desirability of deflating the gold content of the dollar, some wondered how this could be done without creating a panic that would lead to a run on the banks. As rumors of the likelihood of inflationary policies by the incoming Roosevelt administration circulated with more authority in the weeks before FDR's inauguration, a run on the banks did, in fact, occur, which led many to close their doors by inauguration day, leading Roosevelt to declare a nationwide "bank holiday," after which stronger banks were allowed gradually to reopen. Many others, however, remained closed, tying up billions of dollars of depositors' money for months, and adding even further to the deflation.

Despite his early and continued advocacy of the commodity dollar, economist Irving Fisher had by the 1930s come to a belief that the same objectives could be achieved through adjusting the quantity of money rather than the quality of money, through the Federal Reserve Board's management of credit. As he put it in his 1928 book, *The Money Illusion*:

> When my *Stabilizing the Dollar* [1920] was written, I relegated credit control to the Appendix, assuming that all banking, even central banking, would still be conducted purely for private profit. My aim was to make the whole plan of stabilization—both gold control and credit control—as "automatic," that is as free from discretion, as possible.
>
> Since that time, however, as has been shown in this book, discretionary credit control has actually come into existence. This, when duly perfected and duly safeguarded, will greatly simplify and improve the technique of stabilization and will make gold control secondary to credit control.[34]

In *Booms and Depressions* (1932) Fisher reiterated his belief that the Federal Reserve could provide for a stable dollar by effecting changes in the quantity of money, while relegating changes in its quality to a secondary role "when other means proved inadequate."[35] Again, in his book *Stable Money* (1934), Fisher conceded that "a rough stabilization could be obtained by sole reliance on adjusting the price of gold," but that he would "depend for a stable dollar mainly on open market operations and occasional adjustments of rediscount rates [by the FRB].[36] Thus, while Fisher was identified in the press with the Committee for the Nation's efforts to obtain a commodity dollar through manipulation of the "quality" of money, he was clearly putting priority in the New Deal years on actions by the Federal Reserve Board in manipulating the quantity of money to achieve the same result.

After Roosevelt suggested that he see Raymond Moley, Fisher was unsuccessful in getting an appointment to see the brain truster, so he wrote the president on March 2, 1933 that the committee hoped he "would make a ringing declaration against the deflation of the last four years saying that the Democratic platform favors sound money; that you are committed to sound money, but not to a money which, masquerading under that name, is really unsound." Soundness required stability, "that there must be neither inflation or deflation," and judged by that standard America's money over the past four years had "been far from sound." Equating America's deflation with the ruinous inflation in Germany a few years earlier, Fisher wrote that America's prices had "been shooting down to ruin, just as Germany's had been shooting up to ruin." The restoration of sound money, he argued, required the restoration of "the price level sufficiently to let the average debtor pay his debt on a basis like that on which he contracted it, doing full justice to his creditor; that we must have a 'new deal,' one that does even-handed justice." This was the way to restore prosperity and to preserve it in the future. The Committee hoped that Roosevelt would "present to the Congress specific recommendations towards that supremely important end."[37]

In a letter that he sent to O.M.W. Sprague, advisor in the Treasury Department, with a copy to FDR, Fisher pressed a sixteen-point "program for reflation and stabilization," that included: a declaration that the objective of Roosevelt's policy was to restore the 1926 price level "or thereabouts"; permitting a free market for gold, with a temporary minimum price of $30 for U.S. sales of gold with increases if advisable; "Induce friendly suit as test case in Supreme Court to settle validity of gold clause repeal"; unfreezing of deposits in banks closed by Roosevelt at time of bank panic; and

> Make monetary standard of U.S. henceforth potentially independent of other countries. I.e. not wait for action by other countries, nor make our action dependent on theirs, nor tie up our standard to theirs irrevocably. Otherwise we shall again suffer deflation or inflation if they do. Such a declaration of independence is necessary if we are to be sure of maintaining our new level of prices.[38]

The Committee gained an additional friend in the administration in February when Henry A. Wallace, one of its board members, was tapped for Secretary of Agriculture. Wood wrote that he was delighted by the selection, but he told Wallace:

> I also hope that you may be able to have a voice in affairs beyond agriculture. Though a Republican, I voted for Mr. Roosevelt. However, if he is going to let Barney Baruch and some of the New York crowd influence him, we are not going to have anything better. I cannot see any chance except in a change in our monetary unit, through either a devaluation of the dollar or international bimetallism.[39]

In March 1933, the Committee issued an "Interim Report and Immediate Recommendations" that was mailed off to some members of Congress and members of the Roosevelt administration, as well as to the "Executive Heads of One Hundred Large Corporations." The report reviewed the economic situation in America in terms of agricultural conditions, public and private debts, the condition of the banks, the decline of purchasing power (which they put at only 46.1 percent of the 1929 figure), the mortgage situation, and recommended, first, that "a banking bill be immediately passed with an amendment providing an adequate federal guarantee of the deposits of all existing banks upon application for a limited time"; second, an "immediate embargo of gold export and suspension of specie payments to prevent hoarding and foreign withdrawal"; and, third, "a definite program to raise the whole level of commodity prices."[40] Secretary of Commerce Daniel Roper wrote that he was so impressed with the report that he was "placing it before the President for his deliberation."[41]

Roosevelt did take the United States off the gold standard, and the psychology of inflation that had caused the banking panic now continued on into panic buying of raw materials by manufacturers, and of inventories by wholesalers and retailers, all of which created the illusion that recovery was underway and the mistaken impression that it was based on confidence rather than fear by businessmen. But Wood was concerned over the disposition of the Federal Reserve to "close thousands of small banks," a course which he considered "disastrous." He wrote Senator Robert LaFollette that he had "assumed that the President was not afraid of some real inflation, but this is deflation," and it would doubtless check the current rise in commodity prices. Its practical effect, he wrote, would be "a paralysis of business in the rural sections."[42] LaFollette agreed that the developments following the banking crisis and the passage of the economy bill had set in motion "an engine of deflation." He asked the Committee's help in persuading Roosevelt to embark on a program of re-employment as soon as possible.[43]

Wood told LaFollette that he would do everything he could, since he considered a reemployment bill desirable, and "the larger the bill the better," not only because it would put men back to work, but also because it would be, "in itself a large inflationary measure, which will, in my opinion, depreciate the dollar and lead to its ulti-

mate revaluation."[44] To Sidney Weinberg, a friend and member of
the Democratic National Committee, Wood wrote that after the
banking bill was passed and Roosevelt had issued his proclama-
tion on gold, "the feeling was we would have some inflation,"
and commodity and security prices had risen. But the actual effects of the administration's policies had "resulted in a further
gigantic deflationary step in the closing of 5,000 banks." He
explained:

> It is true that they are the smaller banks, but the freezing of $5,000,000,000
> to $8,000,000,000 of deposits constitutes in itself a tremendous deflation.
> Large sections of the country have practically no banking facilities, and
> there is a virtual paralysis of business in the rural sections. The three
> large mail order houses were running approximately 50% below last year's
> sales for a similar period - and the sales last year were very low. Our orders
> to manufacturers are being cancelled, and we are making further and radi-
> cal reductions in payroll, all of which is continuing the process of defla-
> tion. Business is actually getting worse, not better.
>
> Whatever may have been the President's intention, the interpretation of
> his policy is in the hands of the Federal Reserve, headed by Eugene Meyer,
> who is a deflationist, and apparently the new Secretary of the Treasury has
> been won over to the New York point of view.

Wood hoped that Weinberg would bring to the attention of the
administration the way things were working out for business.[45] And
he was hopeful that the new Federal Reserve Governor would be
from outside New York, "for it is difficult to find any one in New
York who is not bound by tradition in his views on monetary questions and on inflation, even when he may be very liberal in other
respects."[46]

Late in March, Rumely wrote Vanderlip and other board members of the promising response that had resulted from the Warren
talk in Chicago and from distribution of copies. The Committee
had compiled a list of 100 economists who had expressed support
for revaluation of the dollar and was sending each of them a copy
at Professor Warren's suggestion. Irving Fisher had also "supplied
a list of economists willing to take membership on the Committee."
More and more prominent businessmen were aligning with the
Committee.[47] A March 30, 1933 letter from Rand to Committee
members told them:

Reports indicate that a majority, both in Congress and the Senate, is in favor of rebuilding the price level, although not agreed upon the best means of accomplishing this purpose. It is hoped that the Committee's program may furnish a common meeting-ground for action. It must be borne in mind that in public matters, leadership even of a national administration cannot progress too far in advance of public understanding. Hence the importance of the Committee's work.[48]

Early in April, Rumely was called to Washington by Professor Warren for consultations going on that included Professor Fisher relative to a bill to be introduced in Congress by Representative Goldsborough. "Professor Warren," he wrote, "thought it wise that he and his associates be given a chance to express their opinion and that discussions be carried on to bring them as completely as possible to the committee's program." In Washington, Warren and Rumely drew up a draft of a bill "on the basis of Professor Warren's notes which he had made in the course of his discussions during the day with the others." Congressman Disney told Rumely that the leadership of the Roosevelt administration would be "the all-important factor," but suggested that the Committee mount pressure on Congress from the grassroots. Despite some disagreements a consensus was hammered out for a bill that included "the essentials of the committee's program," but which included provision for "the issuance of currency in large volume until such time as the price level is restored," after which the new currency would be gradually recalled. A limitation restricting the value of the new notes to double the value of the "profit" on gold devaluation, meant that the new issue would amount to about $4,800,000,000. If used to buy bonds or to finance new projects, it would "put money into circulation." Discussions were continuing on other aspects of the bill. Rumely also reported on "a profitable twenty minutes talk with [columnist] Mark Sullivan who today ran an article on the gold clause and tomorrow's [Herald] *Tribune* will discuss the Administration attitude further." Rumely found Sullivan "open-minded and moving toward the committee's viewpoint."[49]

The next day, Rumely could report that the Committee had an appointment to see the president in the White House, and that they would take up with him the preliminary draft of the bill.[50] That meeting was apparently fruitless, since Roosevelt did not push for passage of the bill. In mid-April, Rumely send the president a state-

ment of his ideas on what the administration should do. Recalling
his earlier letters to Roosevelt, Rumely wrote: "Thinking retrospec-
tively of developments since I first wrote to you of the plan and
outlined such a committee, I am now prompted to give you what I
see ahead." Rumely told the president:

> The distress and injustice that follow a change in the commodity price-
> level are now so evident that our nation cries for a better standard of mea-
> suring value....The destruction in human values resulting from the break in
> price level during the past four years has probably cost the nation many
> times more than the world war itself in both lives and property.
>   Revaluation of gold will be forced by circumstance whether we will it
> or not. Those occupying positions of traditional power in the banking
> field will be forced by events to accept devaluation, but will resist the
> establishment of a social measure of value that will give permanent stabil-
> ity, and the equity between man and man, between economic group and
> economic group, that comes from a stable price value....It is now evident
> that the gamble of fluctuating money—the most dangerous and most de-
> structive gamble of life—must be eliminated....In your hands lies the op-
> portunity to establish a stable measure of value, the measure which con-
> trols the exchange of goods and services, the measure which is the basis of
> equity for dealings between man and man in the present, and from the
> present to the distant future.
>   Revaluation of gold is inevitable for the United States as it has been for
> thirty-one other nations. None of these, however, took the additional step
> of securing a stable base. They all remained upon a one-commodity mea-
> sure of value [gold] instead of adopting the all-commodity dollar, which
> does not change, and gives a base of stable purchasing power for perma-
> nently equitable contracts....
>   The objective...is stability of the measure of value. The political situ-
> ation is such that you hold in your hands the unique opportunity that
> never has come to another President and is not likely to come again in our
> generation.[51]

These recommendations somewhat paralleled those that the Committee had advocated in a release, "Five Next Steps in the Program
of the Committee for the Nation," that was mailed to all members a
month earlier. Pointing out that "a debt contracted in 1918 by a
farmer, in terms of commodities, amounting to 100 in units of produce, rose to 172 in 1921,...and skyrocketed to 351 in 1932," the
Committee insisted that "trading between group and group cannot
to go on." And the cause of the problem was the change in the
purchasing power of the dollar. The Committee then outlined five

steps in a program it had reached as a result of the research of the NICB and others:

1. Reopen the maximum number of banks immediately and release their deposits for use, if necessary guaranteeing their deposits temporarily until confidence in them returned;

2. Continue the embargo on gold exports and the suspension of specie payments ;

3. "Discontinue the efforts to keep the dollar at its former gold parity" in foreign exchange and do everything necessary to depress the value of the dollar "so that foreign countries can acquire it at a lower cost to pay their debts to us and to use it in buying goods from American agriculture and industry."

4. The price of gold should be raised from its present price of $20.67 per ounce to $36.17 per ounce, which should reestablish the 1926 price level in America;

5. "A federal non-partisan Board should be created to stabilize the United States general price-level of wholesale commodity prices at 100"—the average of price levels between 1921 and 1931.[52]

In mailing out copies, Rumely pointed out that the Committee now embraced "85% of the agricultural leaders and about 400 business men on this printing, but actually we have twice as many business firms available for the nest printing in New York." "Step by step," he wrote, "as the program of the COMMITTEE was outlined, the various steps were presented in Washington and have found acceptance."[53] On May 1, Rumely wrote a friend that he had been working fifteen-to-twenty-hour days, putting together the Committee's program, organizing businessmen and farm leaders to support it, and then presenting it "in the most effective way at Washington." The fact that the administration had already adopted much of the Committee's program was, he said, "a source of satisfaction."[54]

Virgil Jordan, head of the NICB applauded the Committee's program, but added that he thought it should be supplemented by some emphasis on devices for encouraging reemployment.[55] Perhaps in response to Jordan's suggestion, the Committee issued a "Sixth Step" in April that proposed a loan of $2.5 billion to employers for the purpose of putting workers back to work. W. J. Cameron, of Ford Motor Company, however, pointed out that the stoppage of business was not the result of lack of working capital but of the absence of a market for the goods they might produce.

Instead, Cameron suggested that the $2.5 billion would more likely "start the wheels a-turning if it were used as undiluted purchasing power." The "game" of lending on good security and at interest was, he said, over, and was being forced out by "the compulsion of events."[56]

In May, Wood expressed his disappointment that LaFollette had voted against the inflation (Thomas) amendment to the Agricultural Adjustment Act when it was in the Senate. He told LaFollette that he was convinced "the monetary unit is the very root of our trouble." If the dollar was pegged "at somewhere between 66 and 75 cents" farm prices would rise and industry would receive an impetus. But he agreed with LaFollette that, in addition to this, there was need for a flood of additional dollars into the economy through "a tremendous program for public works and other inflationary measures."[57]

Looking ahead to the World Economic Conference in London, Wood wrote Secretary of Agriculture Wallace:

> If the President keeps his nerve and goes through with the deflation of the dollar, and on top of that insists on their (the British) stabilizing on a basis which will give a ratio between the two currencies of better than 4 1/2 to 1, we are going to have great prosperity in this country. We must, however, have in our delegation to London alert men, with a liberal outlook, as opposed to the traditional outlook, who can not be swung by the British. When it comes to finance and trading the British are much smarter than ourselves, just as we are much smarter than they in matters of production.[58]

In May, Rumely wrote his daughter that he had "been under terrific pressure in New York but have had the thrill of success with our efforts. The Administration has adopted the Committee's policy and this country is on the way to restoration of the 1926 price level, we believe."[59]

George Warren and his coauthor Pearson were disappointed, however, with the early New Deal for its failure to travel farther up the mountain of price stabilization. Nor did they agree with the analyses of those who, like Chase and Coyle, were preaching the doctrine of overproduction and technological unemployment. Instead, they argued in their book, *Prices*, published in early 1933, that technological advance did not create unemployment, since most such advances "set numbers of invisible men at work back of the new machine," employed in making and transporting the new machines and the power to run them. As for overproduction, when deflation occurred it naturally produced idle plants and idle workers, leading to "two fallacious conclusions: that the nation's output could be increased many times and that the number of plants is far too great. They assume that unlimited labor supply and raw materials are available for each plant, and arrive at the illusion of enormous capacity for multiplying output," ignoring the fact that this would require more labor and raw materials than existed.[60]

The more civilized a society became, the greater the division of labor, and the greater the dependence on "purchased rather than home-made articles," and the greater the tendency of people to act in unison, all of which accentuated price cycles. They wrote: "Many factors combine to make prices what they are. These causes may be analyzed just as a substance may be analyzed chemically, and the proportion due to each cause ultimately may be determined. The science of price analysis is still new but has progressed far enough to be of help."

There were other ways of effecting more stable prices, but "stabilization of the purchasing power of the monetary unit is necessary to solve the most serious of the price problems."[61] The price system was the best mechanism for guiding supply and demand. It did not always work perfectly, they admitted, "but no committee could guide the millions of producers to meet human needs so well as price guided them—provided the medium of exchange functions properly. When it functions badly, the people turn to dictators and social control."[62]

In times of inflation or deflation prices were not a true measure of demand or supply. In deflationary times, such as existed in the depression, efforts were made to protect producers and creditors:

Efforts are made to prevent each commodity from falling in price, at a time when the whole price level must fall. Every country builds its tariff walls higher and puts on import restrictions...to prevent others from selling in "our markets." States devise schemes to handicap nonresident corporations. The government is called on to give bounties for exports, to buy products to be held off the market or to be dumped in the sea....

Groups of producers of this and that commodity organize to hold the price of "our" product up by alloting production or sales territory, price-fixing agreements, dumping of products abroad, and the like....

Corporations make agreements to hold prices up. They discover that they cannot hold up both prices and sales. The government is also called on to organize farmers and other unorganized producers so that they may attempt the same futile procedure....

Since debts cannot be paid, the government is called on take over private debts of banks, railroads, farmers, and home owners....

Inability of unemployed persons to buy, allows stocks of goods to accumulate and results in the illusion of over-production. Exaggerated statements of capacity to produce are made and efforts are put forth to find means to permanently curtail production, under the childish assumption that if each of us produces less, each of us can have more.

Since the exchange system breaks down, so does the form of government and the organization of society based on private enterprise. Since society as a whole does not know what to do, it is sometimes proposed that some individual seize power, assuming that he would thereby become all wise. When there is no knowledge, the people turn to some one who promises everything and accept him on faith. A political faith becomes religion to be accepted without question. When there is no knowledge, the people perish, but dictators flourish.

Such changes the authors regarded as an attempt "not only to bring the mountain, but the universe, to Mohammed."[63]

Warren and Pearson were convinced that it was the world's gold supply that lay behind fluctuations in commodity prices. By graphs they made the point that so long as the world's gold supply rose at the same rate as the world's physical volume of production it was sufficient to support prices, but when gold stocks rose more rapidly than production, prices rose, and when the the obverse, prices fell. After 1915, world gold production had not increased rapidly enough to maintain a stable price level. Warren and Pearson concluded:

The great rise in prices in the United States was due to the fact that most of the gold-using world ceased to use gold [went off the gold standard] and eased to bid for it. This reduced the demand and the value of gold, and commodity prices rose.

The frantic demand for gold [when many returned to the gold standard] carried prices lower than the level that probably would have existed had there been no war. Even without a war, there would doubtless have been some price decline, but since price relationships would not have been adjusted to a price level above pre-war, the result would probably have been no more serious than previous periods of gold shortage.

The major source of the difficulty was low demand for gold for many years, which resulted in having price relationships, debts, and taxes approximately adjusted to a commodity price level about 50 per cent above prewar; followed by a world-wide frantic effort to return to gold, which caused price chaos and made it impossible to pay debts.[64]

No country, or group of countries, could "easily reduce the value of gold except by demonetizing it." Gold prices were set by supply and demand, the same laws that governed the value of all other commodities. The low demand for gold during World War I led to a declining value and higher commodity prices, but in the erratic international trade that followed the war, governments sought more gold reserves than normal to be safe, driving up the value of gold and causing a collapse of prices, while increasing the burden of debt. The debt could be eliminated only through widespread bankruptcies or by a return of the value of money to that which prevailed when it was borrowed. "When the bankruptcies are over, the nation can again be prosperous," they wrote. "If the deflation plan is followed to the bitter end, it will mean the life-time economic ruin of millions of individuals but will not hurt the next generation unless the foolish laws which are being passed remain to plague them."[65] The Depression was not an act of God, nor a business cycle, nor due to unsound business practices or overproduction, nor to lack of confidence, it was purely and simply due to "high demand for gold following a period of low demand for gold." Critics might charge that this explanation was too simple to be true, but: "Truth is always simple. Ignorance is mystical."

It was debts, not wages, that stood in the way of recovery, and little recovery could "be expected until debts are adjusted to the price level, or the price level reflated to the level at which the debts were contracted."[66] Gold production had declined so that a reflation of prices was unlikely to occur through expanded gold stocks, but the production of silver was coming closer to keeping pace with the production of other things, so that a monetary system based on a combination of gold and silver would be more stable than gold.[67]

"An ounce of gold" they wrote, "is, of course, always worth an ounce of gold, and an ounce of silver is worth an ounce of silver." The only reliable way of determining the value of one thing was to compare it with many things. Stabilizing the price level did not mean that individual commodities would be free of the fluctuations in price that resulted from supply and demand, but it did mean that they would not go through fluctuations depending on the value of gold or silver.

Warren and Pearson then pressed their own proposal for stabilizing prices:

> The compensated dollar is a proposal to establish a scientific measure of value. This proposal has been developed in great detail by Irving Fisher. He proposes that the gold dollar shall cease to be a constant weight of gold with a variable purchasing power, and shall become a variable weight of gold with a purchasing power as nearly constant as possible. This is sometimes called a rubber dollar by persons who do not understand it. The dollar has to be rubber as to either weight or value. It cannot have both its weight and its value fixed. This proposal lets the weight rather than the value vary....With such a system, there would no longer be any coinage of gold. The government's gold supply would be kept in gold bars. The actual circulation would be the same as at present, i.e., paper dollars and small coins. All the currency would be exchangeable for gold on demand, as at present, but the amount of gold that a dollar would exchange for would vary with the price level, that is, the price of gold would be allowed to vary with its value just as the price of wheat varies with its value....This would make the dollar have the same value at all times. It would be independent of business cycles.[68]

Borrowers would know that they could repay in dollars of the same value as those borrowed, lenders would similarly know that they would be repaid in dollars of the same amount loaned. The compensated, or commodity, dollar would also "enable one to save for old age or leave life insurance for a family with assurance that the sum would not shrink, and that it would not grow so unjustly large as to cause the bank or company to fail." It would not eliminate business cycles, but it would put an end to "precipices," since it would act as a check to the booms and depressions that accompanied rapid swings in commodity prices. The value of the dollar would be based on an index of a specified list of commodity prices.[69] The English economist John Maynard Keynes, had, they pointed out, advocated something very like the Fisher plan for England, but leaving it to the Bank of England to set the value of gold in order to keep commodity prices stable.[70]

The House of Representatives, they noted, had shown support for the commodity dollar concept in 1932 by passing the Goldsborough Bill by a vote of 289-59. That bill would have directed the Federal Reserve Board and the Federal Reserve Banks to reflate commodity prices by changing the value of gold.[71] The bill had failed of passage in the Senate. One obstacle to changing the price of gold would be the existing "gold clauses" embodied in many contracts, which called for repayment in gold dollars of the same weight and fineness as those borrowed. But Warren and Pearson were confident that the Supreme Court would uphold the invalidation of those clauses, since under a commodity dollar the lenders would be repaid in dollars of the same purchasing power as those they had loaned.[73]

After examining the various remedies that had been proposed for the depression, Pearson and Warren concluded that private enterprise required "a reliable medium of exchange," without which chaos reigned. Such chaos did not signal a breakdown of capitalism, "which is another name for private enterprise," but simply a breakdown of the medium of exchange that needed to be corrected. Capitalism was no more to blame for this "than it is to blame for the failure of a bridge to carry a certain load." The remedy was "to supply a tool that will work," and that tool was "a measure of value that will keep the average price of commodities stable." There were many ways to do that if "the science involved is understood."

As for the despair that some felt over the failure of democracy to deal with the depression, and the suggestions that a dictator was needed, Warren and Pearson wrote: "A civilization based on private enterprise is a very effective but delicate machine. Money is the battery that keeps it going. If this tool functions badly, the thing to change is the tool and not the form of government."[74]

Warren and Pearson then approvingly reviewed the monetary policies of the New Deal that had occurred in the few months before their book was published. First, the banks had been ordered to turn in to the Federal Reserve System all gold and gold certificates, then the order was extended to individuals possessing more than $100 in gold and gold certificates. On April 19, the gold standard was suspended and exports of gold were prohibited. Commodity and security prices promptly rose. On May 26, Roosevelt asked for invalidation of the "gold clause," and Congress promptly responded with a bill that was signed by the president on June 5. This clear indication that the dollar had been permanently divorced from its former gold value had brought a further rise in prices.[75]

From April 17 to 20 [1933], the price of gold rose 12 per cent, and prices of 17 basic commodities also rose 12 per cent. By May 6, the price of gold was 21 per cent above par, and prices of 17 basic commodities had risen 25 per cent. The dollar then strengthened and the advance in basic commodities was checked. On May 26, the President called on Congress to invalidate the gold clause....and commodity prices rose. From May 26 to June 10, the price of gold rose from $24.13 to $25.46 per fine ounce and the indices of prices of 17 basic commodities rose from 132 to 145....The increase in the price of gold from April 17, when the United States departed from the gold standard, to June 10 was 23.2 per cent; in the prices of basic commodities, 45 per cent.[76]

Here, it seemed, was clear validation of the Warren and Pearson theories, and they applauded these initial steps that could lay the foundation for the commodity dollar they advocated.

But this was not enough. They explained:

The price level must be raised to the debt level or the debt level lowered to the price level. Unless the price of gold is raised, the process of bankruptcy and deflation has been only temporarily arrested. There can be no general employment until it is largely completed. This is not a matter of psychology or confidence. It is a grim reality that, at present values of gold and commodities, many of the debts are more than the properties are worth.[77]

This seemed to be the goal of the president, as Warren and Pearson quoted from his statement that:

The Administration has the definite objective of raising commodity prices to such an extent that those who have borrowed money will, on the average, be able to repay that money in the same kind of dollar which they borrowed.

We do not seek to let them get such a cheap dollar that they will be able to pay back a great deal less than they borrowed.

In other words, we seek to correct a wrong and not to create another wrong in the opposite direction....[78]

This was a succinct statement of the goals of Warren and Pearson's policies, and those of the Committee for the Nation. It remained to be seen if the president would adopt their means to that end, and whether their means would work as well as they expected.

Finally, it should be noted that the Warren and Pearson attitude toward the type of international monetary stabilization that was contemplated for the World Economic Conference in London that summer was distinctly negative. What was needed, they wrote, was for each country to "revalue its currency on such a basis as to restore the balance in its internal price, tax, and debt structure, and enough to start employment," with no international considerations allowed to interfere with this process. This meant that the United States should revalue the dollar at a level that was best for its domestic affairs, and other countries should do he same.[79] Thus, Warren and Pearson joined with the planners in advocating economic nationalism for the United States.

2

The Committee for the Nation and the New Deal

The Committee for the Nation quickly emerged as the leading group lobbying on behalf of monetary action, as acknowledged by no less a New Dealer than Rexford Tugwell.[1] In mid-June the Committee wrote Roosevelt:

> In April, after comparing results of its own exhaustive investigations with studies of best informed economists and leaders in finance, Committee for the Nation recommended Treasury price $36.17 as basis for revaluing gold. This was equivalent to a cut of 42.8% in gold content.
>
> Our Committee's recent further investigation confirms these calculations. They indicate that reduction of gold content by only 25 to 30% would check recovery and leave marginal groups under partial deflation. Agriculture would suffer most seriously. The farmer, since 1921, has been in position of disadvantage. We must cut gold content sufficiently to give him such prices for his products that he can again become a buyer....
>
> Time is of the essence. Approximately twelve millions are still unemployed. We are losing two to four billions per month of national income through deflationary conditions. The more quickly the purchasing power of the dollar is reduced to 1926 the stronger the stimulus for price rise and reemployment. Bureau of Labor index of wholesale prices for all commodities has risen only from 59.6 in March to 63.8 in June.

The Committee recommended "the immediate establishment of a free gold market in the United States," and that devaluation of the dollar be undertaken to set the value of gold at $36.17 per ounce, which the Committee estimated would reestablish the 1926 price level. This represented a 42.8 percent cut in the gold content of the dollar.[2]

Two days later the Committee responded with alarm to the nego-
tiations underway at the World Economic Conference in London,
writing Roosevelt:

> The price of commodities and securities throughout the United States fell
> today in response to news of the mistaken policy being pursued by the
> American delegation in London. The [British] pound has already depre-
> ciated 31 per cent. The dollar must be cut, according to our calculations,
> 43 per cent to restore our price-level. This means that if the English pound
> were held stationary at its present gold equivalent, it would have to go to
> $5.70.
> Every attempt to stabilize in the ratio of $4.00 to a pound must raise grave
> doubts as to early restoration of American price-level. Our market prices
> now are supported only by speculative anticipation of a reduction of our
> dollar to its former purchasing power....
> Instead of stabilizing, the United States should act to depress the dollar
> by selling it abroad....Our Committee is convinced that efforts to fix the
> dollar's destiny by conference and compromise in Europe must lead to
> unsatisfactory if not disastrous results here at home.
> Our 10 per cent of foreign trade and international finance must be subor-
> dinated to our domestic price-level which controls the relations of all
> Americans to each other.[3]

A few days later the Committee telegraphed a vacationing FDR
at Campobello Isle that it was "gravely concerned over developments in London." They cited a dispatch from London in the *New
York Evening Post* that reported an effort led by John Maynard
Keynes to induce the British Government to "link the pound with
the dollar and so join and control the American inflationary movement."
Their telegram went on to say:

> A thousand industrial leaders, executive heads of corporations who have
> made a study of these monetary questions, and ninety per cent of the lead-
> ers of organized agriculture represented on the Committee for the Nation
> have viewed with great satisfaction your steadfast resistance until now to
> the efforts of Europe to interfere with the dollar relationship of Americans
> with Americans.[4]

By his "bombshell" message wired to the World Conference in
which he torpedoed the work of the delegates and sent their delib-
erations into oblivion, Roosevelt signaled to the world that the United
States had turned its back on world economic cooperation in seek-

ing a solution to the depression, and would hereafter seek a domestic recovery in isolation from the rest of the world. This was exactly what Rumely and the Committee had sought.

In mid-July the Committee took up again the issue of frozen deposits in closed banks, where "progress in releasing frozen deposits" had not kept up with other features of the recovery program. The areas of the country where business was most lagging behind was precisely in the areas of closed or restricted banks. It was for that reason that the Committee had made the reopening of the maximum number of banks the first of its Five Steps program, and it was now organizing a special Committee to Release Frozen Bank Deposits that would undertake a nationwide survey "to find the exact amount of deposits in restricted and closed banks, both within and without the Federal Reserve System." The Committee sought from its members information on the banking situations in their areas so that the information might be presented to the administration. One hundred and ten radio stations were broadcasting an address concerning the problem by Earl Harding, an advisory member of the Committee.[5]

In August, 1933, Irving Fisher had the first of two personal meetings with Roosevelt in Hyde Park. It was, Fisher wrote his wife, "the most satisfactory talk I ever had with a President and the most important." In talks with Theodore Roosevelt, Taft, Wilson, Harding and Hoover, Fisher had "never felt I got as good a reception of my message before." Roosevelt began their half hour meeting by asking Fisher if he agreed with Warren and Rogers that an increase in the Federal Reserve's prices for newly mined gold would raise commodity prices," and of course Fisher did so. Fisher suggested several other policies, as well, including opening the closed banks in order that the frozen money of depositors might be released. Apparently unaware of Roosevelt's reputation for appearing to agree with everyone who talked to him, Fisher came away convinced that the president was committed to reflation by tying the dollar to the commodity price level.[6]

But a few days later Fisher wrote his son that the New Deal was "a strange mixture." He wrote:

I'm against all the restriction of acreage and production, but much in favor of reflation. Apparently F.D.R. thinks of them as similar—merely two ways of raising prices! But one changes the monetary unit to restore it to normal, while the other spells scarce food and clothing when many are starving and half naked.[7]

In a "calendar of action" it had taken during the summer of 1933, the Committee recalled its opposition to stabilization at the World Economic Conference, despite the fact that it was advocated by Secretary of Treasury Woodin, Budget Director Lewis Douglas, Brain Truster Raymond Moley, and others, and the President's message to the conference, "brushing aside the carefully laid plans for stabilization," in which he had "outlined a monetary program which, when realized, may stand as one of the Nation's historic policies." It also described the Committee's efforts in behalf of freeing frozen bank assets through its affiliated Committee to Release Frozen Bank Deposits, and its radio campaign for this purpose.[8]

The Committee for the Nation also claimed credit for a number of successes in the early New Deal. A 1933 committee pamphlet noted:

In February, 1933, the Committee for the Nation recommended embargo of gold exports and suspension of specie payments as prerequisite to restoration of the American price level. These two steps became accomplished facts early in March.

April 6th the Committee pointed out that the effect experienced in other countries of suspending specie payments could not be realized in the United States so long as the Government continued to peg the dollar in international exchange. April 19th the dollar was cut loose from gold.

May 18th the Committee made the establishment of a free gold market in New York one of its objectives as a means to increase the price of gold and raise commodity prices. August 29th free exportation of newly-mined American gold was permitted.

Through May and June the Committee vigorously opposed currency stabilization at the World Economic Conference. July 3rd the President rejected stabilization.

In June the Committee took to the country the issue of frozen bank deposits. By September a change in Government policy was ordered.[9]

To the above achievements by the reflationists should be added the passage of the Thomas amendment to the Agricultural Adjustment Act. During the winter before FDR's inauguration, rumors were rife that his administration would pursue inflationary policies, and that if it did not Congress would seize the bit in its teeth and do so on its own. A month after his inauguration, Roosevelt invited a leader of the inflationist forces in Congress, Senator Elmer Thomas of Oklahoma, to the White House in an effort to calm the inflationists on Capitol Hill. Roosevelt invited Thomas to draft a bill that would allow, but not mandate, presidential devaluation of the dollar, monetize silver, and inflate the currency. Thomas did so, and the Thomas amendment became law as part of the Agricultural Adjustment Act. Thus Roosevelt cooled off inflationary sentiment in the Congress while gathering discretionary powers and committing himself to nothing. Clearly Roosevelt had not neglected the reflationists in his dispensation of sops to the various factions within the New Deal, but the discretionary powers granted to him under the Thomas amendment cast a pall of uncertainty over the stability of the dollar. While Warren and Pearson attributed rising prices to the rising value of gold, an equally convincing case could be made that the rise in prices was the result of panic buying in anticipation of further inflation.

However, even the Tugwellian "planners" recognized that something must be done about gold. As Tugwell wrote in his diary over a month before inauguration day, and before the bank panic:

> Our policy has been shaped toward a pragmatic handling of prices....I believe in stabilization...—that is in a managed currency and independence from the gold standard. But I am anxious first to straighten things out. There is more currency now than is needed. We need to correct disparities and inflation would not do that....My view is that we ought to go off gold in international exchange so that we can manage internally. The Governor [FDR] asked me some time ago how it could be done. He said some one had told him that a law giving the President power to regulate gold in international exchange in 1918 had never been repealed. If this is true it is important because then it could be done overnight by proclamation without long Congressional debate which would spoil the effect. I promised to look it up.[10]

But while the planners sympathized with much of the program of the Committee for the Nation, the Committee evinced none for the program of the planners. As Tugwell wrote, in a later addendum to his diary, the Committee for the Nation

> pictured those of us who thought regulation and the encouragement of expansion necessary as being hardly less than Russian emissaries. We

wanted regimentation for its own sake, they said. Also they pictured us as running the nation through an unbalanced budget. To inflate by this method was Communistic or something equally radical; to inflate by monetary methods was, however, quite all right.

Tugwell sought to convince Roosevelt that the New Deal policy should be selective—that some industries did need higher prices, but others should have them reduced. In this, however, he was unsuccessful in swaying the president.[11]

The difficulty, as Tugwell realized, was that Roosevelt's friend and Hyde Park neighbor, Henry Morgenthau, who later became secretary of the treasury, was the "go-between" for the "Cornell group," as Tugwell referred to Warren and the others, lending them a standing with Roosevelt they would not otherwise have had. The result was that Roosevelt "was very much interested in the monetary approach to the depression."[12] Tugwell's analysis omitted the fact that the Committee for the Nation also counted the secretary of agriculture among its supporters, Henry A. Wallace having been a member of its board until Roosevelt picked him for the cabinet.

A break in stock and commodity prices that roughly coincided with the implementation of the NRA and AAA in July was, in the eyes of the Committee, "unnecessary and uncalled for," but was caused by "uncertainty over our monetary policy and our unreadiness to apply necessary steps in the recovery program which left us open to mass psychology and foreign manipulation." The price of gold had increased 40 percent when what was needed was an increase of 75 percent. There had been, so far, "no definite foundation under our price rise." Instead, it had been based on "mass psychology and speculative guessing of what our Administration does to reduce the dollar's abnormal purchasing power." The increased value of farm crops had been at least temporarily wiped out. "This restoration of values was releasing productive energies which overshadowed anything done by regimentation or government decree to increase purchasing power." The remedy, the Committee argued, was simple. It was to move the United States toward a dollar that would steadily rise "toward the desired point of its gold value." Psychology would no longer serve the purpose.[13]

Another release by the Committee two days later called attention to what it described as two "divergent philosophies of economic and social organization" that were "struggling for mastery in Washington." The first of these, represented by the Committee, recognized the monetary cause of the Depression and sought to produce recovery through monetary measures. "The other," it said, was "the philosophy of deflation. It frowns upon raising prices by monetary action. Instead of a rapid restoration of price-level and the old balance on an automatic basis, it resorts to government regimentation and aid at all steps of the program." It continued:

> These conflicting philosophies are coming to test in connection with the break in price-level and the temporary check in the progress of restoring our dollar to its normal purchasing power....
>   Psychological measures will no longer suffice. Definite monetary action by the Administration is required.[14]

The lines were being drawn.

In August, the Committee circulated copies of a radio talk by Virgil Jordan, of the NICB, and wrote that "We stand at the crossroads." America could "take the course of monetary action to rebuild our price-level, or follow indefinitely the road which still means continued deflation with its necessary accompaniment of regimentation and state regulation." It added:

> With millions of children undernourished, with millions inadequately clad, with much of our housing a disgrace to our progress, we should go slowly in attributing our troubles to over-production. We know that world production has not increased out of proportion to population; rather it has slowed down.[15]

In August, Warren published an article in *Forum*, on "The New Dollar," in which he argued that ever since April 19, each rise in the price of gold, however small, had been accompanied by a similar rise in commodity prices. For example:

> In the first two days after the suspension of the gold standard, the price of gold rose 12 per cent, and the price of cotton in New York increased 12 per cent....As soon as the price of cotton began to rise, cotton growers and others began to buy clothing. Cotton mills have steadily increased their activities. The rise in cotton, therefore, was due, first, to the depreciation of the dollar and, secondly, to the resulting increased demand for cotton.

But a further considerable reduction in the value of the dollar would be necessary, Warren argued, in order to restore equilibrium in the price structure. The current deflation, Warren argued, was linked to the post-World War I attempt to maintain the pre-World War I gold-based currency. It "had no relationship to any ordinary business cycle nor do we find a comparable situation in our previous history." As for the improvement since going off the gold standard in April, Warren wrote:

> It would be a great calamity to be deluded into thinking that the rise in prices which has come from a decline in the gold value of the dollar is due to currency, credit, or government control of agriculture and industry, all of which came later. None of these can succeed except as the gold content of the dollar is reduced, and if the gold content of the dollar is reduced by the right amount, none of these is necessary.

"The next fight," he predicted, "between the bitter-end deflationists and the reflationists will be over the amount of gold in the new dollar." International considerations should not figure into any decision in that regard. Rather, "The United States should revalue the dollar at the level which is best for our own internal affairs." The Committee for the Nation, he noted, recommended "that the price of gold be raised 75 per cent, or that the gold content of the dollar be reduced 42.8 per cent....This would bring quick recovery, quickly put men back to work, and quickly balance public budgets."[16]

Later in the month, the Committee fired off another salvo concerning the deflationary effects of the closed banks:

> The total of $2 1/2 billions of frozen deposits shown by the official Treasury figures as of June 28 refers only to banks open up to March 5th which have remained closed or restricted since then. It omits the 5,000 banks with estimated deposits of $5 billion closed during the depression but before March 5th. These 5,000 include the great number of large and important banks closed during January and February.
>
> The total of frozen deposits in commercial banks alone is therefore nearer $7 1/2 billion. The total deposits in all commercial banks now operating without restriction has been reduced to $31 3/4 billion.
>
> Thus nearly 20% of the deposit circulating medium of the country is frozen.
>
> Furthermore, to get a true perspective, we must take into consideration $7 1/2 billions of deposits under restrictions in savings banks as of May 31, not included in the Treasury's totals....

Bureaucratic control has made depositors, stockholders and bank management powerless to save themselves from unnecessary losses. Although the salvaging of bank assets is wholly in the hands of the Government, today, after five months, no adequate machinery to cope with this problem exists. The problem is attacked piecemeal, and has been handled largely under the influence of the deflationary interests that have sought to control monetary policy....

There has been some liberalization of policy since this Committee first called attention to the seriousness of frozen bank deposits. But most of the reformation of policy is still to be accomplished. Public opinion must demand it, and support the President in effecting it.[17]

Irving Fisher had for a long time advocated a commodity dollar similar to that championed by Warren, but by the 1930s he had begun to give priority in his writings to achieving that goal by adjusting the quantity of money, rather than the "quality" (i.e., the gold value), and had been busily lobbying the administration, or trying to do so. In the early 1920s, Fisher had been instrumental in organizing the Stable Money League to advocate the commodity dollar. In that year he published *Stabilizing the Dollar*, in which he wrote:

Our dollar is now simply a fixed weight of gold—a unit of weight, masquerading as a unit of value. It is almost as absurd to define a unit of value, or general purchasing power, in terms of weight, as to definite a unit of length in terms of weight. What we really want to know is whether the dollar buys as much as ever. We want a dollar which will always buy the same aggregate quantity of bread, butter, beef, bacon, beans, sugar, clothing, fuel and other essential things for which we spend it.[18]

What was needed, he wrote, was a

gold dollar fixed in purchasing power and therefore variable in weight. By adding new grains of gold to the dollar just fast enough to compensate for a loss in the purchasing power of each grain (and reversely) we can secure a stationary instead of a fluctuating dollar, in terms of purchasing power.

As for the mechanics of doing so:

What criterion is to guide the Government in making these changes in the dollar's weight? Am I proposing that some Government official should be authorized to mark the dollar up or down according to his own caprice? Most certainly not. A definite and simple criterion for the required adjustments is at hand—the now familiar "index number" of prices....For every one per cent of deviation of the index number above or below par at any adjustment date, we would increase or decrease the dollar's weight by one percent.—In other words, to keep the price level of other things from rising or falling we make the price of gold fall or rise.[19]

By the 1930s, the Stable Money League had passed through the National Monetary Association to become the Stable Money Association, headed by President Roosevelt's uncle, Frederic Delano, former member of the Federal Reserve Board, who served the New Deal as head of the National Planning Board, 1933-34, and then as chairman of the National Resources Board from 1935-38. Thus, just as Warren had his entree to the White House through Morgenthau, Fisher had his through Delano. Delano became president of the Association in 1929, only months before the stock market crash, with a distinguished list of founders and advisory board members that included leading economists, bankers, and businessmen. Delano, who served as the Association's increasingly unwilling president through its remaining history, viewed it as an instrument for research into the desirability and possibility of a stable dollar, and his view was shared by most of the more conservative founders and board members. As he put it in 1929, matters had advanced to the point where "we think a currency of uniform purchasing power is of great importance to the lender and to the borrower alike; to the employer, as well as to the wage earner; in short, to every class." However, none of the plans yet proposed had yet "proved sufficiently convincing to warrant adoption," and it was the purpose of the Association "to study the entire problem thoroughly, fairly, and without prejudice, to the end that a correct solution may be arrived at."[20]

With the onset of the Depression, however, the funds for such research dried up, and a more activist element in the Association turned to advocacy of the commodity dollar as a panacea that would produce recovery. By early 1931, Delano had become convinced that the Association, "with its present personnel, is absolutely useless if, indeed, it is not harmful." The people involved were "promoters," unequipped for "the work of thorough and unbiased education." Delano wrote to banker Fred Kent:

If the Association had absolutely no program except the recognition of the grave difficulties which are confronting us and an earnest desire to get at the fundamentals of our troubles, I should be in sympathy with it, even though there are already many research organizations in the field and though I doubt that the Stable Money Association gives promise to make a definite and valuable contribution in such educational work.

The Association, he added, had become "tainted with certain dogmas which willy nilly creep out here and there."[21]

In 1933, Delano appointed a committee to consider the future of the Association. As chairman of the committee, Irving Fisher wrote Delano in September 1933 that it had unanimously recommended "that the Stable Money Association should, in effect, be succeeded by the Committee for the Nation." James Rand, Jr., head of the Committee for the Nation, had agreed to the merger. Fisher continued:

it would be tacitly understood that no objection would be made to the C.F.N. [Committee for the Nation] soliciting the members of the Stable Money Association, and all connected with it in any way, to give their moral and financial support to the C.F.N. in any capacities which the C.F.N. may in each case desire.

This last would be the important contribution of the Stable Money Association. It has assembled the most influential group of sponsors in existence for the idea of stabilization and they can be of inestimable service for bringing about stabilization in the future. In particular their influence may well be enlisted to oppose and prevent any wild inflation beyond the limits set by Mr. Roosevelt.

As to inflation (or "reflation") up to those limits, the Stable Money Association, as such, is not concerned. It is concerned only with stabilization. The C.F.N., on the other hand, is concerned both with reflation and stabilization. Up to the present time it has been principally occupied with reflation; but the time will probably soon arrive when it will feel that that half of its job will have been finished. Up to that time it has the support both of the moderate relationists and of all inflationists. But the instant the C.F.N. calls a halt it may encounter opposition from many, especially in the west, who would go further. Then will be the time when most of those who have constituted the Stable Money Association can furnish the reinforcements needed in the interests of sanity and conservatism.

As to the problem of how to stabilize, that also is no concern of the S.M.A. as such. By its constitution it is stopped from advocating any particular plan. The C.F.N., on the other hand, aims at specific proposals, so that each member of the S.M.A. will have to decide for himself whether he approves of these proposals before accepting any invitation he may receive from the C.F.N.[22]

Thus, the activist element in the Stable Money Association could now join their counterparts in the Committee for the Nation in advocating reflationist policies based on the theories of Fisher and Warren.

In September, after a Rand meeting with Roosevelt, the Committee took up "a study as to what should be done with silver," since "very strong influences are pressing for some action and there are indications that it may have to be dealt with in some way."[23] The question was how could silver be included in a monetary program without interfering with the future of the stable dollar. New York international bankers would want to stick to gold alone, but the silver states had "representation far out of proportion to their population in the Senate" and held "important seats in the Senate and in the councils of the Administration." It was likely that Roosevelt would seek to placate these interests in both the Senate and House, and the supporters of a stable dollar could use their votes in its behalf in Congress. Bimetallism had been found impractical. Rumely concluded that

> The Committee can tie the silver support into the stable dollar only in one way—namely, making silver part of the metallic base into which the future commodity dollar is exchangeable. Such action is not merely a concession to win silver support. It is recognition of a fundamentally desirable and advantageous step for the following reasons.

For one, the value of two metals fluctuated less than one, and silver was more stable than gold, thus providing greater stability to the stable dollar. Since silver was a monetary metal in much of Asia, its use by the United States would promote trade with that part of the world. Rumely added:

> Professors Warren and Pearson are believers in symmetalism. They define this as a metallic base in which fixed and pre-determined proportions of silver and gold shall underlie the monetary unit.
>
> This fixed proportion does not, however, preclude a stepping up gradually of the proportion of silver as it becomes possible for the United States to accumulate a reserve stock of silver without upsetting the world's markets.[24]

Robert Wood agreed that "some method must be adopted to put silver in the program," and also that the "only practicable method" he saw for including it was through "the symmetalism plan proposed by Warren, and the only immediate program that I see is the authorization of the building up of a reserve and the purchase of a certain amount of silver by the government."[25]

Veteran progressive Amos Pinchot wrote Rumely in September that he felt at any moment the Committee was "due to go over the top, that is, it and circumstances will succeed in making the government take the needed step" toward the stable dollar. "Yet," Pinchot added, "I still have the feeling that something has got to bust, that a worse situation than now exists must arise before Roosevelt will use his real weapon."[26] A day later Rumely wrote his daughter that "The whole inflation drive is coming to a head. The President hesitates to use his powers but pressure is accumulating. It is probable that he will act before long."[27]

To further this along, the Committee sent its recommendations to Roosevelt on September 21. These included devaluing the dollar "to full limit of 50 percent, increasing price of gold to $41.34." The recommendation of $36.17 per ounce of three months earlier was no longer considered adequate to restore the price level. The implication was clearly that the economy had slipped during those three months. They also included announcing that the administration would "introduce a Bill to assure stability of normal purchasing power of the dollar that will hold average price-level at 100" (United States Bureau of Labor, 1926).[28]

In mid-October 1933, the Committee sounded the alarm, writing to its members:

> A major crisis threatens business and agriculture. Our price structure is collapsing because the Administration has returned control of the United States dollar to New York banking and Federal Reserve advisers.
>
> In a few days the gold value of the dollar has risen 8 cents and, in consequence, $10 billion of security and agricultural values were wiped out.
>
> No society, except in a period of disintegration, has ever allowed such irrational and destructive fluctuation of the purchasing power of its monetary unit....
>
> If the financial policies that have again become dominant are not overthrown, the producers of the country face years more of deflation, and the institutions of our free society are in jeopardy.
>
> The Directing Committee is exerting its influence in many different ways. Every member who endorses its program must help.[29]

"The opposition," wrote Rand, was "entrenched and powerful." Deflationists, who called themselves advocates of "sound money," were acting "in concert with those who wish by regimentation to socialize our institutions."[30]

In an October 16, 1933 memorandum for its members, the Committee drew the issue even more clearly:

In mid-July, certain advisers of the President threw their influences with the deflationists and gained the upper hand over monetary policy. This group holds the mistaken view-point that the free institutions of private property and private capitalism should be curbed and superseded in part by a regimented and regulated economy. This group felt that the farmers would not willingly submit to the controls that have been planned in connection with the establishment of a regimented, regulated state. Under this advice, the restoration of price level was checked....

Ever since the passage of the emergency legislation in March, the Administration has had it within its power to restore the price level of basic commodities within 90 days and, allowing for lags of slower moving factors, the general price level within a 6-months period. Since mid-July monetary policy has been dominated by a combination of those who desired to supersede capitalism by planned economy and a regimented state, the Administration's deflationary advisers and the Federal Reserve Bank of New York, cooperating with and reflecting the viewpoint urged by the bankers of London and Montagu Norman, Governor of the Bank of England.

Thus, despite the political victory of the South and the West, the same influences that dominated the policies of the Hoover Administration, again resumed control of U.S. Treasury policy....

Despite the Administration's early profession and announcement of a policy to restore the price level, the sweep of deflationary forces since March 4th has created greater damage, greater social and economic hardship and injustice than during the entire period from 1929 to March 4th....

There is but one hope — and that lies with the President. Will he free himself from the influence of those whose advice in the previous Administration brought the credit structure of the country to the brink of ruin?[30]

On October 21, the Committee dispatched a telegram to Roosevelt aboard the yacht, *Sequoia*, in Chesapeake Bay. Addressing the wave of farm discontent in the Midwest, the Committee wrote:

Farm strikes are merely symptoms of a general condition both critical and dangerous to our institutions. Ever since the founding of our republic, prosperous, land-owning farmers have been the real backing of our national stability....Only when his economic existence has been threatened, in periods of long deflation, has the farmer shown resentment.

Never in history has the economic position of the farmer been so deeply undermined. Never have so many farmers lost their homes.

The cause, as the Committee had pointed out time and again, was the loss of farm purchasing power and the necessity to devalue the dollar in order to restore it.

From April 18 to July 18 while the price of gold was increasing and the country believed that your Administration would go through with a program of monetary reform, the price level for farm products continued to rise. Prices reached levels which, had they been sustained, would have averted present farm unrest.[31]

A month later, the Committee totaled up the damage since July, when the dollar had been allowed to rise in value by 8 cents, equivalent to an increase of 12 ½ percent, causing by mid-July the destruction of "15 to 20 billions of restored values" of all types. "Only our worst enemy could plan for such irrational and unnecessary swings in the purchasing power of our money....Formulating plans to release 1 billion of bank deposits and putting seven cabinet members on the radio to explain the benefits of NRA will not neutralize such destruction of values." The only solution was to carry through the devaluation of the dollar. "Delay has cost us billions. How much longer must the producers of this country suffer from a senseless deflation senselessly prolonged?"[32]

In October, Fisher pleaded with Roosevelt to speed up reflationary actions, telling the president: "Delay is helping the opposition gather momentum and is fast becoming ruinous to business."[33] A few days later, responding particularly to agrarian unrest over the failure of the AAA, Roosevelt sought a "white rabbit" by acceding to the monetarists. In a fireside chat on October 22, Roosevelt told the nation that he was

going to establish a Government market for gold in the United States. Therefore, under the clearly defined authority of existing law, I am authorizing the Reconstruction Finance Corporation to buy gold newly mined in the United States at prices to be determined from time to time after consultation with the Secretary of the Treasury and President. Whenever necessary to the end in view, we shall also buy or sell gold in the world market.

It was, Roosevelt said, "a policy and not an expedient," another step "toward a managed currency."[34]

The announcement of the new policy aroused a storm of criticism in the press and among economists. Critics watched commodity prices as avidly as did Roosevelt and the monetarists, looking for evidence of its effect. After four days it had shown so little effect that Roosevelt expanded the program to include purchases of gold in foreign markets. *Newsweek* took a look at George Warren, to whom the "role of the Devil in the miracle play that furious dissenters seem to think is being staged around America's currency," calling him "the demon of the rubber dollar." Warren, they reported, occupied an office "buried somewhere in the magnificent labyrinth of the Department of Commerce Building," where the phone was never answered and knocks on the door evoked, at best, "a voice saying: 'Not in!'" The "invisible" Dr. Warren was never seen entering the White House, and speculation had it that he traveled between the friendly confines of the Treasury Building and the White House using the tunnel that connected them. *Newsweek* wrote:

> Mr. Warren knew Franklin Roosevelt as a farmer and as Governor long ago. He has had some of his most important talks with the President while they were on railroad trains rolling over farm land. Whenever these meetings are observed they are apt to reach the headlines. "Roosevelt confers with Warren, observers believe currency change imminent" got to be an old story last Summer [1932][3]

Amid the storm of criticism, Frank Vanderlip, Wall Street banker and one of the organizers of the Committee for the Nation, went to the defense of the policy with a radio talk in which he told his listeners that the commodity dollar offered "the one feasible defense against the danger of unlimited currency inflation." He explained:

> Fear of currency inflation is one of the chief reasons why I should like to see the commodity dollar tested, and if the test proves satisfactory, adopted. The commodity dollar provides a definite stopping place for inflation. The price index, rather than a printing press, dominates. Rising prices would be corrected by it with the same methods that falling prices were brought back to the agreed level.
> If we can escape the dangers of currency inflation through the commodity dollar, and at the same time insure a stable currency, which will perma-

nently have a level purchasing power for the average run of goods, we shall have created a new mechanism which the whole world be likely to adopt.[36]

A week later, James H. Rand of Remington Rand, one of the founders of the Committee for the Nation, complained to Warren that:

> The President has not used many of the powers of the Thomas Amendment....The one measure that he is using is the gold buying measure; IT SEEMS TO ME AS AN OUTSIDE OBSERVER THAT THIS OUGHT TO BE USED WITH MAXIMUM SPEED; certainly, in any event, to get to $41.34 [double the previous price of $20.67] by December 15, so that there will be a few weeks before Congress convenes to see the effects of dollar devaluation before we are pushed for further action.[37]

The Committee instantly wrote its members asking them to "wire President Roosevelt immediately" to commend him on the step, because he would "need all the support and encouragement which members of this Committee can give him" against the influence of the deflationists.[38]

A few weeks later, Robert Wood wrote Rumley to suggest that the Committee support Henry Morgenthau as a candidate for treasury secretary. Morgenthau, it will be recalled was a student of George Warren at Cornell. Wood also wrote that he had talked to Forbes Morgan, "who was active on the Democratic National Committee, who is a personal friend of the President and who is with us heart and soul in this monetary matter. He is connected with the Farm Loan Board, is close to Morgenthau and is a powerful ally in Washington."[39]

Late in November, Rumely released a long interoffice memorandum to members of the directing committee in which he wrote that they were "now at that critical moment when resistance has been broken down but when, in mopping up, we can easily lose the fruits of a whole year's work." Rumors were in the air of compromises. "Most serious, however," Rumely wrote, "are the reports of intended temporary stabilization by the Administration and of reported assurances...to European central banks that the gold price will not be raised beyond a certain point." Rumely had heard from a usually reliable quarter that Roosevelt "did not believe public opinion ripe for going through with his program" and that he was preparing to "retreat to a compromise position." Rumely went on:

Henry Morgenthau, Jr., has the advantage of complete insight and intellectual understanding of Professor Warren's work. He is a pupil of Cornell,
firmly convinced of the soundness of Warren's theory, is a long, close friend
of the President, and this friendship is one of the major national assets,
tending as it does to cement the President to the sources of right knowledge and understanding on financial matters. Mr. Morgenthau has not had
administrative experience on a vast scale. He and Professors Warren and
Pearson are highly intellectual. Men of that type are not usually the tough,
tenacious, fighting and administrative type needed to carry through. Our
whole program can now be crippled or partly defeated by the absence of
the tenacity and administrative ability in carrying it into effect.

Rumely was also concerned over the interpretation the administration put on public opinion. He was convinced that they were
overestimating the importance of the press, which tended to be
against the monetary policy, but seemed to be unrepresentative of
public sentiment, which supported it.

Rumely wrote, with emphasis: "WE SHALL NOT HAVE PO-
LITICAL REST AND CONDITIONS OF STABILITY FREE FROM
RADICAL AND COMMUNISTIC TENDENCIES UNLESS WE GET
FOR THE FARMER A PRICE OF GOLD HIGH ENOUGH TO RE-
STORE TO HIM FULL PROSPERITY. THEN, INSTEAD OF A
FOCUS OF RADICALISM, FARM OWNERS WILL BE THE BUL-
WARK OF CAPITALISM." The administration must be brought to
realize that "the overwhelming strength and numbers are on the
side of its announced program....Vacillation, delay and hesitation
will lose the position that has been gained. Today prompt, decisive
action, with rising prices, is the best indication of the President's
program."

Rumely went on: "The Committee's telegram yesterday to Messrs.
Henry Morgenthau, Jr., and Jesse H. Jones analyzed the consequences of the indecision of the previous week as reflected in the
sagging markets." The telegram read as follows:

Reports current in high financial circles suggest that monetary program
will be superseded by unannounced stabilization as it was last July. Also
that foreign bankers have been informed that price of gold will not be
raised beyond predetermined figure which is specified as substantially
under Forty-one Dollars needed to restore 1926 prices stop. The fact that
the dollar has been allowed to regain seven percent of its abnormal purchasing power and that gold price has remained unchanged gives unfavor-
able significance to these reports stop. If feeble execution or failure to

proceed with announced program prevent a substantial price rise public will attribute this failure to unsoundness of program itself stop. Hesitation has already been seized upon to undermine support of the President. New York Evening Sun tonight says "Gold buying called failure." Instead of rising prices which should furnish most powerful support in public opinion, supporters of the President's program are confronted with seriously adverse influences which are developing as a result of failure to act.[40]

That same day Rumely had sent a long letter to presidential confidante, Louis McHenry Howe, on the propaganda battle that was raging between opponents and supporters of Roosevelt's gold buying initiative. He wished, he told Howe, that the latter could have been present in New York City to see "two meetings on the monetary question—one held in Carnegie Hall by the Crusaders organization, financed for this special purpose by wealthy opponents of the President's program." They had used, Rumely said, "the ballyhoo methods of a circus, having siren cars with banners running through the streets and substantial paid advertising," but Carnegie Hall was no more than two-thirds filled, with many of those supporters of the president. The meeting in support of the gold buying program had been organized around Father Coughlin. Rumely wrote that newspapers had estimated the attendance at 20,000, and that a veteran newsman said he had never seen so much enthusiasm at a meeting of any kind—both during and after it. Coughlin's speech had also been broadcast on the radio. Concerned that the Roosevelt administration was gauging public sentiment from the newspapers, Rumely wrote:

Radio is interpreting this issue instead of the newspapers. Never since radio was born has there been an issue as vital and close to the interests and as moving to the masses of our people as this issue of rebuilding prices and purchasing power. To the whole United States, it means freeing them from bondage of debt and fixed charges to the creditor classes.

Within the present weeks, as I told you, we are running 500 fifteen-minute electrical transcriptions, after running about 500 some weeks earlier. In addition, we have had five national hookups for radio broadcast and have mailed all newspaper editors, financial editors, Washington correspondents, etc. of daily and agricultural press, weekly and sometimes several times a week. The clippings from the press and the vast mail that we receive give us an index of public opinion.

The press does not begin to reflect this issue as the radio does. Our thousands of letters, Father Coughlin's 750,000 letters tell the real story. Were we to rely upon the clippings, we should get a most inadequate picture....

So far as the farmers are concerned, their very existence as a prosperous economic group is at stake in getting a price of $41.34 for gold, which is that to which the English colonies were restored long ago. With the greater debt and fixed charge burden, our American farmer should really have a price of $45 to put him on equality.

The danger that now exists is that the Administration may not recognize that it has won its victory and move to decisive action. The most powerful force in the world is self-interest. A rising price level will convince all who are being benefited. There are six millions of farm owners and farm operators who will gain enormously as the market for basic commodities rises with the price of gold. There are more than millions of home owners and 15 millions of security owners who will benefit. A rising price level always means rapidly increasing jobs. A rising price level means profit to the two or three million individuals who are the mainsprings of our capitalistic system. All these will be with the President, provided only the price level is rising.[41]

But by mid-November it appeared that the gold-buying program was causing weakness in the government bond market and a flight of capital from the United States, and it had caused important and well-publicized departures from the Treasury Department, including Undersecretary Dean Acheson and Dr. O.M.W. Sprague. Acheson left quietly, convinced that the gold-buying program was illegal, but, as New Dealer Thomas Corcoran observed, "F.D.R. was stubbornly arbitrary, didn't give a damn for the law." Sprague, in particular, left with a blast at Roosevelt's policies for threatening "a complete breakdown of the credit of the Government." He intended, he said, to play an active role in arousing public opposition to inflation.

So did other economists, who soon formed the Economists National Committee on Monetary Policy to oppose Roosevelt's monetary policies. They were, thereafter, able to checkmate much of the influence of the Committee for the Nation.

In mid-December the prestigious Brookings Institution concluded that "no definite predictable rise in the commodity price level can be assumed to follow a given depreciation of the currency," nor could commodity prices "be automatically controlled by altering the price of gold." the *Economist*, too, concluded that the program had produced no effect on commodity prices, and had only served to weaken Government securities.

For the Committee of the Nation, however, the lack of success was only evidence that Roosevelt had not gone far enough. As J.H. Rand, Jr. wrote to Warren:

Instead of making chalk marks on the blackboard with the daily announcement of a theoretical price for gold, we must establish the machinery that
will make the price set by our government a mandate controlling the purchasing power of the dollar the world over.

We must have an unlimited buying market....

The moment we declare ourselves willing to buy all the gold offered,
the anomaly of having the world abroad disregard the theoretical price that
we set and of having foreign financial centers hold the purchasing power
of our dollar at a higher price to suit their interests, will cease.

Our gold buying policy up to now has been a fiction with limited psychological influence. It must be made a reality.[42]

Certainly Roosevelt's approach to setting the price of gold devi-
ated considerably from the "scientific" approach that Fisher had
insisted upon in *Stabilizing the Dollar.* Roosevelt's approach was
capricious and light-hearted. Rather than tying changes to the price
index, Roosevelt chose "lucky" numbers and whims as the basis
for increases that were made daily.

The *Nation* found in December that within "Wall Street lurks a
dissension in the ranks which belies the apparent unanimity of opinion in the financial world in opposition to experiments with the
currency." There were, it wrote, "genuine differences of opinion
on the respective merits of inflation and deflation," as well as the
"conflict of special interests." The "orthodox bankers and conservative business men" were unified against the "soft dollar," but the
"speculative and gambling fraternity of Wall Street" was not so
nearly opposed. The *Nation* went on:

The fight for the soft dollar in Wall Street has...been abandoned to a group
of business men who have thrown off the discipline of orthodox economics and turned toward the activities of the Committee for the Nation to
Rebuild Prices and Purchasing Power. This organization...has embraced as
its main doctrine the theory of the managed dollar propounded by Professors Warren and Pearson, a circumstance which probably explains a good
part of the committee's success in transforming its policies into established
governmental procedure. Its record presents an interesting corollary to the
development of the Roosevelt monetary program.

"The committee's technique," it pointed out, included "extensive use of radio broadcasting and newspaper publicity and circulation of its reports among Congressmen and members of the Administration, supplemented by personal and individual pressure."

Its members were, for the most part, businesses that maintained "a large export business," or which were heavily dependent on "farm purchasing power, or with the commodity and stock prices."[43]

Veteran banker Frank A. Vanderlip was receptive to many of the ideas floated by the Committee for the Nation. In his book, *Tomorrow's Money*, published in 1932 and revised in 1933, Vanderlip took a position somewhat closer to the "quantity" reflationists than to the "quality" ones. The nation, he pointed out, had been "experiencing a financial and economic chaos unexampled in the world's history," one whose events had "so intimately clutched the lives of every man, woman and child as to become a universal, although utterly abnormal, experience." One product of it all was that:

> Orthodox theory and orthodox practice in financial matters seem no longer to fit the facts. Outdated economic principles still linger in superstitious attachment to fetishes. Such solid handgrips as the gold standard, "sound money," the sacred integrity of contracts, have become insecure.[44]

A primary difficulty, Vanderlip concluded, lay in the "old" gold standard, and the delusion that by fixing the value of the dollar at a specified amount of gold, a dollar of standard value was created. In fact, of course, the value of gold fluctuated as wildly as did any other commodity, meaning that the dollar, too, fluctuated widely in value, even though those fluctuations were generally expressed in terms of the fluctuating prices of the things that were purchased by the dollars. It was not, however, the price of wheat, for example, that was fluctuating, Vanderlip pointed out, but the value of the gold-based dollar with which the wheat was being purchased.

Advances in statistics in the 1920s, and particularly in the creation of price indexes, had made this much clearer than before. Vanderlip wrote:

> On the testimony of these compilations the purchasing value--which is the real value—of the old dollar, instead of being a fixed standard, has fluctuated wildly in recent years....The gold dollar had long been defined by law as consisting of 23.22 grains of gold. But that unvarying weight of gold has not behaved at all like an unvarying measure of value. Between 1896 and 1920 the purchasing power of this 23.22 grains of gold declined two-thirds....It is an amusing illustration of the way this so-called gold yardstick shrinks and expands to take prices that were average for 1913, just before the outbreak of the Great War to be a standard yardstick 36 inches

long. On that basis the gold dollar yardstick in 1920 had shrunk to less than 20 inches and was something over 50 inches long in 1926. In 1932 it had contracted again to about 27 inches.[45]

After reviewing the failures of the old gold standard in the face of uncontrolled international capital movements and domestic hoarders, Vanderlip concluded that the old gold standard had been made as outmoded as trench warfare had outmoded cavalry.

Regarding the Roosevelt administration's gold-buying program of late 1933, Vanderlip wrote:

> It first made a higher price for domestically mined gold. That naturally had little or no effect on the world gold price. Then we made some quite tentative purchases of gold in England and France. The object, of course, was not to acquire gold, but to reduce the value of the dollar measured in terms of gold....The Treasury marked up on its black-board a daily price for gold and, for a time, daily increased that price. It bought some gold at the published price, and so we saw the spectacle of a nominal price for gold named by the Treasury but a lower price in the foreign exchange market. The only way for us to have made an effective gold price was to have offered dollars unlimitedly for gold, wherever located and of whatever origin. That would have instantly harmonized the price as exhibited in the foreign exchange market with our dictated price.[46]

However, Vanderlip recognized that the legality of purchase of gold by the RFC was suspect.

Vanderlip advocated a new gold standard under which paper money could be redeemed in gold only when used in settling foreign trade balances. It would be managed by a non-partisan Federal Monetary Authority, which would absorb many of the functions of the Federal Reserve Board and Treasury. Among its powers would be that of adjusting the nation's money supply in order to stabilize the purchasing power of the dollar. In January, 1934, he noted, Roosevelt had depreciated the dollar by revaluing it at 13.74 grains of pure gold. Vanderlip explained:

> The motive for devaluating the dollar and reducing the number of grains of gold for which it is exchangeable lies in the belief that a general rise in prices is necessary in order to make the country solvent, in view of the enormous debt structure which was incurred, in the main, on a level of prices far higher than the present level.

The year 1926 has been rather generally accepted as offering a price level to which it is desirable to return. The 1926 price level is regarded as "normal" because it happens to be about the average of the decade from 1920 to 1929.[47]

Vanderlip, however, did not agree that the gold value of the dollar should be altered in order to bring it into accord with the 1926 price level, since his Federal Monetary Authority would be able to accomplish the same objective through adjustments in the quantity of money in circulation.[48] Reviewing what he called the Fisher-Warren theory, Vanderlip wrote that alterations in the gold content of the dollar would doubtless affect the price level, but he did not believe "that the reaction on the price level would be prompt, nor would there be a mathematical correspondence between the change in the gold content and the change in the price level, although over a long period there might be an approximately close relation."[49] Roosevelt's gold-buying experiment had been only "partially successful" and had "demonstrated that the process of price change takes time." Vanderlip wrote that even if the gold content of the dollar "had been more steadily and firmly depreciated than has been the case, the price level certainly would not have immediately responded with mathematical accuracy."[50]

An unstable dollar was destructive of the instinct for thrift and provision for one's old age. Where was the incentive to save when there was no guarantee that the dollars put away today would be worth anything when needed?[51] A "reasonably efficient government," Vanderlip wrote:

> should provide its citizens with three things in the way of economic machinery with which to carry on the business of living: First, a monetary system that is free from dismaying fluctuations; second, a banking system stable enough to make it reasonably certain that depositors can get their money back without damming up the flow of credit that makes jobs and wages; and third, a long-time stability in the purchasing value of the dollar and system of investments that makes it desirable and safe to save money.

These were "the backbone of thrift, and thrift is the backbone of the world as we have known it."[52] As for the popularity of the commodity dollar concept, Vanderlip wrote that it resulted precisely from the "great public demand for a dollar that will remain approximately the same in value from one year to the next," but he was convinced that by giving his envisaged Federal Monetary Authority control over currency and credit, the same objective could be achieved "without resorting to such radical expedients as the various commodity dollar schemes present."[53]

Like other proponents of a monetary solution to the Depression, Vanderlip was disturbed by the tendencies he witnessed in the New Deal, writing that the times were filled with confusion into which

> there have been injected into our political, economic and social order such unprecedented expedients as the plowing up of growing crops, government payments to individual farmers to induce them to let land lie fallow, the wholesale slaughtering of more than five million hogs, the enforced adoption of hundreds of industrial codes, the projection of huge public works to be paid for at government expense and the employment of millions of men at public expense for civil works of doubtful economic value and at wages frequently higher than the current industrial scale. For the first time rates of wages and hours of work have been sweepingly dictated by government edict.

To this was added a governmental effort to "reform the moral code of the business world" by removing traditional practices through "the surgical knife of government dictation," chief among which was the Securities of Act of 1933, which had been "drawn on the new principle of caveat venditor."[54]

All of this had created "the great conundrum of the times." Vanderlip explained:

> Is it the object of the effective political power to restore the opportunity for business profits in order that capitalism can be repaired and continued? Or is its real object a regimented, managed economy which spells the end of the capitalistic system? The destruction of the capitalistic system need not mean tearing it down brick by brick. Business profits are the foundation of capitalism. Remove them and the whole giant structure, apparently firmly established up to the last moment, would crumble into a cloud of dust. The possibility of an attack upon the foundations of capitalism has raised fundamental fears in the minds of those who believe that the old capitalistic order has borne fruit in the highest material civilization ever attained and who fear that its destruction will be followed by an unworkable communism.[55]

The "general belief that there is something wrong with our social and economic system which can be cured through our own efforts" was the basis for the "astounding acceptance of President Roosevelt's leadership, an acceptance so complete that Congress hardly has the courage to discuss, much less vote against legislative proposals originating with the Administration." The delegations of power by Congress to the President early in 1933 were "unquestionably necessary," and there was broad support for the administration's subsequent actions. What was now needed was the creation of "an adequate mechanism for a new, permanent and logical gold standard. The need for a managed currency and the methods for its management are emerging more clearly." For the future, Vanderlip envisioned

> an order in which the hand of government will have greater force in our business life. That by no means indicates that we are facing the necessity for socialized banking and a regimented life. It has merely become obvious that there are some things that business cannot do for itself, and that a wise and restrained government can do those things to the great benefit of business and of all the people. We should accept, and accept gladly, some extension of government powers and give up, also gladly, some of the old laissez faire "rugged individualism" which was, in some cases, really piratical anarchy."[56]

While the monetarists could rationalize the failure of the gold-buying program among themselves, for others that failure had discredited the movement. Leo Pasvolsky of the Brookings Institution noted that numerous devices were being used in an attempt to raise prices—the AAA, NRA, public works, relief expenditures, and cheapening of credit:

> Even if one were to argue that these policies, singly or conjointly, have had no effect whatever in raising prices in the United States, and that the rise which has occurred is the result solely of the depreciation of the dollar, it still remains true that the extent of the rise in the general level of prices shows little correspondence with the rise in the price of gold. The great disparity between the two movements furnishes conclusive evidence that the theory of automatic adjustments between changes in the price of gold and changes in the commodity price level is without scientific validity.[57]

Former Democratic presidential candidate Al Smith was more succinct in suggesting that professors of agricultural economics should stick to educating their students.[58]

Late in December the noted English economist John Maynard Keynes responded to a request from the *New York Times* that he write an "open letter" to Roosevelt. In his letter, Keynes suggested that the president introduce some stability into the monetary picture by announcing that he would control the dollar exchange at a definite figure. Scarcely two weeks later, Roosevelt moved to introduce the monetary stability Keynes had recommended. The Gold Reserve Act gave him the authority to devalue the dollar to a point between fifty and sixty cents in gold, and Roosevelt set the value of the dollar at 59.06 cents by establishing the price of gold at $35, the figure which the reflationists had recommended heretofore. But the failure of prices to rise commensurate with the devaluation of the past weeks had led the reflationists to conclude that the price of gold should be raised even further.

Still, Fisher and the reflationists took some satisfaction from the president's action, Fisher writing his son that Roosevelt's signing of the bill into law had been a "proud moment." He wondered how much the president realized "that his monetary policy goes back to me in large part—through Warren and Rogers and Rand, as well as directly."[59] But Fisher couldn't "help feeling that the president could have gone much faster if he hadn't mixed in so many things which were holding us back instead of getting us out of the depression." In this category, he included the NRA, agreeing with economist Willford King that it was "a National Retardation Affair."[60]

The gold-buying episode was the high tide of influence by the Committee for the Nation. The failure of the effort, for whatever reason, to live up to the claims and expectations of its backers tended to discredit the entire issue of monetary reform among all but its most devoted supporters. While they would continue to advocate the commodity dollar to an unlistening administration and public, the focus of the Committee hereafter would be primarily defensive rather than offensive, negative rather than positive, agitating against those pieces of legislation that they opposed, and offering the commodity dollar as the preferred alternative.

Looking back at the ten months of "struggle over monetary policy" in the United States, economist Bernhard Ostrolenk found it had been waged between "the forces of entrenched wealth" who included "the holders of $40,000,000,000 of riskless bonds, who can now get more for their interest coupons than at any time since 1914," along with a legion of "hard money economists," on the one hand, and a variety of influences on the other, that included Warren and Pearson, who had "indoctrinated with their ideas thousands of students who have gone out as farm leaders," including Treasury Secretary Henry Morgenthau, "a close friend of the President," the Farm Bureau Federation, and the Committee for the Nation, "headed by bankers, industrialists, exporters and others." The Committee's program, based on Warren's studies, "had a way of gradually unfolding itself as administration policies during the Summer and Winter of 1933." Roosevelt, he found, had clearly embraced the views of those "who believe that deflation is an unjust form of economic adjustment," who wanted "to re-establish a price level that will, as nearly as possible, repair the injustice of the deflation and then keep the price level constant." When Roosevelt had embarked on his gold-buying program late in 1933, the "hard money advocates," including business associations and college professors, had "launched a vigorous campaign for the immediate stabilization of the dollar." Discussion had reached a "fever heat" with the resignation of Dr. O.M.W. Sprague as special advisor to the Treasury Department, but Roosevelt, said Ostrolenk, had shown "no sign of being perturbed," and despite "the flood of propaganda which poured upon the country from great financial houses, orthodox economists and conservative publicists, public confidence in the President remained unshaken." The result, he said, was that the debate had shifted from one between hard money and inflation to one over the "various methods of dollar depreciation and the point at which stabilization was desirable."[61] This growing acceptance of the necessity for devaluation must, it would seem, be largely attributed to the educational and lobbying efforts of the Committee for the Nation.

3

The Decline of the Committee for the Nation

In 1934, Harry Elmer Barnes published "A Candid Analysis of the Inflation Controversy," entitled *Money Changers vs. The New Deal*. In it, Barnes took a position on the causes of the Depression that was similar to that of David Cushman Coyle, in arguing that the rich had cornered too much of the wealth in the 1920s, but had not spend it, leaving little to the working classes who would have. Thus, purchasing power was moved from those who might have spent it, and concentrated in the hands of those who didn't, depriving the capitalist engine of the fuel that could maintain it "in a state of health and growth." Worse than this, as Coyle was pointing out elsewhere "the rich ultimately spend the sums they have saved to intensify some of the worst evils of the capitalistic system," by investing it in the

> construction of industrial plans with which we are already gravely over-stocked, to advance credit to speculative enterprises that jeopardize legitimate industry, to promote the accumulation of debt through installment contracts, and for over-construction in apartments and skyscrapers which are either unneeded or beyond the economic reach of those who do need them.[1]

The United States, Barnes noted, was "faced by a more persistent demand for inflation than has existed at any time since the momentous campaign of 1896." The reason was "the increased value of the gold dollar and the corresponding fall in prices," which had created a "Utopia for those who owe no debts, pay no taxes and have a high fixed salary which has not been cut," but an "Inferno for those who are in debt, must pay ever increasing taxes and find their income menaced by wage cuts, a decline in the prices of farm products, and the like." The only class seriously harmed by inflation were "the vested creditor interests, absentee owners and the like." "It is too bad," Barnes wrote, "if these groups are injured, but their interests hardly transcend those of the rest of the community."[2] "The plain fact," he wrote, was that "if some degree of inflation is necessary for recovery, then it is bound to help everybody to some extent."[3]

Indeed, Barnes wrote, nothing that even the most extreme inflationists advocated could do as much damage to the economy "as did Hoover and Mills by their deflationist policies" from 1929 to 1933.[4] Those who opposed Roosevelt's inflationary policies were "chiefly the money changers whom he promised to drive from the temple, though he has thus far notably failed to make good this promise."[5] "If anybody is to run printing presses," he wrote, "the money changers wish to be in charge," but Barnes reminded his readers that when the bankers had been in charge their "follies and chicanery brought about the failure of over 16,000 banks since 1920, losses of more than $5,000,000,000 in deposits," and these were "the men who are now raising their voices for soundness, stability, caution, conservatism, the welfare of widows and orphans and the like."[6]

Roosevelt, Barnes wrote, seemed "to approach no major problem with any impregnable dogmas," but rather to have surrounded himself with men drawn from many schools of thought," which accounted for some of the inconsistency and lack of continuity in his policies. But for his monetary policies, the president seemed to have relied primarily on Warren and Professor James Harvey Rogers of Yale. Roosevelt, however, did not seem willing to put all of his recovery eggs in the Warren basket, but preferred to use monetary reform as but one part of his strategy for battling the Depression. Yet, in Roosevelt's monetary policies one could "easily detect the deep influence of Professor Warren's doctrine and advice." Barnes cited Roosevelt's message to the London Economic Conference: "Let me be frank in saying that the United States seeks the kind of dollar which a generation hence will have the same purchasing power and debt-paying power as the dollar value we hope to attain in the near future." That he had not changed his mind was clear from his address to Congress on January 3, 1934, in which Roosevelt had said that he was desirous of "arriving eventually at a medium of exchange which will have over the years less variable purchasing and debt paying power for our people than that of the past."

But in actual practice the president had been timid and indecisive. Such improvement as had taken place, Barnes pointed out, had been triggered mainly by anticipation of inflation rather than by the real thing.[7] Barnes wrote: "We shall over the next year have an opportunity to judge the validity of Professor Warren's theories. As we have seen, he believes that there is a direct and positive relation between the value of gold in terms of the dollar and the commodity price level." Prices needed to be raised 67 percent over those of March, 1933, to reach the 1926 level. According to the Warren doctrine, this could be accomplished by raising the price of gold by 67 percent over the fixed legal price of $20.67—or to $34.52 an ounce.

> On January 11th [1934] the price paid by the Reconstruction Finance Corporation for gold was $34.06—an increase of almost 67 per cent. But commodity prices have not yet risen in any close relationship to the jump in the price of gold. They had only been boosted about 20 per cent by January 11th. The dollar is still worth about $1.40 in terms of the 1926 dollar.
>
> It is only fair to wait for a time to see if commodity prices will slowly but surely follow the marked rise in the price of gold. If they do not, the Warren doctrine will suffer a severe blow in prestige. Even if it should prove a failure, however, the discrediting of this particular device to produce reflation would have no bearing upon the merits of the inflation issue viewed as a whole.[8]

Barnes concluded that none of the inflationary proposals current in America would "be likely to jeopardize seriously the economic foundations of the nation." On the contrary, "Deflation and sound money, in the conventional sense of the term, are Public Enemy Number One in the monetary realm." Most of these proposals were, in fact, reflationary, rather than inflationary, since they sought only the limited goal of "restoration of a practicable price level which would enable capitalistic enterprise to resume activity and function smoothly....They aim to help us escape in part from the crushing burden of debt to a past full of folly and injustice—without which escape there is no hope for our capitalistic economy."[9] He concluded:

The sensible way in which to regard the whole inflation controversy is to recognize that decisive reflation is an incidental but indispensable item in a broad gauge assault upon rugged individualism and the dominion of the money changers.

If we wish to reform and preserve capitalism for any considerable period, we must concentrate our efforts upon assuring mass purchasing power and conserving the interests of the consumer. Finance   c a p i t a l i s m must be ended.[10]

In this way, Barnes straddled the positions of the reflationists and David Cushman Coyle.

In January, the Committee broadcast a letter to members of the House and Senate and to presidential advisors that commended Roosevelt for his "leadership in formulating the aims of a new national monetary policy." "His action to nationalize our gold is the first fundamental step to a unified currency system." What was now needed was an "arm of the government" that would make those policies effective. Once again the Committee was supporting a bill in Congress that would provide "the mechanism for giving stability to the purchasing power of money." Rand wrote:

The pending gold bill concentrates monetary authority in the hands of the Secretary of the Treasury. Such concentration raises serious doubts in the minds of many, as it combines the functions of currency issue in the same hands that must borrow for and meet government expenditures.

The draft bill attached hereto creates a Federal Monetary Authority, coordinate but entirely independent of the Treasury, responsible to the Congress, but free from political control. In such an institution the best monetary knowledge of the country could be centered and a body of experience developed such as is possessed by the central banks which serve other nations.[11]

To Senator Duncan Fletcher, chair of the Senate Committee on Banking and Currency, Rand wired that stabilizing at 60 percent, such as New York and London bankers expected to happen after the gold bill was passed, would leave America in "serious deflation and our price level may be kept permanently so low that it will endanger our institutions." Congress was entrusted by the Constitution with the power to regulate the purchasing power of the nation's money, and that function should not be relinquished permanently by Congress to one cabinet member. The Committee asked permission to appear before Fletcher's committee to testify against the bill.[12] Meanwhile, the Committee had asked the NICB to study the bill for its possible deflationary aspects.[13]

In March 1934, the Committee mailed out a form letter signed by James H. Rand, Jr., in which he wrote:

> Secretary [of Agriculture] Wallace says America is at the fork of the road and must choose—"fated for grave adjustments, with no chance to turn back."
>
> He recommends taking the "planned middle course" of regimentation on which the Department of Commerce has started. We believe that course leads inevitably to the extreme "LEFT," to abandonment of our inherited institutions, to a completely socialized state. Is that America's choice? Do we realize what it means?
>
> The alternative is prompt restoration of our price level through immediate increase in the price of gold ($41.34 an ounce is needed). That would end the need for regimentation. That course leads back to our historic institutions of freedom that gave us the greatest wealth and power ever enjoyed by any nation.[14]

The credibility of the Committee was, however, further rocked by the publicity that accompanied the Wirt incident in April 1934. William Wirt, a distinguished educator in Gary, Indiana, where he was superintendent of schools, was also a member of the Committee for the Nation. Deeply disturbed over the collectivist tendencies in Washington, he arranged a meeting with a number of lower-echelon New Dealers, including David Cushman Coyle, and reported on it in a letter to James Rand. Rand produced the letter while testifying against the Stock Exchange Bill before the House Interstate Commerce Committee and it immediately created a furor and a Congressional investigation of Wirt's charges that the New Dealers were bent on thwarting recovery from the Depression in order that they might carry out the collectivization of the country using Roosevelt as their "Kerensky." One of the New Dealers had allegedly said: "We believe we have Mr. Roosevelt in the middle of a swift stream and that the current is so strong that he cannot turn back or escape from it. We believe we can keep Mr. Roosevelt there until we are ready to supplant him with a Stalin." In the ensuing testimony before the committee, however, the other participants insisted that it had been Wirt, himself, who dominated the conversation, giving the others little opportunity to get in even a word.

Still, Wirt's letter expressed misgivings and suspicions about those around Roosevelt that were becoming more widespread as the New Deal completed two years without any visible improvement in the number of unemployed and those drawing welfare benefits. Columnist Walter Lippmann concluded that "the conviction that recovery is being held back is the basis of the outcry against the Brain Trust, and the reason why, in spite of the collapse of Dr. Wirt's charges, the Brain Trust is increasingly unpopular." It was certainly true, as Wirt had charged, that all of the New Deal legislation, "from A.A.A. to the Stock Market Bill," had the effect of constricting enterprise.[15]

Interestingly, after Wirt died in 1940, former Congressman John O'Connor, who was a victim of Roosevelt's purge in 1938 after years as a loyal New Dealer, issued a statement on the Wirt matter. O'Connor had been one member of the three-man New Deal majority on the committee, and he recounted in his statement, "Confession is Good for the Soul," how they had prevented the two Republicans on the committee from conducting a fair investigation of Wirt's charges, how they had denied Wirt's lawyer the opportunity to cross-examine the six participants (including the correspondent for Tass, the Soviet news agency), and how the testimony had been "staged," it being well known that they had met and "rehearsed their denials of what they had told Dr. Wirt."[16] Nevertheless, the alleged quotes were little different from what many of the New Dealers were saying in private correspondence and public conversations. In January 1932, for example, George Soule of the *New Republic* wrote to Rexford Tugwell soliciting an article, telling the brain truster that "if we began to plan at all, as we must, we should have a bear by the tail and could not let go, until at some time in the future we should find that we had set up a Socialist economy."[17] And once the New Deal was underway, Bruce Bliven of the *New Republic* quoted a New Dealer as having told him:

> Two things to remember. First, that what is now being done can never be undone. If the New Deal succeeds we can't go back; if it fails, we can't—no matter who wants to or how much. The command is forward, from now on, and the movement is certainly toward the left.[18]

In May the Committee for the Nation circulated a Lippmann column from May 3, 1934, in which the noted columnist pointed out that in February 1933 cowhide in Chicago was selling at 35 percent of its 1926 price, but men's shoes were selling at 96 percent of 1926. During the next twelve months the price of hides rose from 36 percent of 1926's price to 78 percent, while the price of shoes did not rise at all. "This meant," Lippmann wrote, "that the hide, leather, and shoe industry was really recovering: the different prices were coming into balance, and the producer of hides could therefore buy from the producer of shoes." Lippmann continued:

> There is no other way that recovery can take place. Trade is an exchange goods. If some products fall violently in price and others do not, the exchange cannot take place. If men have been buying two dollar shoes with 15 cent cotton, they cannot buy as many shoes with 5 cent cotton. Either the shoes have to come down or the cotton has to rise to the shoes.
> That is why the monetary policy and not N.R.A. has been the really effective instrument of recovery....This is reflation, the re-building of the price structure. While it is by no means completed, very great progress has been made, and to it we owe what recovery we have achieved.[19]

In mid-May, Rand addressed another letter to Roosevelt concerning the dangerous monetary situation. The gold value of commodities was once again dropping, from 48 percent of the 1926 value in March 1933 to 40 percent in March 1934. To restore the 1926 price level would now require a gold price of $51.67. The present gold value of basic commodities was dragging down the general price index. The only way to "restore purchasing power and economic balance between groups" was through increased prices for agricultural good and raw materials. "These basic commodities as a group have risen almost exactly as the price of gold has been raised. The evidence is so positive, we believe, as to leave no doubt that the PRICE OF GOLD CONTROLS THE PRICE OF BASIC COMMODITIES." Rand continued:

> If the dragging down of prices by our 147 per cent dollar is checked, the following factors may help to close the gap between the now authorized $41.34 price for gold and the indicated requirement of $51.67:
>
> A—The gold value of commodities in the United States has dropped a few points lower than in other countries. A slight rise in gold values of commodities in the United States to equalize this could reasonably be looked for.

B—There is evidence that the world-wide decline in gold value of commodities has ceased during the past few months, and there is some tendency to stability. If recovery proceeds, the world value of commodities in terms of gold should rise somewhat in the next few years.

C—If silver is introduced into the monetary basis and used to release substantial amounts of gold, the value of gold itself may be somewhat diluted.

D—Currency issued against revalued gold, if placed in circulation, would save interest to the Treasury. This would increase non-earning bank reserves and help to drive them into commercial lending. Profitable credit would follow a definite and protracted commodity price rise.[20]

In June, the Committee wired Secretary of Agriculture Wallace that the leaders of the major farm organizations wanted the Roosevelt administration to know that "farmer interests now require the action requested in the following resolution:

Resolved: that there should be an immediate and substantial increase in the buying and debt-paying power of the farmers and people generally of the United States. To this end we urge the President of the United States to at once raise the price of gold to the highest point permitted by law—$41.34

Recalling Wallace's "early recognition that the cause of this depression was primarily of monetary origin and that the chief remedy must arise from monetary action," the Committee felt that he was the one to impress upon Roosevelt the importance of raising the price of gold. The telegram ended:

We stand at a critical time. The farmer's return for this year's crops and his power to buy from urban industry are at stake. We appeal to you as Secretary of Agriculture to reflect to the President the viewpoint upon which the leaders of agriculture have united. Early action is necessary to give to the farmer the benefit in this year's marketing.[21]

When Congress passed the Frazier-Lemke Farm Mortgage Moratorium Act, the Committee wired Roosevelt that farmers did not want repudiation of their debts unless driven to it by the continuation of deflationary monetary conditions. Instead, they wanted and expected "price restoration that will enable them to pay their debts." It was the advice of the deflationists to hold the price of gold low that had led "to the social chaos and disintegration of which this

Frazier-Lemke bill is only a symptom."[22] In July, Senator Thomas's support for raising the price of gold was given considerable publicity in the press, as were his letters to all congressmen urging them to take control of the nation's money.[23]

Late in July, amidst falling economic indices, the Committee wired Roosevelt who was leisurely vacationing in Hawaii:

> Near panic in markets with no bids for many sound listed securities impels us to urge your immediate action. Only you can order steps to insulate us against Europe's political and economic repercussions.
>
> Since your departure the public has come to believe NEW YORK TIMES and other published statements that we have de facto stabilization of dollar at one thirty-fifth of ounce of world commodity gold. This leaves us at mercy of international forces acting upon gold and unfree to protect domestic price level by increasing price of gold.
>
> Leon Fraser states in report of Bank for International Settlements that you have retreated from position of year ago. WALL STREET JOURNAL published that Governor Harrison assured Fraser's directors that you will not alter price of gold.
>
> This has created impression that your Administration has abandoned its purpose of making restoration of domestic price level supreme consideration....
>
> Our internationalists who constantly suggest entangling financial relations forget that we are no longer a colonial dependency. With only 8% international trade with 40% of entire world's producing capacity to care for only 8% of its population we have the strength to build prosperity for our people....
>
> Immediate increase of price of gold will be notice to world of your intention to use monetary powers delegated by Congress to insulate United States against destructive foreign developments. During last ten days we have had nationwide decline in commodity and security values amounting to more than $10 billion. Therefore, we urge action at once. Believe it more needed and more helpful than year ago.[24]

That same day the Committee issued a press release that tied "the market collapse" to the "consequence of sidetracking domestic recovery for international exchange stability and thereby unnecessarily submitting our markets and our recovery program to foreign political and economic repercussions."[25]

In August, Amos Pinchot joined in the attack on Roosevelt's inaction, sending a letter to 200 editors for publication. Roosevelt, he recalled, had pledged on May 7, 1933 that he would restore the dollar to its normal purchasing power, thus enabling Americans to repay their debts in dollars of the same value they had borrowed. Pinchot then continued:

> Armed with ample powers given him by Congress, Mr. Roosevelt has taken some steps of a reflationary kind. But he has not carried through. The dollar still is a full third larger and harder to earn than when most of our debts were contracted. The debts still remain a crushing burden that holds down recovery, impoverishes the public and decreases the buying power of all but a comparatively small and unjustly favored creditor class. Every moment of delay on Mr. Roosevelt's part puts off recovery.

There was, Pinchot pointed out, nothing "radical" about restoring purchasing power, as over half a dozen nations had already done, nor was there anything unfair about it to creditors, since it was "difficult to argue that justice demands a creditor shall be paid in a bigger dollar than he loaned." Pinchot concluded that with "ten million people idle we need quickly the rising price level promised last year by the President."[26]

In the midst of widespread strikes and falling economic indices in late 1934, James Rand, Jr., head of the Committee for the Nation, was invited by *Scientific American* magazine to comment on the situation. In an article, "Strikes, Business, and Money," Rand wrote that "The greatest danger is that, in blind resentment against some ill-advised policies, we might overlook the corrective steps that are indispensable to America's recovery."

> It should have been apparent for a long time to our financial leaders that we had gone beyond the limits of "safe" deflation. They should have realized that unless we restored commodity prices and taxable values and employment before the economic cancer of deflation reached the vitals of American institutions, the profit system could not survive.
>
> Our financial leadership, clinging to its gold standard traditions, has been slow to realize, slow to admit, slow to face this challenge, and quick to oppose all who did recognize and did face it. Some still appear to believe capitalism and our free American institutions would be safe and that all would be well if we simply would vote this fall to return to what we had in 1932.

Showing Warren's influence, Rand added:

> Many farm leaders and some business men have taken the trouble to find out that the depression came from monetary causes. The five-year fall in

commodity prices resulted simply from the increase in the purchasing power of our gold dollar. This threw economic groups into disparity, killed purchasing power, created unemployed, destroyed for business the opportunity to make profits. The evils that flow from monetary derangement can be corrected only if the monetary system is soundly rebuilt....Because the United States was the last of 34 nations to raise its price of gold and then hesitated to raise it far enough to restore economic balance, we had been rushed into socialistic experiments in government control that undermine American industrial leadership.

If industry wished to be free, it "must insist upon reflation. It must insist that the half-executed program to restore and thereafter keep stable the value of our money shall be carried through." If price levels were restored, it would "cut the ground from under the argument that regimenting industry and agriculture is necessary." He hoped that Roosevelt would steer the ship of state away from the influence "of the deflationists and internationalists" and act "on the gold price with the same forthrightness he displayed when he put domestic price level recovery ahead of international exchange stabilization at the London Economic Conference in July, 1933." If he would use the authority under the Thomas Amendment to revalue gold further, he could "immediately restore 1 1/4 billion dollars of additional farm buying power. From $35 to $41.34, a rise of 18 percent, should bring a corresponding rise over last year's seven billion dollars of farm income." The only two ways to do this were by revaluing the price of gold or by printing press inflation. The gold pricing policy so far had worked, he insisted, with commodity prices rising "as much on average as the rise in our price of gold," but they could go no higher with gold stuck on $35 per ounce. What he proposed, was not inflation, Rand insisted. It was, instead, "the surest way to avoid the printing press—which every sensible American knows can be more deadly than the machine gun." Rand closed by saying: "Can we awake industry to realize that it must act to save itself—to keep out European ideas, and preserve our American system"[27]

In 1934 and 1935, the Committee successively agitated against the Bankhead Agricultural Bill as "a fate-changing turn on the road to regimentation," the regimenting aspects of the Fletcher-Rayburn (SEC) Bill, and the Eccles Banking Act of 1935, while supporting passage of the Silver Purchase Act of 1934.[28] Mixed with the attacks was a drawing of the line between the forces of regimentation and the "American" alternative, in the form of the commodity dollar. As Irving Fisher put it, in an address before the Chicago Federated Advertising Club in mid-April, 1934, the Depression could still be defeated by the commodity dollar, while he viewed with alarm the "Russian" experiments with the SEC, NRA, AAA, CWA and the other elements in what he described as the "alphabet soup" of the New Deal. There were two very different approaches to dealing with depressions, he told his audience, the Russian way of the government running everything, and the American way of letting businesses make profits and reemploy labor. The Roosevelt administration, he said, had been "trying a little of both, and I think it has already gone too far toward the Russian way and not far enough, nor fast enough, in the American direction."[29] What he objected to "mostly violently," he told Roosevelt, was "the philosophy of wealth destruction and limitation of enhancing the money values for certain classes at the expense of the nation as a whole. On this matter some of the 'brains trust' do not seem to have brains to trust."[30]

In August, the Committee alerted its members to a radio address to be given by Senator Thomas over a national network in which Thomas would take "an aggressive stand for rescue of creditors as well as debtors." It told its members that "The crisis confronting agriculture and industry is set forth by the Oklahoma Senator so effectively that this address should command national notice."[31]

Meanwhile, Fisher was telling Roosevelt that recovery could come only through profits, and "the N.R.A., P.W.A., C.W.A., A.A.A., despite certain good points have set recovery back." He wrote:

> We are slowly recovering perhaps, but not yet back to last July. You may soon have to choose between the regimentalists and the money-stabilizers. Capitalism, if it is to be retained, must have the lure of real profits, to justify its either seeking or getting the financing needed for formal re-employment of labor.
>
> I believe that monetary reflation and stabilization are your best ways out, and that you need now to put profits near the top of your list of objectives.[32]

Fisher's letters to the president began increasingly to take on the tone of a professor lecturing a somewhat slow student. As the economy turned downward in the second half of 1934, approaching the levels of the summer of 1932, he wrote Roosevelt that in his opinion, "irrespective of its reform possibilities, the N.R.A. has retarded recovery and especially retarded re-employment." He reminded the president that: "In a capitalistic economy, employment depends on the employer, lured by the prospect of high profits. When as now, he fears he won't be allowed more than say 6% or 7% profit but runs the risk of 100% losses, he doesn't dare extend himself and employ labor as he would if reassured." Without the fears on the part of employers and investors that had been created by parts of the New Deal, he was certain the United States would "have been practically out of the depression many months ago." Roosevelt should, Fisher said, "reassure business with unmistakable decisiveness."[33] Invited to Hyde Park a week later for a meeting with Roosevelt, Fisher found the president "very cordial" and anxious "to get all the unemployed at work as soon as possible," but thinking mainly "in terms of employment by the Government rather than reemployment in private industry." Fisher told him he "thought the best way was to stimulate reemployment in the old industries as fast as possible, that public works were slow, clumsy, inefficient and costly." He offered Roosevelt an eleven-point plan for stimulating private industry, which the president proclaimed as "Perfectly grand," and he scheduled a meeting between Fisher and Secretary of the Treasury Henry Morgenthau for the following week.[34]

Included in Fisher's program was "an immediate raising of the price of gold to $41.34," which would "help the farmer particularly," and an announcement by Roosevelt "that you aim to free business, not to fetter it; that honest profits will not be taboo, however high, except as just taxes necessarily reduce them," and that the other items in the program were "designed to help business and employment; that the government intends to withdraw from its depression activities as fast as private business absorbs the unemployed; that meanwhile, it will pay wages below those paid by private industry, so that labor will not be tempted to refuse private jobs offered." In addition, Fisher's program included unemployment insurance, increased public works, and an announcement of Roosevelt's readiness to use greenbacks, if necessary, as authorized by the Thomas amendment to the AAA.[35]

Nothing having happened, Fisher pressed for another meeting with FDR in December, noting that unemployment was "still excessive," and that the president still had Fisher's recommendations from their September 6 meeting. Fisher called the president's attention to a chart in *Barron's* magazine that compared U.S. recovery with that of Canada. The chart, he told Roosevelt argued "mainly for pursuing your monetary and against pursuing further your wealth-destruction policies," since it showed that "at first, while you pushed your monetary policy, the recovery of U.S. was faster than that of Canada and that later, when the NRA and AAA had their effects the U.S. receded relatively to Canada."[36]

Warren had already expressed his own pessimism to Herman Oliphant, general counsel to the Treasury Department, in December, when he wrote that the NRA and AAA would "require a control of everything, a greatly lowered standard of living, and an end of democracy and freedom." Although he was a "confirmed optimist," he was "becoming fearful of what may happen to us if this point of view is not changed and changed quickly."[37]

Robert Wood remained optimistic after a February 1935 trip to the Pacific coast, writing Rumely that he had recently lunched with Marriner Eccles and found him "opposed to what he considers the trend toward socialism in this country," and convinced that "if the government takes over all credit facilities, the nationalization of credit is much more dangerous than anything else." He did not, however, "have a correct idea on the gold question." He told Rumely that the increase in the price of gold was increasing its production in the west and he felt that the "effect of that new money will be felt sooner or later." He continued:

> Referring again to Eccles, I do not disagree with a spending policy within reasonable limits except that I believe as you do, that the spending is merely a corrolary [sic] of the increase in the price of gold and would have little or not [sic] effect without it.
> I think the world is working irresistibly toward further increases in gold, that if the gold block goes off gold or if Great Britain is forced to increase its price, which I think is possible in the very near future, it will force us to go to a $41. price. I think everything is working in line with this.[38]

When the Supreme Court upheld the invalidation of the gold clause in contracts in February 1935, the Committee welcomed the decision as a "victory for our policies," since it opened "the way to managed currency and to the completion of the program for which the Committee has pioneered and fought during the past two years."[39] A few months later they mobilized against the so-called Eccles Banking Bill that was being debated in Congress, joining most of the nation's bankers in opposition, though for different reasons. Part of that bill would have delegated to the Federal Reserve Board the authority to alter the value of the dollar whenever to do so would, in their judgment, "promote conditions conducive to business stability and to mitigate unstabilizing fluctuations in the general level of production, trade, prices and employment." While the Committee obviously had no complaint with altering the gold value of the dollar, this was vesting too much discretionary power in the FRB to suit them. The committee, therefore, opposed passage of the bill unless it included an amendment offered by Congressman Goldsborough that would have required any changes to be linked to commodity prices, thus producing the commodity dollar they had sought.

Rumely's wife wrote of their reaction to the bill in a letter to their children:

The country is now gravely concerned over the Administration's Banking Bill which was written by Felix Frankfurter's Hot Dogs. Neither Eccles nor Morgenthau knew what was in it. It is before the House Committee. They closed their hearings after hearing only those Roosevelt wanted heard, but the Committee for the Nation forced them to hear Rand and Vanderlip. There is to be a big fight on Part III which gives the President power to decide whether any individual may receive credit or not at a bank, and other unlimited powers which will enable them to spend all they want without the public becoming aware of it. Senator Glass will stage a great fight against increasing the powers of the Federal Reserve and against ratifying Eccles for the post of Federal Reserve Governor, but he is against Vanderlip's "Monetary Authority" and the farmers' "1926 dollar."[40]

A few days later Amos Pinchot, who had begun to cooperate increasingly with the Committee, wrote to Rumely about the banking bill, but told Rumely "the subject on which I would especially like to get your reaction is more important than the banking bill." He explained:

It is the effect which placing vast, permissive and undefined powers in the President's hands, to be used at his discretion, will have, and, for that matter, is having, on business and farming and on the government itself.

The fact is that New Deal legislation has given the President more discretionary power than any ruler has had, in peace-time, in any constitutional government. This element of enlarged executive discretion is found in practically all the important bills that have come to Congress as administration measures. It is found in the Thomas amendment which empowers, but does not require, the President to devalue the dollar. It is in the National Industrial Recovery Act's permissive, but not mandatory, wage and price fixing. It runs clean through the enforcement of the codes....

Executive discretion is preponderant in the Works Relief bill, that empowers the President to spend nearly five billions just about as he pleases. It is in Section 9 of the NIRA, which authorizes the President to divorce oil producing companies from pipe line companies whenever he believes such divorcement necessary in order to restore competition.

All of this discretionary authority, Pinchot pointed out, involved both the right to do things or not to do them, as Roosevelt saw fit:

To attack or not to attack, to approve mergers, prices wages, and practices, or not to approve them—these are questions to be answered by the Executive and his appointed aides. And the answer is dictated, not by law, nor by any known rule or standard, but, in the last analysis, by a man and his appointees, whose course in any given case cannot be foretold, because it depends, to a large degree on personal opinion, experience, and background.

The new banking act of 1935 was typical, in which "through control of the personnel of a revamped Federal Reserve Board, the President is given huge powers, not one of which is authorized by the Constitution."

Under [the banking bill], and the Thomas Amendment of '33, the President can move the domestic price level either up or down. He can change the size of the dollar, and thereby alter the terms of every mortgage, lease, or contract so that a long-term engagement to pay in dollars becomes in essence a gamble. He can make farms profitable or the reverse. He can change the buying and debt-paying power of every savings account and the value of every insurance policy. He can expand, contract, or allot or withhold, credit according to his judgment.

Through his power over the reserve banks, he can change the rediscount rate and alter the reserves which banks must carry against loans. And he can expand or contract the volume of currency.

All of these, Pinchot pointed out, were constitutional powers, but were vested in Congress, not the president. He added:

Taking the entire body of New Deal legislation together, and keeping in mind its permissive, in distinction to mandatory character, we have a picture of Congressional abdication on the one hand and executive usurpation on the other that is exceedingly disturbing. I am more than sceptical about this kind of government. It is based on the exploded socialist and fascist idea that there can be found an all-wise and all-powerful personal leadership, that will prove experienced enough and competent enough successfully to fix price and wages, to regulate the amount of production, to decide which mergers shall be allowed and which forbidden, to approve or forbid monopoly, to encourage or condemn competition, and finally to control banking, money and credit, and to fix the price level and the size of the dollar. This, as it seems to me, is too big an order by a long shot.

Pinchot noted Tugwell's observation in a recent book that it was the purpose of the New Deal to shift the United States "to a new design for government," one in which Congress, "by legislative delegation" would turn over its powers to a strong executive. This "new design," Pinchot argued, was "creating an immense, inefficient bureaucracy," was "discouraging competition and encouraging monopoly, thereby raising prices and decreasing consumption, production and employment."

"Today," Pinchot wrote, "almost everyone with property of any kind stands to a greater or less extent in awe of the government." He explained:

For, by its newly forged personal and discretionary powers the Executive can withhold or extend financial help, and grant or deny immunity from the new laws and innumerable regulations. Banks, railroads, industrial and financial corporations fear the RFC. Farmers fear the AAA, even as they accept favors from it. Landlords, manufacturers, and business men fear the NRA....and other people, who are dependent on the government's loaning agencies, hesitate to take a stand on public issues that may offend the administration....

It may be said that the dictatorship, into which Mr. Roosevelt has inadvertently drifted, has a string to it, that Congress gave it and Congress can take it away. But, with an executive possessed of a mammoth-sized pork barrel and supported by an incredible host of bureaucrats, Congress may find it a hard matter to come back. And a further difficulty is that, having patriotically disarmed itself during the crisis, Congress is as much afraid of the Executive as anyone.

The struggle in Congress over the Banking Bill would "disclose the President's true attitude toward the deeper issue between democracy and autocracy." If Roosevelt insisted on executive control of the monetary system, he would, "so to speak, cross his Rubicon." "Today," Pinchot wrote, "the nations of the world may be divided into two classes — the nations in which the government fears the people, and the nations in which the people fear the government. It is the New Deal's tragedy that it is moving this country into the second class."[41]

Frank Vanderlip wrote to Louis McHenry Howe that without the Goldsborough amendment the banking bill was, in his judgment, "both dangerous and unconstitutional," since it delegated to the FRB "the vast powers of Congress over the dollar to a board without defining what the dollar measure of value must be." He wondered if Howe would "vote to empower the Bureau of Standards to change the gallon measure or the yardstick whenever they thought that such changes" were desirable. That was what the banking bill proposed to do to the dollar, he told Howe.[42] The veteran progressive, Amos Pinchot pressed his support for the Goldsborough amendment in more positive terms, telling Howe that he believed "the passage of this amendment will restore confidence, create business activity, cut down unemployment and relieve the government from the pressure that is driving it toward regimentation."[43] While the Goldsborough amendment failed of passage, the banking bill that passed was minus some of its worst features.

"After 1935," writes a historian of the Committee, "relatively little was heard from the Committee for the Nation" except for "occasional speeches and releases."[44] In part this was no doubt due to the fact that the regimenting tendencies of the New Deal had been set back by the Supreme Court decisions on the NRA in 1935, and on the AAA in early 1936. While the Committee was not as active after the fight over the banking bill, it was not entirely silent. But there was clearly a sense of futility. Rumely wrote to his son in early July of a visit with Vanderlip.

> Senator Borah is working with us in Washington. We have some hope. Yesterday I visited Mr. Vanderlip for about an hour at his beautiful Scarborough home. He said rather sadly, "What a tragedy that so few minds understand and that men like the American delegation to the International Chamber of Commerce Convention should plead so ignorantly for a return to a fixed weight of gold — the very thing that has brought the deflation and almost destroyed our economic order." He said, "Sometimes I become discouraged, feeling it alone," and then he gave me the warmest handclasp and seemed to say, "We have had a good fight."[45]

When the export manager of General Motors supported stabilization at $35 gold, Rumely described it as "hari-kari for American agriculture." If General Motors was going to throw its support behind the deflationists, Rumely said, Ford's help would be indispensable for "this side." He told Edsel Ford:

> We are sending out thousands of pieces of literature today to support Senator Borah and the farm organizations - and sending them largely on nerve.
> We need money. Even more help would be the prestige of the Ford name in the business and banking world.[46]

Rumely planned, he told Robert Wood, "to have about 100 farm leaders bear down on Mr. Ford." If the General Motors position was put into circulation, Rumely thought Ford might support the Committee's position, since "it's a First Principle with the Ford organization to do the opposite from General Motors." Still, Rumely wrote: "If I could split myself into 4 or 5 people and park one in Detroit for a systematic campaign of weeks or a month, there might be a chance of accomplishing something. But the chance is so slim that I dare not risk putting more energy in that direction than I am giving."[47]

When the director of the Cotton Section of the AAA called for amending the Constitution in order to give the AAA more authority, Rumely sent a copy of the newspaper clipping to members of the directing committee and wrote:

> the Department of Agriculture is already beginning to sell the idea of changing the Constitution to farmers, presenting to them the viewpoint that the only way to get more money for what they raise is to give the government control over private property; that is, break down the constitutional protections which have been the guarantee of our free enterprise system.
> If the business world throttles monetary action and drives the farming population into alliance with the regimenters the Farmer Labor Alliance will outvote business interests....Once the constitutional protection is broken down to make AAA possible, the Government will be supreme and our private property guarantees subordinate.[48]

If there was a problem with cotton, the Committee wired Roosevelt, it could be solved simply by the president "using powers vested in you to increase at once the price of gold to $41.34 overnight," a move that would "add 1,250 million dollars to United

States farmers income during next 12 months and would increase prices and buying power of other basic producers as much more."

> These two and a half billion dollars of increased buying power in the hands of the 55 million producers of basic products in the United States would increase business activity, restore employment to two million men in private industry and by helping lift real estate out of deflation would stimulate building and general business upswing.
>
> Our Committee adds its urgent recommendation for immediate action to that of the National Grange, the American Farm Bureau Federation, the National Grain Corporation and the National Cooperative Council in asking you Quote at once to raise the price of gold to the highest point permitted by law — $41.34 per ounce unquote.[49]

It was a lost cause.

By September, Rumely had divided the work of the office of the Committee between two outside projects: the "Gannett project," which involved accumulating "a large list of Republican leaders throughout the country, and Mr. Gannett, sending letters to them from time to time," work with a "political tinge," and a magazine that Rumely was promoting called *Leadership and Labor*. But the Committee continued its work. In October, Rand wrote Roosevelt:

> Business is on the upgrade. Security prices, stimulated not only by business recovery but by easy money, may be outrunning recovery as they did in 1927, when an easy money policy was initiated at the request of Europe while basic commodity prices were allowed to remain low.
>
> There will be danger of repeating the disaster of 1929 unless the position of our basic producers is lifted simultaneously with business recovery. The 32 3/4 millions of our population on farms are still short $5 billion of their normal income....You have it in your power immediately to make a substantial correction of this inequality by increasing the price of gold to $41.34 per ounce.

"Public opinion," he told Roosevelt "may still need preparation for such a step," but the Committee, farm organizations, and many industrialists would back him in such a step.[50]

By the beginning of 1936, the Committee had begun to shift from its identification with James Rand to a closer relationship with the political activities of Frank Gannett, while trying to retain its non-partisanship in monetary matters. As Rumely put it, there were "certain inherent differences of opinion" that had to be "bridged over to find a program that would make possible a united effort and still enable us to bring along our support." The invalidation of the AAA by the Supreme Court early in 1936 seemed to open a new opportunity for the Committee's program. As Rumely reported matters to the directing committee:

> When Secretary Wallace called farm representatives together after the demise of AAA, farm organizations met and re-passed vigorous monetary resolutions. A suggestion to appoint special monetary committees in each of the national farm organization was discussed.

The Committee for the Nation was lending the farm organizations the services of Earl Harding, and underwriting his salary, so that he could man an office in Washington as a lobbyist for the farm organizations in behalf of monetary policy.[51]

By March, Rumely was actively engaged in raising funds for Senator William Borah's candidacy for the Republican presidential nomination, Borah being the only candidate in either party who supported the Committee's program of monetary reform. Rumely pointed out, however, that the Committee could not involve itself in politics, since it was "non-partisan and merely tries to educate all in public life on the monetary question." Therefore, Rumely could not use Committee time for the Borah campaign.[52] To Robert E. Wood, Rumely wrote later in the campaign that "We are scrupulously careful not to take any political stand by the Committee. When the Committee was formed, this resolution was passed and the policy established." In fact, he pointed out, the Committee had devoted "an enormous amount of energy in supporting the President's monetary policy leading toward a managed currency." All of his time spent working with Gannett was done off the Committee payroll.[53]

Still, though, the Committee was maintaining its voice. A speech by Secretary of State Cordell Hull endorsing a return to the international gold standard prompted a long telegram from the committee scolding him for turning the administration's "back upon the unanimous request of American agriculture for a monetary policy in the interest of American producers and consumers." The Committee went on:

> You say this is needed to assure "stability." Stability for whom? Certainly not for American agriculture. Certainly not for American producers of lead, zinc, copper, petroleum, lumber, etc. Certainly not for American labor.

The gold standard ruined agriculture and basic raw material producers everywhere. The gold standard never gave stability of prices, excepting over brief and fleeting periods.

If you have been so far misled by the mumbo-jumbo of international finance that you have overlooked these facts, let us call your attention to the actual figures on what you describe as the "stability" of gold.

The telegram then repeated the familiar figures on loss of purchasing power under the deflation. Hull now proposed, the telegram went on, "that the power vested in Congress to regulate the value of the dollar shall be usurped by the Treasury and State Departments and by them delivered over to the mercy of foreign—and too-often secret—conferences, dominated not by the interests of American producers and consumers, but by international finance." It went on:

> The National Agricultural Conference, representing 3500 cooperatives, 8000 Grange locals, 1800 Farm Bureaus and 300,000 cooperating grain growers, met in January and unanimously passed resolutions against the gold standard which you wish to make permanentby international bargaining. These farm organizations, after careful investigation, ask for "a dollar with constant purchasing power, regulated on an index of basic commodities."
>
> This is the stable dollar which Mr. Roosevelt promised in 1933, and which is unattainable under the international gold standard....
>
> In behalf of agriculture and of American business men who have investigated monetary policy at home and abroad and who understand what the consequences of your program would be, we protest.[54]

Robert E. Wood disagreed with the telegram, writing Rand that he "thought the program of the Committee this year was to be more or less quiescent and that it would limit its activities to a little educational work among the industrialists and bankers." He did "not think it wants to get into controversies at this time."[55]

Later in the month, Rumely sent Wood a copy of a Frank Kent column stating that the tax bill showed "the continuing great influence of Tugwell on the White House." Rumely went on:

> We know [Federal Reserve] Governor Eccles. In 1933 he was a contributing member of our Committee. We were in frequent contact. Stuart Chase met him, won him, brought him to the attention of Tugwell and Tugwell brought him to Washington. Mr. Vanderlip and I attended a private meeting at the Harvard Club where Eccles was a speaker to a selected group of

about two hundred. He expounded his and the Roosevelt Administration's philosophy regarding the Federal Reserve System. In this talk he expressed the viewpoint that the economic machine would not function smoothly unless the government stepped in and by taxation takes away property from some and redistributes it to others.

After the Eccles talk, I walked home with Mr. Vanderlip. He was dismayed at the collectivist viewpoint that Mr. Eccles had presented.

During the discussion of the Banking Bill, Mr. Vanderlip, Mr. Harding and Mr. Rand spent an evening with Eccles. He wholly disagreed with our viewpoint that control over the price of gold is a vital factor in managing money to keep it stable in purchasing power. He resisted the idea of a monetary unit of stable buying power, and urged the viewpoint that would enable the appointees of the Executive to raise and lower the price level.

Governor Eccles is personally an agreeable, friendly chap and has proved himself a capable business man in the enterprises and positions of power which he inherited from his father. The difficulty is that he lacks a fundamental understanding and allows himself to be made the advocate and agent to help establish viewpoints that will in the end undermine a money economy of free enterprise....His special pleading helped more than that of any other single individual to defeat the Goldsborough amendment.

In a postscript, Rumley added that in bringing Eccles into the administration Tugwell doubtless "knew that Governor Eccles' thinking would fit in with his program of a planned economy."[56]

The campaign of the Farmers' and Business Men's National Committee for Borah was unsuccessful, when Alf Landon of Kansas won the nomination. Both Borah and the Committee opposed the monetary plank of the Republican convention.[57] At first leery of Landon, Rumely embraced him when he straddled on the monetary issue, pledging not to return the United States to the gold standard "unless and until it can be done without hurting the interests of agriculture."[58] Through the balance of the presidential campaign, Rumely busied himself with giving advice to the Landon camp. It was obvious that Landon would get the business, taxpayer and property owners' vote, he told Gannett, but he needed to get the votes of liberals and farmers "by showing that the so-called New Deal is not Liberal but a reaction toward despotism and arbitrary government from which our forefathers were striving to escape when they came to this country and set up our Constitution."[59]

In September 1936, General Robert E. Wood terminated his and Sears Roebuck's relationship with the Committee, writing that he had "felt for some time that the work of the Committee for the Nation should be brought to a close." He went on:

I have never changed my opinion as to the great value of the work the Committee did in assisting in the devaluation of 1933. I felt that was a vital and essential step. I have also felt that the Committee could perform a valuable, educational work in getting the business men of the country at least to think about the monetary question regardless of their views. In this, the Committee has done some good.

However, you [Rand] personally have been able to give but little time to the affairs of the Committee. The whole conduct of the Committee has devolved on Dr. Rumely. I like Dr. Rumely personally very much, but I do not trust his judgment. He got the Committee into a bad mess in regard to the Dr. Wirt matter. During this past year I have been out of sympathy with his insistence on a higher price for gold. I do not believe that anyone in the world today knows what the right price for gold is.[60]

By October 1, Rumely had lost hope that Landon would be elected. The problem, he told Gannett, was that the Republicans had "thrown out the window" the one issue on which they might have won, adopting instead a "weak straddle" on monetary policy. "Instead of a courageous, strongly affirmative stand for restoring farm prices, they hushed the thing up and delivered in private meetings interpretations of telegrams and platform planks that the banking group viewed as commitments to their standpoint."[61] Later in October, he wrote Gannett that he should spend the next four years hammering the monetary issue as a road "to national leadership in the next four years." He told Gannett, "There is no other answer to the charge of the collectivists against the capitalist system except to make it work and give full employment, and that cannot be done in a rational way except by rationalizing our monetary system."[62]

After the election, Gannett congratulated Wood on the pro-FDR position he had taken during the campaign, avowing that he had shown "wise discretion and good judgment" in his attitude. Gannett continued:

Now that the election is over, we face a great task. The ballot has not solved our problems. I go back to the position we of the Committee took a year ago. We must solve the farm problem and the unemployment problem if we are to save America from the fate that has fallen on the countries of Europe.

From "inside sources" he had heard that the Roosevelt administration was "sympathetic with the position we have taken on the money question." Gannett thought the Committee "should drive harder than ever for wise action on this question, strive for a managed currency both foreign and domestic." Moreover, Borah's "outstanding victory" in Idaho put him in a position "to render great service in the Senate in the way of getting real monetary reform."[63]

Wood responded that he had been convinced that neither Landon nor his running mate Frank Knox had understood the money question. He agreed with Gannett that much could be accomplished through Borah on the monetary question, "particularly as the Administration has at least been sympathetic with our views." But he would not change the decision he had made about the Committee and Dr. Rumely.[64]

Rumely, too, wrote to Gannett after the election, arguing that the monetarists' position was seriously hampered in its efforts to influence national opinion because it did "not control a nationally syndicated article." Rumely suggested forming a syndicate that would sell columns by men like Amos Pinchot and William Hard, both of whom were widely and favorably known. "If we want to exert future influence," he wrote, "we must get the reins of power into our hands."[65]

Shortly after the election, Treasury Secretary Morgenthau indicated that Roosevelt would seek an extension of the powers previously granted him by Congress, including the power to fix the price of gold. This meant, Rumely argued, that "our monetary questions will be settled, not as the Constitution requires, by the Congress, and not from the all important standpoint of the restoration to normal of the buying power of our dollar, so that we may have our normal price level and its maintenance thereafter as a stable measure of value." If Congress ceded him the power, it would lose control over money. Rumely had in mind gathering the opposition of Senator Borah, the farm organizations, and some Democratic leaders to any such extension unless it included "a mandate to the 1926 price level in connection therewith. In other words, the Goldsborough Amendment to the delegation of powers asked for.[66] If the Republican Party did not take a stand on this issue, Rumely said, "it will have thrown away the most important issue at its disposal and possibly, its own future."[67]

However, 1937 would bring even more momentous issues, beginning with Roosevelt's proposal to pack the Supreme Court. The Committee for the Nation now rapidly was transformed into a National Committee to Uphold Constitutional Government under

Gannett, with Rumely as executive secretary, operating out of the same offices that the Committee for the Nation had used. The purpose, as Rumely put it, was to organize a nonpartisan educational campaign. People must be educated as to "what the courts have done to protect liberty...and the country aroused to an understanding of the fundamentals of democratic government on this issue as on no other issue in a decade."[68]

After an immense public relations campaign by the National Committee Roosevelt was defeated. In mid-June the Senate Judiciary Committee reported out the bill with a report so negative that, as one columnist observed, it read like "a bill of impeachment except that [it] refers to [the] bill instead of Roosevelt by name."[69]

Another challenge in 1937 was the Black-Connery wages and prices bill, which was also opposed by the National Committee to Uphold Constitutional Government. This bill was rushed through the Senate with scarcely any debate. While it was being considered by the House, the National Committee released a press statement saying:

> The Black-Connery Bill, with its jokers and hidden purposes, is now before the lower house, where more dangerous provisions may be added unless nation-wide protest is instantly made to Congress.
> We must not stop with our fight for constitutional government half won. In the closing hours, Congress must not rush through half digested legislation that is a radical departure from the constitutional American way. It would be far better for Congress to adjourn and give the nation time to stop and think.

The National Committee appealed for telegrams and letters to congressmen, and added: "If the committee's work to resist dangerous trends toward one man, personal government is to continue, it must have immediate financial support."[70]

Rumely wrote to Senator Borah asking him to push for early adjournment of Congress, since it was "a negation of Democratic process to rush bills through without giving time for deliberation and without giving public opinion in the country an opportunity to follow the proceedings in the Congress and make up its mind." During the "emergency" of early 1933 there had been some rationale for rushing legislation through Congress, but now, when there was no longer any need, the Roosevelt administration seemed determined to make "the rush act proceedings of '33...into standard practice." Borah should make a plea for "a restoration of full discussion," since the bills before Congress—executive reorganization, wages and hours, and farm legislation—each represented "probably the greatest departure in the particular field from the experience and practice of the preceding 150 years."[71]

Rumely and the National Committee realized that they could not rest. Roosevelt's clear determination to "purge" those Democratic senators who had voted against the court bill by defeating them in their 1938 state primaries, meant that if he were successful the challenge to the court could be remounted in 1939. Thus, the National Committee continued its fund-raising efforts, not only to head off the legislation pending in Congress, but to prepare to defend those targeted Democratic senators against Roosevelt's purge attempt.

Late in 1937, the economy plunged into renewed depression. Initially, Rumely and the other monetarists seem to have been so concerned about opposing the legislation before Congress that they neglected this opportunity to once again push their reflation proposals. But with all indices plummeting and unemployment rising, the Committee in October urged once again that Roosevelt raise the price of gold to $41.34 per ounce in order to raise security and commodity prices. A few days later, Rumely admitted to the press that several of the Committee's leading figures had severed their connections with it. These included not only the aforementioned Robert E. Wood, but also Lessing Rosenwald, chairman of Sears, Roebuck, as well as William Wrigley and William Bendix. The *New York Times* reported that the Committee's October 1937 telegram to the president "came as a surprise to some of those, formerly identified with the committee, who thought the organization was moribund."[72] Irving Fisher, meanwhile, also wrote the president once again to urge upon Roosevelt "the importance of having the Treasury and the Federal Reserve apply measures for increasing the circulating medium in order promptly to secure recovery." He added:

As you know, you have been more than once accused of delaying recovery in order to obtain reform. In the present case I think the events indicate the opposite order even to secure some of your reforms.

A quick recovery which is entirely feasible I believe, would, at this time, I think, greatly help you toward the long time goals you have in mind.

He would not bother Roosevelt with "a bill of particulars," however, since he had "indicated them before."[73]

In March 1938, Senator Sherman Minton's committee undertook an investigation of the National Committee's lobbying activities in a clear effort to intimidate it. Included in the attack on the committee was new publicity given to Rumely's imprisonment during World War I as part of the "smear." Minton sought to subpoena all of the records of the committee, a call that Gannett refused as unconstitutional. Rumely wrote of his own experience:

> The Committee was called by the Senate Lobby Committee last Thursday. I was subpoenaed with the demand to produce all records, which I refused. I appeared on Friday in Washington. Senator Minton's plan was to get me first, try to smear on War record...and then, through me, to smear the Committee. He did not succeed.
>
> For two and a quarter hours he and his committee tried to put on a grilling, but they could not make the thing stick, and I was able to get into the record, the real facts of the Committee's activities and enough of the truth about the War period so that that did not go.
>
> The press and radio are with us and it now looks as if this discussion is going to be the most valuable thing our Committee ever had happen to it.[74]

When the White House in early 1938 sought to reverse the downturn by a return to spending—"pump-priming"—the National Committee did not offer a monetary alternative. Instead, the committee took the position that

> First, we can agree that the needy and involuntarily unemployed must be fully cared for. Next attack "pump-priming" as an economic fallacy because it brings misuse of taxpayers' billions for political purposes. If continued, it will lead to the building up of a corrupt political machine that will be almost impossible to stop. In the end this must inevitably lead to destruction of democracy and to one man government.

Therefore, the committee insisted that Congress should issue no more blank checks to the White House for billions to be spent under executive discretion, and Congress "should make it a criminal offense" for relief officials to use the money for political purposes.[75]

During the summer, the committee's effort heated up to aid threatened "constitutional" Democrats and to help defeat those who had voted for the court-packing bill. As Rumely put it, it was impossible for the Republicans to elect enough men to Congress to uphold constitutional government, and so the "job of upholding constitutional government has to be done between now and 1940 if it is to be done at all, by a coalition of Constitutional Democrats and Republicans."

> It was not easy for men like Wheeler, Burke, Van Nuys to turn their backs upon party loyalty, and it would hereafter be less easy if the record made in this summer's and fall elections, proves that, rejected by their party machine, no other force cares enough to turn a hand for them.[76]

Rumely was also involved in the effort of Congressman J.J. O'Connor in New York, who was battling a Rooseveltian purge attempt.[77] As Gannett defined the issue, O'Connor, as chairman of the House Rules Committee, had been mainly responsible for the defeat of the "President's dangerous Reorganization Bill." By "misuse of relief funds and patronage," Roosevelt had been successful in defeating O'Connor in the Democratic primary. It now behooved Republicans to rally behind O'Connor in the general election to restore him to Washington as a "constitutional Democrat."[78]

In November, as the economy continued in the doldrums, Rumely returned to a popular theme, writing the head of Zenith Radio Corporation that

> The private enterprise system is doomed if we remain in deflation much longer. By that I mean if we keep an amount of gold in the dollar which causes the dollar to buy about one and a half as much of farm products as it did all through the 20's, which means that farmers who got $12 billions for their products, now get only $8 billions....
> This destroyed buying power prevents urban industry from selling to the 55 million basic producers and, therefore, we cannot have as many jobs as there are men nor opportunity for our youth....

But, Rumely lamented, "it is not possible to drive home this thought against the resistance that exists."[79] It was a fitting epitaph for Rumely's six years of efforts on behalf of the managed dollar.

4

The Emergence of Stuart Chase

Edmund Wilson in 1932 described Stuart Chase as "perhaps the vividest writer of the liberal camp; he has an unusual knack of making statistics take shape as things and people."[1]   In 1936, *Time* magazine wrote of Chase:

> Among U.S. economists, Stuart Chase has a reputation for being the best story teller of the lot. Master of the art of leading audiences up the mountain, he has held out bold and attractive visions of happy economic figures, plausible-sounding and easily-attained, in most of the sprightly, bright, informal, argumentative volumes he has written in the past eleven years. Interspersing his books with anecdotes, personal reminiscences, moral tirades against waste, he has always discussed human problems as an economist, economic problems as an evangelist, political problems as an engineer, and philosophic problems as an irascible citizen who wants to know why something is not done.[2]

Paul Douglas described Chase as "at once accountant and artist. Without much formal training in economics and therefore frequently liable to technical slips, he is a constant irritant to the orthodox. But with an artist's eye he nevertheless was 'shaping fantasies, that apprehend more than cool reason ever comprehends.'"[3]

Like so many amateur "economists" of the 1930s, Stuart Chase was educated as an engineer, but unlike the others he abandoned engineering for his father's profession and became a certified public accountant. As an accountant he was privy to the inside operations of businesses, and much of what he saw clearly appalled both his engineer's and accountant's dislike of waste. His service in the federal government, first with the Federal Trade Commission, then with the Food Administration during World War I, and then with the FTC again, brought him into intimate contact with the operations of the meat packers and led to *Profits of the Packers*, a volume he wrote for the FTC, and an article he wrote for the *Journal of Accountancy* in 1920, "What Is a Reasonable Profit?" In both works he was critical of business accounting for its inaccurate reporting of profits.

Launched on a career as a social critic, Chase became involved with the Technical Alliance, a group of engineers inspired by Thorstein Veblen who sought the elimination of waste through industrial coordination, and the Labor Bureau. In the 1920s, he expressed his misgivings about the economy through magazine articles, many of them published in the *Nation*, and books. The 1920s, as William Barber has pointed out, was a decade in which engineers made the study and elimination of waste an item of social service, largely under the leadership of Secretary of Commerce Herbert Hoover, himself a noted engineer. For most, like Hoover, the elimination of waste could be carried out within the existing capitalist system. For others, like Chase, waste in all its forms could be eliminated only by an overhaul of the economic system that left engineers in charge. By the end of the decade this belief would find its major expression in the Technocrat Movement.

In two 1921 articles he wrote for the *Nation*, Chase excoriated the existing waste and drew contrasts between the present system and what could be achieved in an economy directed by engineers who would not be primarily motivated by profits, as businessmen were. He called for an alliance of labor unions and engineers to operate the economy for maximum production and minimum waste. A 1925 book, *The Tragedy of Waste*, developed further his criticism of waste. In 1927, he attacked the subject from another direction, co-authoring with F. J. Schlink, the book *Your Money's Worth*, which tried to educate consumers to look for real value rather than be misled by marketing hype, and co-founding with Schlink Consumer's Research, Inc., the forerunner of the modern *Consumer Reports*.[4]

Chase was particularly critical of advertising and salesmanship, writing of the former that two quadrillion words came off American printing presses in a year—11 billion linear miles of words, or enough to circle the solar system—and well over half were advertising copy.

Advertising, he observed, was "the life blood of quackery, and the patent medicine industry." Over $1.25 billion was spent on advertising every year, and it made up 40 to 75 percent of the contents of newspapers, meaning that over half the nation's consumption of newsprint pulp went into advertising, with all the hewed timber that represented. An estimated 80 percent of the nation's mail consisted of advertisements, much of which ended up in the wastebasket unread. Advertising employed an estimated 600,000 workers from copywriters to psychologists.

Chase complained that the purchasing power of the nation was not increased by advertising and that it, in fact, drew workers away from productive employment. Advertising only moved purchases from A to B, making B rich and bankrupting A, and in the meantime reducing purchasing power by the amount spent on salesmanship. While admitting that some advertising was essential in a functioning society," Chase estimated that only 10 percent of the 1925 level was necessary, since the remaining 90 percent consisted only of "largely competitive wrangling as to the relative merits of two undistinguished and often undistinguishable compounds—soaps, tooth powders, motor cars, tires, snappy suits, breakfast foods, patent medicines, cigarettes." Moreover, much of advertising was devoted to the packaging and not the product it contained — the "glitter of a shaving stick holder, the unique shape of tonic bottles, the gold foil about a cigar, monogrammed cigarette boxes, powder puff containers," all of which focused attention away from the product and on "the splendor and the glitter of the container."

Pointing out that one dollar was being spent in America on advertising for every seventy cents spent on all levels of education, Chase concluded:

And yet when all is said and done, advertising does give a certain illusion, a certain sense of escape in a machine age. It creates a dream world; smiling faces, shining teeth, school girl complexions, cornless feet, perfect fitting union suits, distinguished collars, wrinkleless pants, odorless breaths, regularized bowels, happy homes in New Jersey (15 minutes from Hoboken), charging motors, punctureless tires, perfect busts, shimmering shanks, self-washing dishes, backs behind which the moon was meant to rise.[5]

Having attacked advertising, as earlier noted, Chase charged a few years later that the "Age of the Salesman" was creating flaws in the American character. He wrote:

The final objective of the salesman is to put it across, to get away with it, to secure the order. The signature on the dotted line becomes the Supreme Good. It follows that any methods involved in this consummation, are, ipso facto, good methods. The new ethics is thus built on the ability to get away with it, by whatever means.

For most people, Chase wrote, "the doctrine of the main chance is part and parcel of the law of economic survival." It required becoming a "yes man," and "for a yes man to have a sense of honor is unthinkable." As for the consumer, caught in a "net of primitive stimulus and response," and "stripped of all standards of judgment, his native sense is overwhelmed with psychological reactions which reduce him almost to an automatic idiot, and he never knows whether the thing he buys is worth the money he pays for it, whether it is a good product ridiculously overpriced, or whether it is just so much junk."[6]

But the "most curious and the most significant item in the whole phenomenon of changing ethics," Chase wrote, was

the ever growing number of barrels of holy water with which business is being sprinkled—nay drenched. Commerce is taking upon itself all the sanctions of the church, and so slowly but surely transforming its common street behavior into a semisacred cult whose rituals are not to be profaned....To the older ethics this alliance between business and religion appears as cant and hypocrisy, but to the new it is accepted as sound and self-evident doctrine. The unbridgeable chasm between behavior animated by selfishness...and behavior animated by the true spirit of unselfish service—is utterly ignored.[7]

What were the effects of machines on American culture? Had that culture become so mechanized that it had become standardized, regimented, a "lock-step culture?" Chase doubted if American culture had become any more standardized than those of non-machine societies like those of traditional China, medieval Europe, and others. In fact, Chase wrote, "One of the outstanding facts governing a machine culture is its restless and remorseless change." If American culture was standardized, it was "the standardization of infinite variety and perpetual change—and thus uncomfortably close to a contradiction in terms." "The machine," he wrote,

having destroyed the bulk of our old folkways, has forced us to experiment with a host of new ones, none of which have crystallized; and none of them can very well crystallize so long as our technology continues to change.

No sooner do we adapt ourselves to traveling at the rate of thirty miles per hour on earth than we are compelled to take to the air at two hundred miles an hour. And what is this going to do to the family, religion, the etiquette of visiting and entertainment, habits of recreation, education, relations with other races and nations?

Varieties of behavior had become legion, with no standard religious code. Chase wrote:

If religious standards are in disorder, sexual standards are even worse. Unless we happen to live in the Bible Belt, we may select orthodox marriage, trial marriage, companionate marriage, marriage of convenience, or no marriage at all. We may divorce at random. We may practise birth control in all circumstances, in specific circumstances, in no circumstances—again with authority to sanction each decision. We are urged to have small families, large families, no families; to marry when we are young and poor, to wait until we are old and rich; to marry within our class, to marry above or below it. Nor is sanction altogether lacking for the advantages, cultural and economic, of a "sugar daddy." The psychoanalysts have lifted the curtain on a variety of matters long held suitable for discussion only in a brothel—if at all—and have made them current coin at every "modern" dinner table. In brief, the only dependable standard in sexual affairs seems to be that any sort of reticence connotes a serious, not to say perilous, internal conflict.

As for the work world, Chase concluded that every American was convinced his place belonged at the top and was devoted to clawing his way there. "In theory," he pointed out, "no man is fixed, however much he may be in fact; and because this doctrine is so generally held, the organized labor movement can make no great headway in America."

Chase continued:

Through all this welter of modern life many old behavior patterns still survive, but the indirect effects of mechanization have shaken us loose from ancient mental certainties. We are never adequately prepared for change and resist it when it comes, but we are beginning to realize with some bewilderment that almost anything may happen. And that mental attitude is slippery ground on which to build a case for one dead level of behavior.[8]

To attempt to assess the positives and negatives that had resulted from the "new industrialism," would, Chase observed, take "a congress of the best living minds, fortified by many tall portfolios of facts, together with certain basic data....which, alas, has never been collected." But Chase drew up what he called "a preliminary balance sheet," that listed more negatives than positives. The life span and standards of living had improved, he conceded, hours of labor and superstition were declining, class distinctions had broken down, while cruelty had probably decreased and social sympathy increased as a result of the cable and camera. But the negative side included the specter of mechanized warfare, natural resources were being depleted at an "alarming" rate, "monotony and wearisome repetition" had invaded many jobs, recreation tended to be second or third hand, technological unemployment, a greater accident rate due to machines, workers being "scrapped" at younger ages, congested cities, and pollution, among other things. To these Chase added others that combined positives and negatives: the mechanization of the home, which deprived the housewife of her old skills, but also "launched the whole phenomenon of economic independence and equality for woman," the debasement of the quality of some goods combined with improvements in the quality of others, and the loss of economic independence when the workman left the cottage for the factory, with the production of more goods with less labor as a result.

Any assessment of the positives and negatives was, however, "purely academic," since there was "not the slightest possibility of our age remaining static. Technology is in a fury of change, and civilization, willy-nilly, must change with it." It would continue to change, Chase predicted, "until we cross all earlier lines and stand surrounded by the noblest civilization which the world has ever seen—provided the menaces can be controlled." And of these, the greatest was the menace of mechanized warfare, but there were the others listed as negatives as well: overspecialization, waste of natural resources, and unemployment. If these could be overcome "it may well be that we shall find no limit to the greatness of the civilization before us."[9]

In 1929, Chase published *Men and Machines*, which dealt with the impact machine production had exerted on mankind in general, and Americans in particular. Citing Austin Freeman's *Social Decay and Regeneration*, Chase noted that before machine production consumer demand had driven production, but with Watt's invention of the functional steam engine, the machine had begun to "develop in accord with its own laws regardless of the needs and conveniences of man. It continually increased its efficiency of rapid production with corresponding decrease of efficiency in elasticity and adaptability, which were not its mechanical functions. Very soon it had supplied the original demand and ousted the craftsman. But still production continues to increase, not in response to any demand, but under the compulsions of mechanical evolution...." "The relations of supply and demand," Chase wrote, "have become inverted. Under the regime of hand production the problem was to supply consumers with commodities. The problem now is to supply commodities with consumers, thus the 'need' for advertising and salesmanship." Factory workers, moreover, had begun to steadily decline, since "Mass production and the automatic function are relentlessly substituting machines for machine tenders. Between 1923 and 1928, total factory employees declined by 1,250,000." The savings that resulted from machine production were, moreover, being eaten up by promotion and distribution costs, as competitors battled for the available consumers. It was also apparent that consumer purchasing power had not kept pace with the increasing production, as the number of productive workers declined.

It was the automobile that Chase found at the heart of the phenomenon of the 1920s, writing:

How far is the whole phenomenon of prosperity, progress and mass production, since 1920 in America, but the shadow of the automobile? Without it, should we have had the phenomenon at all? It was the motor car which brought installment selling to perfection, and so created some six billions of temporary purchasing power out of nothing at all. Then the technique welcomed radios, phonographs, player pianos, electric refrigerators and the rest, into the fold. If we should cease to buy automobiles at the present rate, what would happen to "prosperity"; would it go down like a house of cards?

Moreover, it was the automobile that dominated the recreation of Americas in the 1920s "the most powerful prime mover we possess; it is the outstanding exhibit in mass production; it is the rock upon which the whole structure of American 'prosperity' is founded; it is the chief creator of the new labour burden; the mightiest reason for the congestion of cities and the desolation of the countrysides; and the leading national plaything."[10]

Even before the crash and the Depression that followed, Chase was concerned about what he saw as rising unemployment, particularly among men over forty, caused by three factors prevalent in the late 1920s: (1) mergers, which always resulted in reductions of the work force; (2) mechanization, with hundreds, even thousands of workers, now being replaced by a handful of operating machines; and (3) the stopwatch, that resulted in tasks being timed, and higher standards of speed that displaced workers unable or unwilling to work at the dictated speed. Men over forty were the most likely to be laid off, and the least likely to find new jobs. As Chase put it, "never until the last few years, and in no other country save America, have age limits been set up—written or unwritten—in quantity lots; never have older men, often skilled and competent, had so much trouble finding new work; never has the threat of old-age dependency for both manual and white-collar jobs, assumed an uglier aspect."

The problem was in part due, Chase observed, to "an excess of philanthropy." More and more employers had begun to offer group life insurance plans for their workers until by 1929 "some eight billions in policies covering about 6,000,000 workers" had been adopted by every business above the size of a "peanut stand." Alas, every year that the coverage had grown the more tenuous had grown the position of the older employee. Why? "Because," Chase wrote, "the older the average age of the factory or office force, the higher the premiums under the group insurance schedules." Thus, when hiring, employers preferred to see the average age of their workforce going down, rather than up. The United States was one of the few major nations, Chase pointed out, that did not have government-financed old-age pensions, which eliminated any incentive by employers to discriminate on the basis of age. This factor in employment decisions could only be eliminated if the United States, too, enacted old-age insurance legislation.[11]

In that same year (1929), Chase looked even more critically at America's alleged prosperity of the 1920s in a book entitled *Prosperity: Fact or Myth?* The book was written shortly before the stock market crash in October, but was not published until a few months later, giving Chase the opportunity to look at the crash and its likely

effects in an updated introduction. Of the crash, he wrote: "Confident that no man understands the sublime process of the money
and credit system, I have not the slightest hesitation in affirming
that I do not understand it, and know no more where it is going
than I know where a hurricane is going." The market, he concluded, had been take over by gamblers as opposed to investors.
Investors he defined as those who were in the market in search of
income, who would pay $100 for a stock paying in the neighbor-
hood of $5 per year in dividends. Gamblers, on the other hand,
cared nothing about the income of a stock, but only the prospects
that it would gain in value. During the two years before the crash,
they had "completely routed the investors," driving stock prices up
to the point where "no investor in his senses" would touch them.
The crash meant that the investors had their market back again,
"with prices yielding ten and twelve per cent." In Chase's view, the
crash meant that "a reasonable price structure in the market has
been reached" and "the logical reality of the relationship between
principal and income has reasserted itself, rendering the entire structure more sound and more coherent than it has been for many
months."

As for its likely effect on the economy, Chase reviewed the economic statistics for 1929 and found no basis for pessimism. Except
for "a small spasm of gastritis" in the auto industry, there had been
no severe slackening in production. The "underlying structure of
prosperity was proceeding at par, or a little better than par, when
the stock market collapsed," so it was not declining business that
was responsible for the crash. There had, however, been declines
in the weeks since the crash, and Chase found "widespread uncertainty tinged with fear." None of this boded well for the future,
particularly in the view of someone like Chase, who had discounted
the reality of the 1920s prosperity. As he put it, it escaped him how
"a prosperity founded on forcing people to consume what they do
not need, and often do not want, is, or can be, a healthy and permanent growth."[12]

In *Prosperity: Fact or Myth?*, Chase examined the evidence for
business prosperity in the 1920s, and concluded that from the
businessman's point of view, at least, the decade had been prosperous. But the prosperity "chorus," he found, had "concentrated on
the high lights and forgotten the more somber shadows" of the

economy. The major highlight and contributor to the appearance of prosperity had been the automobile, "something which people really wanted with a desire that amounted to a passion." It had "sent the credit structure spiraling upward, and it certainly made us look prosperous." It unleashed "the whole phenomenon of competitive social standards," stimulated by "aggressive salesmanship on the part of the automobile manufacturer," which made one's social standing in the community dependent on the "make, cost and model of one's motor car." Mass production and high-pressure salesmanship soon spread into other articles: "Radios, washing machines, refrigerators, oil burners, vacuum cleaners and the rest, sought to find and capitalize the same passionate interest which turned the public to the automobile."

Adding to the appearance of prosperity had been higher wages, caused in part by the restriction of immigration in the early 1920s, a flattening curve of population growth, and the growing use of machines in production. There were other contributing factors, as well, but Chase could not shake the feeling it was the automobile that was primarily responsible:

> When all is said and done, I come back to the motor car, and the psychological reactions it has engendered, as the chief factor in the creation of what we call American prosperity. One of the first results of the October 1929 stock market crash was the cancellation of many orders placed for new cars. If this movement, initiated by losing margin account speculators, spreads to the general buying public the curtain may be run down on Act V.

Reviewing the statistics of the 1920s, Chase could find little evidence of improvement in the condition of the people, despite impressive evidence of technological progress and productivity. If one defined prosperity in dynamic terms, as a rate of advance, then clearly the 1920s had been prosperous. But if it were defined in static terms, as a state of affairs that included security and happiness, then conditions did not qualify as prosperity. Reviewing government income tax figures, Chase found that less than 10 percent of the 27 million heads of families earned enough income ($2,500 for a married person, $1,500 for a single one) to require the preparation of a tax return.[13] Such advances as had been achieved in living standards had been accomplished by many people only at the cost of increased indebtedness.

In a chapter titled "Balancing the Books," Chase wrote:

We have let us say an onion. The onion represents the total economic life of the United States at the present time. The heart of the onion is prosperity. How large does it bulk?

First, we must strip off all the states not included in the Middle Atlantic, East North Central, and Pacific states. The National Bureau of Economics find that by and large these states have not prospered.

Second, in the prosperous belt, we strip off most of the farmers; they have not prospered.

Third, we strip off a large section of the middle class. The small business man, the independent storekeepers, the wholesaler, many professional men and women, have failed to keep income on a par with the new standard of living.

Fourth, we strip off all the unemployed. Machinery appears to be displacing factory, railroad, and mining workers—and recently mergers are displacing executives, salesmen and clerks—faster than they can find employment in other fields. The net increase in "technological unemployment" since 1920 exceeds 650,000 men and women.

Fifth, we strip off the coal industry which has been in the doldrums throughout the period.

Sixth, we strip off the textile industry which has been seriously depressed.

Seventh, the boots and shoe industry. Ditto.

Eighth, the leather industry.

Ninth, the shipbuilding industry.

Tenth, the railroad equipment industry.

Eleventh, we strip off the excessive number of businesses which have gone bankrupt during the era.

Twelfth, we strip off those millions of unskilled workers who were teetering on the edge of a bare subsistence in 1922, and by no stretch of the imagination can be called prosperous today. But the core of the onion still existed, and it included:

1. A 20 percent increase in the national income per capital from 1922 to 1928.
2. A 30 per cent increase in physical production.
3. A 100 per cent increase in the profits of the larger corporations.
4. A housing program expanding faster than population.
5. An increase in average health and longevity.
6. An increase in educational facilities greatly surpassing the growth of population.
7. A per capita increase in savings and insurance.
8. A booming stock market up to October 1929.
9. A 5-hour decline in the average working week.

10. A slowly rising wage scale against a fairly stationary price level.
11. An increasingly fecund, alert and intelligent science of management, resulting primarily in an ever growing productivity per worker.[14]

Nevertheless, Chase was not convinced that this represented anything more than progress toward prosperity—a prosperity that might be achieved by the end of another similar period of progress.

Chase ended with another plea for the replacement of management by the engineer:

> Prosperity in any deeper sense awaits the liberation of the engineer. If the owners will not get off his back—and why should they; they pay him little enough and he fills their safe deposit boxes?—I, for one, would not be sorry to see him combine with the wayfaring man to lift them off. A complicated technical structure should be run by engineers, not hucksters. But the technician is the modern Prometheus in chains.[15]

With the onset of the Depression, Chase wrote that America still possessed the raw materials, the labor force, the "beautiful technic of management," and capital, so business would go on. "It may stagger for a time, but it is inconceivable that it is permanently crippled." The Depression would pass, and "the emergency bread lines fade away." But technological unemployment would remain, with men losing their jobs by the thousands even after the Depression. Chase wondered how "near to saturation are the filling-station industry, bond selling, insurance, hot-dog stands, spear carrying in Hollywood, and other 'blotting paper' trades?" He feared they were getting "soggy." Chase had concluded that the "logical, sensible, and only final answer to technological unemployment is to shorten working hours," thus permitting the whole nation to share in technological advances, with more jobs and "undiminished purchasing power." Chase referred to it as the "regularization of industry," and found it already being practiced by some firms. Another solution was the regularization of construction projects, public and private, so that they were "nursed in the good years and brought forward when a cyclical downturn threatened." Companies, Chase observed, had developed many ingenious devices for protecting the "dividends and equities of stockholders." It was high time that they did the same for "the flesh and blood" that provided those dividends and equities.[16]

Later in 1930, Chase took up overproduction as "The Enemy of Prosperity." In both agriculture and industry, he wrote, Americans had been too successful in producing abundance, largely as an outgrowth of the stimulus provided by World War I. Still, for most Americans there was a shortage of the goods that they needed "to maintain a comfortable standard of living," because they lacked the purchasing power with which to buy them. The problem, therefore, was not only of overproduction, but also of underconsumption, and this stemmed, in large part, from the unequal division of income in America. Sounding like David Cushman Coyle, Chase explained:

> The living expenses of the rich have absorbed only a small fraction of their total incomes. The balance has flowed into new enterprises, some of them extremely necessary enterprises, many of them only adding to an industry already overequipped. If more of the gross receipts had been returned in wages, industry would have stood on a more solid base, with less loose capital seeking even looser investment. In brief, a bad distribution of income has done much to foster excess plant capacity. Instead of being used, capital has been abused. It used to be widely held that if profits were tampered with, "capital would leave the country." We might have been better off to-day if it had. We have altogether too much capital in relation to purchasing power.

The situation might not have been so bad in the absence of rampant competition. As Chase put it:

> Great monopolies articulated to consumer demand, producing according to the latest findings of the technical arts, running at approximate capacity the year around, might mean monopoly profits (if unregulated), but would also mean no waste of capital, far less unemployment, no excess plant capacity, no overproduction —even as the Telephone Company now functions. But alas, competition, far from declining, has accelerated.

The result had been overproduction, the increased use of salesmanship, and the "whole gaudy phenomenon of modern distribution." Half of the consumer's dollar was going for "advertising, selling, and transportation." Installment selling had temporarily increased purchasing power, but now, with the Depression, the worker was burdened with debt and even less able to "buy simple food and clothing in the volume that would be good for him, and especially good for industry at this time." What the nation needed at this point was "a deliberate nation-wide fostering of a high-wage policy, and a better distribution of income," and "planned production." Production must be oriented to "consumptive needs." This would probably necessitate a

> drastic revision of the anti-trust laws; an alliance between industry, trade association, and government to control investment (i.e., plant capacity) on the one hand and to guard against unwarranted monopoly prices on the other; universal system of minimum wages and guaranteed hours of labor to frighten off fly-by-night entrepreneurs and to stimulate purchasing power; and finally, and perhaps most important of all, the setting up of a National Industrial Planning Board as a fact-gatherer and in turn an adviser to Congress, President, industry, trade union, bankers, state government, on every major economic undertaking in accordance with a master blueprint.[17]

A year into the Depression, Chase published a short pamphlet entitled *Out of the Depression and After—A Prophecy*. He began by lauding a new emphasis on the behavioral aspects of economics revealed by recent textbooks in the field:

> We arrive precisely nowhere in our understanding of the total scene without taking into account psychology and anthropology, subjects which textbooks of economics hitherto have tended rigorously to neglect. Indeed, most of the vast library of "business literature" built up to towering proportions in the last decade or two, is so much waste paper because of its neglect of the springs of human behavior.[18]

Chase had taken a trip to the Soviet Union in 1927 as a member of an unofficial trade union delegation that included Rexford Tugwell and had obviously been impressed by what he was shown. Complimentary references to the Soviet experiment now began to appear in his works as he confronted the apparent failure of capitalism in the United States. What was to be the result of the "struggle" that was shaping up "between Russia and the United States; between the economic behavior very loosely designated as communism and that called capitalism?"

Chase did not foresee a revolution in America "during the next few years," since the "folkways" of capitalism were too deeply embedded. The Depression did not "mark the end of the world," but was, in fact, simply another of the usual business cycles, made to feel "worse than it actually is because we cascaded from such an exalted peak in 1929...and because the Prosperity Chorus had sold us the idea that the business cycle had been permanently exorcised." Typically, the business cycle would begin an upturn "within the next twelve months" (i.e., 1932), when consumers began again to buy, retailers bought from wholesalers, wholesalers ordered from manufacturers, and the latter began to rehire employees to meet the new orders. Chase saw "no outstanding reason why the old story should not be told again" in the United States, irrespective of whether Europe recovered or not. In the meantime, however, conditions were likely to grow worse, but that fact was likely to produce some reforms, perhaps a system of state unemployment insurance, and an advisory planning board. Such reforms might do much to mitigate the effects of the next downward turn in the cycle, which Chase expected in 1940.

The competition between the Russian and American economic systems would continue, Chase predicted:

> American experience seems to indicate that an industrial unit, such as, say, a stee mill, is more efficiently managed by private parties animated by the hope of profit, but owing to the serious lack of correlation between competing steel mills, and between the steel industry and all other industries, the economic structure as a whole operates with enormous loss, leakage and friction, reflected particularly in over-production and unemployment. Russia, while she has less efficient units, by directing their operations from a central conning tower, is able to avoid overproduction, unemployment, undue exhaustion of natural resources, excessive costs of distribution, crosshauling, labor struggles, and various other wastes inherent in an uncorrelated system.

Chase's own preference for a "correlated" system was obvious.

Peering into his "crystal ball," Chase foresaw an America increasingly alienated from its "machine god" as it grew "surfeited with noise, speed, dust, skyscrapers and gadgets." Sounding Brandeisian, he expected this to lead to "industrial decentralization" from the diffusion of cheap electric power, "clean, noiseless, adapted to small scale, even handicraft production." The alternative was to begin to control the machines through national planning, to "make the cogwheels mesh—or else retreat, after a frightful cataclysm, to the stability of the handicraft age." As Chase put it:

> Russia today is carrying on a magnificent experiment in the purposeful control of the machine. We of the West must follow with experiments of

our own, and that shortly. The gods—as this terrible depression proves—are not prepared to grant an indefinite stay of sentence to the policy of muddling through.

The United States had already experienced a degree of national planning under the War Industries Board during World War I, only to see it dissolve when the war ended. Since then the emphasis had been on "industrial coordination" as distinguished from planning, as manifested in the merger movement. Strangely, Chase did not mention the trade association movement, which was the most notable effort in behalf of that coordination in the 1920s.

In advocating planning, Chase saw the "best unit" as the economic region, such as New England, the Corn Belt, or the Northwest. It was the only scale of planning that was likely to "some day arouse the emotions of the wayfaring citizen" and awaken a competitive effort. The most important feature of any master plan must be control of new investment:

> In a so-called prosperous year in the United States, we may release as much as ten billion dollars. This sum goes anywhere, on a glorious hit-and-miss basis—into woolen mills when there are already three times as many woolen mills as the market needs, into highly dubious foreign enterprises where the size of the banker's commission is the primary magnet, into surplus cement plants, into new oil pools, when we have a 50 per cent excess of producing wells, into miniature golf courses, into skyscrapers and subways to compound the discomfort and danger of existing in Megalopolis, into land reclamation projects when bankrupt farmers are streaming from the land, into a huge advertising campaign to make us athletes'-foot-conscious, into developing house lots in the swamps of Florida.

The intent was to show the unwary investor where money was genuinely needed and where it was not, since:

> The whole wheel turns on the allotment of capital to new enterprises. This is what balanced economy means. Just enough coal mines and iron mines to supply the steel industry; just enough blast furnaces to supply the rails, structural shapes, tractors, and pitchforks that the plan calls for, year by year.

Recalling Thorstein Veblen's distinction between "business" and "industry," Chase expected business, the buying and selling aspect, to oppose planning, while he anticipated that industry, the engineering aspect" to favor it and to provide much of the stuff of any planning agency.[19]

Leisure had, itself, become an "industry" in the 1920s, Chase wrote:

> We have here in the whole country something in the order of thirty million radio listeners a night. Fifty million people pass weekly through the gaudy doors of our moving picture palaces. Thirty-five million copies of tabloids and newspapers are distributed every day, and fifteen millions of the popular magazines make their rounds every month. Our pleasure motoring bill, excluding the automobile as a commercial or business vehicle, runs to the astounding total of five million dollars a year. Our whole bill for recreation, play, and leisure time activities very broadly defined, I have calculated at twenty-one billion dollars, which is about one-quarter of our national income.

The result had been a huge industry, with a huge investment, and many thousands of businessmen involved in it. The result was that the "play industry" was cutting into the "essential industries." For example, Chase pointed to Middletown, where families had been found "giving up needed clothing, for their children, and...even giving up food...in order to buy gasoline." Without high-pressure salesmanship to sell them, traditional leisure time activities like camping, hiking, gardening had given way to the more mechanized pastimes. Americans, he concluded, were like children with new toys, and must go through a period of picking them to pieces, of examining them, of admiring them, of trying them." To fight against the trend was to pit oneself against "twenty-one billions of dollars devoted to commercializing and mechanizing our leisure time."[20]

Reviewing Harry Laidler's book, *Concentration in American Industry*, Chase wrote that the author had shown many examples of the breach of the Sherman Anti-Trust Act by American industry. In this, the trade associations of the 1920s had been particularly guilty:

> Are you aware of what price cutting is now called in trade-association circles? It is called a crime. The price cutter should be incarcerated; he should be lynched! Let your mind rest on this nugget for an instant. To lower prices is a criminal offense. To lower them from what? Obviously from some standard price level. Since when has free competition known standard price levels; since when has it been a crime for a man to sell his own goods at any price he jolly well pleases? What else does free compe-

tition mean? If you take away individual freedom to fix prices, you put a depth bomb under the whole institution. Trade associations are in effect setting or trying to set price standards, and are putting bitter pressure on those who undersell the standard. This price maintenance they call "constructive competition," but they might equally well term it noncompetitive competition.

Laissez-faire, attacked by the bacilli of mergers, interlocking directorates and trade associations, is at the point of death, and it is about time we threw open the windows and called honestly for the mortician.[21]

Late that year, Chase issued what he called his "Declaration of Independence." The Depression, he observed, had to its credit the fact that it had exploded the "American formula which all but blotted out the sun as the last decade marched," a formula based on

mass production, huge volume, high wages, high interest rates, high-pressure selling, installment purchasing, soaring stock prices, brokers' loans, investment trusts, corporate mergers, boom towns, subdivisions, four-dimensional speed, riotous destruction of natural resources, the virtue of rapid obsolescence, gathering technological unemployment, the complete disregard of the farmer, emphasis on luxuries as against necessities, the duty of spending rather than saving, the extension of leisure only on the distinct understanding that the margin be devoted to the consumption of more leisure-time goods.

"To-day," he wrote, "a growing battalion has realized that a nation devoted to the exclusive cultivation of such things as these is a nation lost in the wilderness." As for Chase, his "declaration of independence" included a determination to abandon "keeping up with the Joneses" and cultivating "sales resistance as an exact science," to research the products that he did buy, and to patronize local handicrafts, while also reducing the tempo of his life. "We shall deny," Chase wrote,

the necessity of tumultuous hurry, bustle, spinning about in circles. This catching trains by an eyelid, flying three hundred miles to save an hour and thirteen minutes, this being pumped back and forth in subway pipes, these obscene spurts in outboard motors, these four hundred and sixteen miles torn from the speedometer between dawn and dusk, these utterly devastating week-ends where one rushes in turn through air, water, carbon monoxide, jazz and alcohol, are not pastimes for civilized adults. We shall be profoundly suspicious of the amusement value to be achieved by sheer speed. For a decade, America has been a nation of children shrieking down a roller-coaster. This applies not only to aircraft, motor cars, and speed boats, but to stock markets, mergers, skyscrapers, and salesmanship.

It would also involve a lot of resigning from clubs, boards, and committees. It was time, Chase argued, "that the intelligent minority should realize that it cannot serve God and Mammon," and America was "too fine a land to be longer drugged by the infantile slogans and dazzled by the glittering gadgets of shoddy speculators."[22]

Chase's prediction that the bottom of the business cycle would be reached in 1932 was in fact realized when a variety of economic indictors turned upward in the summer of that year, only to be dashed a few months later as an apparent result of uncertainty over the presidential election in November and the policies that might follow. Even before the upturn, however, he had turned in despair to writing yet another book, *A New Deal*, that was published months before Roosevelt used the term in his acceptance speech at the Democratic National Convention. In his new book, Chase took a more radical turn, asking in the opening chapter "What Is An Economic System For?" It might better have been titled with a "Who" replacing the "What." While in previous works Chase had weighed the pros and cons of capitalism and found them of about equal weight, he now found the cons clearly to be dominant.

The problems of production, he admitted, had been solved, but the great deficiency of the system was in distribution, in the inadequate purchasing power of American consumers. "Why," he asked, "is purchasing power inadequate; why do we Western peoples fail to gain the full benefits of the economy of abundance; why must we go through such scarifying periods of mental panic and physical deprivation as the present? How can they be avoided? That, my friends, is a long and complicated story," and it was the purpose of *A New Deal* to "attempt its telling in broad outline." One fundamental problem was in the prevailing views of what the economic system was for. "By and large," he concluded, "it is regarded either as a means to achieve power and prestige, or as an amusing game to be played, the counters being those same pieces of paper which form purchasing power." Every level was characterized by gambling, the reward of risk, and a belief that in the process some social good was being achieved. Yet few, if any, had the social good in mind when they embarked upon a business career. Considerations of how their actions might affect the business cycle or the adequacy of purchasing power were "normally undreamed of," replaced by questions of profit or fun.[23]

This striving for wealth Chase found taking mainly sixteen forms under capitalism: the creation of an artificial monopoly and the raising of prices; the tying up of a patent or a secret process and charging the maximum possible for its use; raising interest rates to flagrantly high levels; manufacturing "useless, adulterated or even vicious" products and selling them through "high-pressure selling and advertising"; creating a demand for a product that inflated its price beyond what it was worth; "creation of new fashions in costumes, fads or novelties and the astute manipulation of social pressure to market them"; creating and marketing "more or less dubious stocks and bonds" through high-pressure salesmanship; speculating in stocks and bonds; speculating in real estate; speculating in commodities; promoting "parasitic industries" that feed off areas with cheap labor; manipulating political decisions through graft; business corruption; "racketeering"; dumping products in foreign countries; "rushing blindly to compete when excess capacity already threatens the industry." In short, the economic system seemed to be primarily a device "to be manipulated for some individual's profit, power or amusement," with resultant waste and maladjustment to the system. But, Chase argued,

> When used as a channel for personal aggrandizement, a system's function and meaning collapse. It becomes an industrial whirlpool, throwing out a certain amount of goods and services as a byproduct, but susceptible to frightful stoppages, reverse twists, and even complete draining out. We have come in 1932 perilously close to the last....To go on stumbling through economic pits and mires, under a sky recurrently black with the horror of insecurity and even starvation, is tragic and needless waste.

Like David Cushman Coyle, Chase regarded American industry as overbuilt, and savings a harmful tradition that endured from expansionary times.[24]

Surveying the American economy in 1932, Chase found areas in which "a corrupt (i.e. impure) laissez-faire flourishes," others where varying degrees of collectivism existed, and some in which there was "a most unseemly hodgepodge of both." In general, he found collectivism growing at the expense of free competition. Collectivism included the absorption by government of many social functions not envisioned under laissez-faire, including regulation of hours and minimum wages, child labor, safety and sanitation codes, and other things of this nature. It also included much of the function of government, which included the mails, schools, public highways and bridges, public lands and forests, oil reserves, public hospitals, and so on, to the tune of an annual payroll of $6.6 billion. There was also the regulation of business by government through such agencies as the Federal Trade Commission, Interstate Commerce Commission, Federal Power Commission, and various other federal and state agencies. The federal government had also intruded into banking, through the Federal Reserve System, Farm Land Banks, and Post Office Savings, not to mention the legislation then being debated for the creation of the Reconstruction Finance Corporation, with its "two billions of collectivism." The tariff was also a governmental interference with free trade.

Outside of government, Chase argued that free trade no longer existed within the great corporations, and especially within the range of the 7,000 trade associations in the country which were promoting "non-competitive competition." Labor unions, too, had no part in a competitive system, nor did producers and consumers cooperatives, in which private profit had been replaced by mutual profit. While not pure collectivism, these various characteristics of 1932 America were dealing "sledge-hammer blows at laissez-faire and the natural rights of the entrepreneur. They occupied "a point half way on the road to socialization." True competition tended to exist only in retail shops and stores, in some wholesaling and jobbings, and in the manufacture of "novelties and new commodities," farming, construction, and "the production of soft coal and petroleum." For the most part, however, "modern industrialism, because of its delicate specialization and interdependence, increasingly demands the collectivism of social control to keep its several parts from jamming," and government was meeting that need "by continually widening the collective sector through direct ownership, operation and regulation of economic functions."[25]

An expanding population required continual increases in capital investment in housing, factories, and new equipment. But surveying the statistics of the 1920s, Chase concluded that American population was fast approaching a plateau that it was likely to reach within a decade or two. Birth rates were not keeping pace with death rates, even though the latter were falling, and immigration had been substantially reduced by the restrictive legislation of the 1920s.

With America's industrial plant already overbuilt, the "slackening population curve" would only make a bad situation worse. Contrasting the shoe industry in the Soviet Union with that in the United States, Chase reported that under communism the building of shoe factories ceased when enough shoes could be made to supply the Russian population, while in the chaotic conditions prevailing in the United States shoe factories were capable of producing 900 million pairs a year for a population that bought approximately 300 million pairs per year.[26] Investment continued to flow into the overbuilt establishment, but the plants were "increasingly incapable of earning a profit because of inadequate utilization." Technical progress was only adding to the problem of overproduction and simultaneously to the technological unemployment that reduced consumer purchasing power even more. "It would be a jolly good thing," Chase wrote, "to declare a moratorium on inventions for at least a decade, and treat all inventors as dangerous lunatics, with proper care and supervision....One of the best hopes for securing some real progress in the future is to bottle up technical progress, and feed it out with a measuring cup."[27]

One way to increase consumer spending and to reduce debt was, of course, to initiate a modest rate of inflation. But the very word evoked images of a Germany in 1923 when paper money was so worthless that it took a trillion paper marks to equal one gold mark.[28] In addition there was the opposition of the vested interests who would be hurt by inflation—particularly bankers, bondholders, and other creditors. "In general," Chase wrote, "inflation tends to wrench away the dead hand of the vested interests, and to give the underlying community, and particularly active business men, a fresh start." But so long as the United States remained on the gold standard and the gold supply remained constant, it followed that "the total money supply is limited" and purchasing power could only go so far. Chase noted with approval the proposals being made for a "managed currency," which would mean "the end of the metal standard as such, the end of laissez-faire in the whole structure of money and credit, the end of alien and 'natural' causes generally, and the deliberate control of the money supply in line with production, invention and the requirements of purchasing power."[29]

The "prosperity" of the 1920s had not solved the problem of distribution, and eventually the house of cards had collapsed. "High wages and installment selling," Chase wrote, "helped for time to fill the gap between purchasing power and the capacity to produce, but the gap yawned wider in the end; nothing fundamental had been done about it, and the New Era disappeared under a memorial wreath of ticker tape on a certain October morning in 1929." Moreover,

> Toward the close of the period, purchasing power was perceptibly reduced by the freezing of a large fraction of the available supply in the stock market. As much went into brokers' loans as installment selling had earlier released—six billions—while huge additional sums were paid for outright stock purchases at figures which bore no relationship to earning power. The seller in turn repurchased stocks. It has been estimated that between 1922 and September 1929, more than fifty billions was added to stock market values. A good fraction of this came to represent congealed purchasing power. Even before the October crash, business was beginning to fall off, sales were slackening. The public could not buy both goods and stocks. It chose stocks, vociferously assisted by all the frock coats and high hats from the President down.[30]

Thus did Chase now make a connection between the stock market crash and the Depression that had been absent from *Prosperity: Fact or Myth?* Now Chase was convinced that the Depression would have come even without the crash, although "not so violently and not quite so soon," for absent "a functional economic system and a controlled money supply, down we must have come in due time." The Depression, he concluded, had actually begun in the summer of 1929 when industrial production had begun to slacken. "Purchasing power, impounded in brokers' loans, foreign advances, and unproductive investments generally, was running low. Installment selling had reached its limit of swelling the pyramid of purchasing power."

> By October, the facts, though publicly unadmitted, penetrated to certain speculators on Wall Street—where stocks were still gaily selling for fifty times their earning power, instead of the normal twenty. The word was not

passed around, it got through, by some strange telepathy. Suddenly men began to sell; suddenly the whole world began to sell; in a few days fifty billions of paper values went whistling out of Wall Street, and the depression became news.

Thus, Chase now took the position that the Depression had actually preceded the stock market crash, rather than following it. But the crash accelerated the downswing by adding "four definite gravity slides." Chase explained:

> It made people afraid; it continued for a long period to keep purchasing power tied up in brokers' loans; it forced the last buyers in the boom period to pay for their stocks out of income, which impounded more purchasing power. The boom had fostered an unhealthy growth of luxury industries— patronized by the paper profiteers—which, when the crash came, were left stranded.

Now industrial production had been "slashed below the money supply," although both were "enormously shrunk." According to the experts, an upturn in the business cycle could now occur.

Chase agreed with David Cushman Coyle in ascribing much of the blame for the Depression to the glut of savings among the higher income groups, who could not spend all of their income on consumer goods and who, in an overbuilt economy, lacked attractive investment opportunities. Had this surplus income gone, instead, to the lower income groups it would have been spent on consumer goods. The imbalance had seriously reduced consumer purchasing power, and, when joined with the other reductions in purchasing power caused by such phenomena as speculation in Wall Street, had triggered the downturn in business. As Chase put it:

> The rich cannot spend their incomes on consumers' goods; they must save, and often they have difficulty in finding profitable investment. The worker spends most of his wages on consumers' goods. If he received a fairer proportion of the national income, the pull of purchasing power would be steadier and stronger....Too much money in the upper brackets and not enough in the lower, helped to bring on this depression as it has helped to bring on others in the past.

Chase distinguished between savings and investment. Savings were moneys taken out of use, while investments, unless for wasteful purposes, found their way back into the economy. America was "saving too much and not spending enough on consumable goods."

In sum, the principal reason behind the Depression was an absence of control at the top of the economic mechanism, a "failure to ask what an economic system is for." Until that question was answered, the economy would continue to be plagued with business cycles. But Chase suspected that "the end of the economic system as we have known it—and suffered with it—in the past" had come. A "new deal was in order," and that prospect he found "stimulating and exciting."[31]

In seeking a solution, Chase had by now espoused virtually every recipe thus far advanced by reformers. He had advocated engineering control of the "conning tower" of the economy, like a good technocrat. He had approved the remedies of the inflationists and managed money advocates. And he had championed the planning and increased collectivization of industry. He had even made a half-bow in the direction of the Brandeisians in encouraging decentralization of industry and regional planning, as well as by his antipathy for big business and Wall Street. He now also began to sound Keynesian in advocating a massive program of public works, financed by borrowing or inflation, that would absorb "two or three million of the unemployed directly—thus feeding a huge new stream into the river bed of purchasing power—thus stimulating industry—thus causing more of the unemployed to be absorbed as food and clothing workers—thus adding to the purchasing power again—thus checking the domestic price fall—thus strengthening the banks...." The deficit thus accumulated could be liquidated from the taxes of a revived nation later. Ironically, such a course was likely to bring about a traditional rise in the business cycle and make all of the other reforms unlikely. Yet even Chase wondered if a $5 billion public works program would be as effective in 1932 as it might have been a year earlier.[32]

Chase's "new deal" would take what he called "the third road," eschewing violent revolution or business dictatorship. His third road would entail:

> the drastic and progressive revision of the economic structure avoiding an utter break with the past. It must entail collectivism pushed at last to control from the top, but control over landmarks with which we are reasonably familiar. It may entail a temporary dictatorship; I do not know. But it will not tear up customs, traditions and behavior patterns to any such extent as promised by either the red or black dictatorships.

Chase was convinced that a growing number of Americans had grown disillusioned with the economic structure, particularly "the general run of educated people, whether in business, agriculture, government service, or in the home." The system was "impoverishing and shaming them," offering them "no abiding sense of economic security" even in good times. In particular, they had lost their respect for the "American plutocracy." He assumed that this disaffected and intelligent minority was now prepared to countenance more change than at any time in America's history, to "swing to the left, but only for a certain distance."[33]

The major agencies of change that Chase envisioned were:

For money
- A managed currency, ending fortuitous inflation and deflation.
- A stiffening of income and inheritance taxes in the upper brackets.
- Higher real wages.
- The elimination of tariff barriers.
- The control of foreign investment.
- A drastic curb on speculation, particularly stock markets.

For machines
- An industrial budget of national requirements and industrial capacity to meet them.
- A progressive shortening of the work week.
- Unemployment insurance.
- The education of the consumer.
- The promotion of industrial decentralization.

For both
- Reserve and continuing programs of public works, particularly housing and rural electrification.
- Long-term government budgeting.
- The control of domestic investment.
- National and regional planning boards to coordinate the whole.

While not specifically addressed, the problems of the farmer would be ameliorated by every item in the last, but particularly by the public works program, which "aid the farmer through rural electrification, highway construction, afforestation, flood control, technical methods." Chase was convinced that all of the measures he proposed could be "instituted without serious change in the Constitution, or profound violation of existing political or economic machinery."

The most radical item on the list Chase had saved for last, and he recognized that the "loudest alarms will come when the planning board devises a procedure for controlling new capital investment." But this would come later. Chase envisioned only three items on the list coming to fruition in the next three years, by which an impressive beginning could be made. These were:

- A managed currency.
- The drastic redistribution of the national income through income and inheritance taxes.
- A huge program of public works.

The income tax he considered "one of the divinest engines for rectifying the maldistribution of national income ever invented."

Although he did not include it within the initial three listed, Chase foresaw the early enactment of a minimum wage law, such as was already in effect in several states covering the employment of women. It should be extended to all classes of labor in businesses employing ten or more workers. Firms driven out of business by the requirement to pay a living wage deserved their fate, since they were "parasitic and uneconomic." It would help to create purchasing power "and above all help human beings." Tariffs were "an anachronism" and should be abolished. They made no more sense, in Chase's view, than would tariffs between the states. "The whole monstrous edifice," Chase wrote, "should be leveled, and as the biggest boy in school, we should take the lead." Speculation on Wall Street should first be attacked by drying up the sources of brokers' loans. Conceding that humans love to gamble and that Wall Street was "the best gambling joint in the world," Chase suggested closing it up as a gambling joint and opening a new one in Washington that would deal in "huge state lotteries," with at least half the proceeds going to "some worthy public project." The scheme, he argued, would accomplish three things: "It would drain off the gambling instinct into a less devitalizing channel; it would provide revenue for the state; it would keep money from congealing in brokers' loans, stopped from useful service, and thus help to steady the business cycle."

As for economic planning:

The drive of collectivism leads toward control from the top. A managed currency demands a board of managers; long-term government budgeting demands expert technical supervision with special reference to the income tax; a minimum wage law demands economists and statisticians to set the minimums; the control of foreign investment demands a competent authority on which investors and the public can rely. The regulation of hours of labor, of minors in industry, the creation of a scheme for unemployment insurance, an augmented public works program, the control of domestic investment, indeed nearly every plank in our platform leads directly to a conning tower or series of towers which must see the nation steadily and see it whole. All planks are related parts of one central project—to build a sturdy bridge from production to distribution.

All of this was to be done by a National Planning Board, which would give its advice based on "a steady flow of facts and statistics covering all significant aspects of the country's economic life." It would be supplemented by "Regional Boards in major economic areas." While the boards would have the requisite distinguished figureheads at the top, the real work and thought would be done by technicians, the "class most able, most clear-headed of all in American life, hitherto only half utilized in technical detail and in college class rooms." Chase speculated that some moribund industries that were beyond hope of efficient private operation would have to be socialized in some way. He mentioned the railroads, coalmines and oil fields, electric power, steel and meat packing as examples, as well as wheat and cotton production.

Public works could undertake a lengthy menu of needed and useful projects, including housing, highways, rural electrification, development of Muscle Shoals (which would become the Tennessee Valley Authority under Roosevelt), reconstructing the forest reserves for all the good effects it would have on soil preservation, climate, rainfall, and scenery. To protests from some businessmen that such projects were "uneconomic," Chase responded:

> Presumably patent medicines, Tom Thumb golf equipment, cigar lighters, loans to non-existent railways in Brazil, two cents worth of perfume in a five dollar urn, Eugenie hats, Florida swamp lots, broker's loans, tooth pastes which remove the enamel, Cadillac cars, Beauty Shoppes and nine out of ten Hollywood films are more economic.

Besides their "prime function of providing essential services which the people of America desperately need," public works would have the added benefits of providing employment, and would be "a second line of defense to a managed currency in mitigating the business cycle," since they would be geared to the rise and fall of prices

Chase's third road, he said, sought to "dissolve capitalism with a minimum of governmental interference," by shifting purchasing power into the hands of consumers and ending new investment in socially destructive fields for socially useful ones like public works. The forces were growing in America, Chase believed, who were ready to embark upon such an experiment. He added:

> And woe to Supreme Courts, antiquated rights of property, checks and balances and democratic dogmas which stand in its path. We shall have plenty of exhilaration on the road if we have the will and courage to take it, even if it lacks the drama of red dictatorship and the imperial eagles of the black.[34]

He ended his book by asking: "Why should Russians have all the fun of remaking a world?"[35]

5

Stuart Chase and the New Deal

When asked some years later if he was the father of the term New Deal, as used by FDR in his speech accepting the Democratic nomination later that year, Chase responded:

> People are always asking me if I am the author of the phrase "a new deal." The facts are these: in February 1932 I completed the manuscript of a book to be published by Macmillan to which I gave the title "A NEW DEAL." It had some preliminary publicity of course and in May and June of 1932, the New Republic ran five articles taken from the book under the caption, A NEW DEAL. In July 1932, Franklin Roosevelt flew to Chicago and on the floor of the convention first used the phrase. In his acceptance speech were one or two sentences which had a faintly familiar ring leading me to wonder out of idle curiosity whether those who had helped him on the speech had been reading the New Republic.

However, Chase wrote, he had not "the faintest desire to claim paternity," although he was "in favor of much of the legislation which passes under that label."[1]

In a June article for *Harpers*, Chase called for the creation of a "Peace Industries Board" modeled after the War Industries Board of World War I, as the first step in planning the economy. Its purpose would be to draft a ten year plan for the United States and to execute the plan once it was completed. The target of the plan should be to provide "a minimum family wage of five thousand dollars by 1943." Chase wrote that the task before the Peace Industries Board was simpler than that faced by the WIB during the war:

> It is easier to make a dwelling house than a tank, a plow than a field gun. The old Board had to create the vast paraphernalia of the wastes of war, both in man power and materials, while at the same time raising the stan-

117

dard of living. The new Board need concentrate only upon the latter....It is challenged with the opportunity to abolish the human misery which flows from economic maladjustment, to liquidate the agony of unemployment, to keep both men and machines steadily employed raising the standard of living in line with the growth of the technical arts, to conserve the precious natural resources of America, to stamp out poverty itself.

In deciding which industries should fall under its supervision, the new Board would distinguish "between the area where unadulterated laissez faire does more harm than good and the area where it may do more good than harm," but the Board "must know statistically all about everything," because even unregulated industries required raw materials, and the "industrial structure is so interwoven and interlocked that planning, even in highly restricted areas, is a game of blind man's bluff without such knowledge." In the interests of efficiency of investment, bank loans would have to be "more carefully allocated," and stock values must be not allowed to "pitch up and down like a canoe on the heaving level of market quotations." The new Board would be organized much like the older one, combining business and government, but with an engineer as chairman and competent technicians staffing all levels. Two principal tasks must be achieved by the new Board: "The national income must be more equitably divided so that purchasing power may be maintained. Second, ways and means must be found to steer the investment of new capital into something more enduring than the swamps of excess plant capacity and overproduction."[2]

In that same month, Chase published an article in *Atlantic* that similarly extolled the War Industries Board, lamenting that its lesson had been lost on America when "normalcy" became the slogan. The "wild horses" of industry were turned loose and the depression had resulted. It was time now to "harness" them again through a master plan. An "advisory commission drafting a plan and submitting recommendations...would undoubtedly be a move in the right direction, but would accomplish, one suspects, little beyond oratory and beautifully bound reports." "Somewhere," Chase wrote, "there must be a set of teeth, perhaps not too many teeth to begin with, but at least two or three sound and articulating molars. The War Industries Board, you remember, controlled fuel supply and freight cars, without which most business men are helpless." A key element must be "the orderly control of new investment," as in Russia, where "the whole wheel of the Russian Five-Year Plan turns on the allotment of capital to new enterprises." Chase went on to add:

> The second great task of master planning is to bring purchasing power into alignment with the growth of the technical arts, to give citizens enough income to buy back the goods which citizens make. The failure to do this hitherto has been the bitterest paradox of the whole industrial revolution. It means tinkering with the credit system, tinkering with wages, tinkering with hours of labor.

Yet Chase recognized that the "psychological imperative" to re-fashion the industrial system was still lacking in America. He was hopeful, though, that another year of depression might yet produce "the emotional crisis that drove us almost willingly into the arms of the War Industries Board."[3]

Late in November, Chase described what he would do if he were temporary dictator, unfettered by a Supreme Court, Congress, or the shared powers of federalism. He would eliminate the tariff, dissolve the army and navy, raise taxes on high incomes and inheritances, spend $3 billion to $5 billion on public works, create a system of unemployment insurance and old age pensions, abolish child labor for those under eighteen, legalize beer and wine, and recognize and resume trade with the Soviet Union. A planning board would be assigned the task of deciding how best to coordinate "all basic industries into state trusts, under government supervision but operating as independent units so far as possible—utterly removed from bureaucratic control." Such trusts were, he wrote, "particularly needed in oil, coal, iron and steel, electric power, meat-packing, textiles, lumber, railroads." The Sherman Anti-Trust law would be "declared a piece of antiquated timber." All corporations above a certain size, perhaps $1 million dollars, would be subject to federal incorporation and required to submit detailed reports that would furnish the grist for a comprehensive system of industrial statistics that would be used for "wise measures of coordination, guidance, and control," including the elimination of unwise investment, and methods for "expanding and contracting credit so that purchasing power may be kept in alignment with production." The planning board would also decide whether to mandate compulsory labor unions and a minimum wage scale, would examine ways to decen-

tralize industry into new regional areas following natural boundaries whose self-sufficiency could be improved. Meanwhile, Chase
would indulge himself in "a few private ukases" unrelated to recovery, including the establishment of "a nation-wide system of
birth control clinics," and "sun-bathing reservations near all great
cities." Those who attempted to erect signboards on public highways would be deported, and "menagerie cages" would be used to
incarcerate all those who sought "to use the radio for advertising
purposes." The manufacture of "chewing gum, outboard motors,
corsets, steam riveters and derby hats" would be forbidden. "Vul-
gar and moronic" movies would be forbidden.[4]

The Depression of the 1930s was not only the most severe ever,
but it was also the first to produce "such general agreement that
drastic steps must be taken to control the business cycle in the future. Men and women from all walks of life," Chase found, "are
willing and eager to promote such control." People who had heretofore paid no attention to anything "beyond their own front fences
are now pathetically trying to grasp the essentials of national and
international economics," a fact which, of course, contributed to
the popularity of Chase's own essays and books. The choice seemed
to lie between the competition championed by "Mr. Broadback"
and the state socialism of "Mr. Redbonnet." Collectivism was already a fact of life in American industry, since "modern industrialism, because of its delicate specialization and interdependence, increasingly demands the collectivism of social control to keep its
several parts from jamming." Government was meeting that demand, "unconsciously and clumsily, to be sure—by continually
widening the collective sector through direct ownership, operation,
and regulation of economic functions," and industry, agriculture
and business were, themselves, involved in various forms of voluntary collectivism. "Collectivism," Chase wrote, "is peradventure,
on the march....Should we encourage voluntary collectivism or state?
In what fields? Here are real problems, not a war of ghosts."[5]

In a July 1932 article for *Harper's* the ubiquitous Chase returned
to the topic of inflation that he had examined in *A New Deal*, reviewing again the advantages and disadvantages and the advantaged
and disadvantaged. Nodding approvingly in the direction of John
Maynard Keynes, Chase wrote:

If the United States Government borrowed or inflated for a bold program of public works which absorbed two or three million of the unemployed directly—thus feeding a huge new stream into the river-bed of purchasing power—thus stimulating industry—thus causing more of the unemployed to be absorbed as food and clothing workers—thus adding to purchasing power again—thus checking the domestic price fall—thus strengthening the banks...we should come close to the situation found in the upswing of the business cycle.

The imperative need, he wrote, was to "put at least five billion dollars in ultimate consumers' hands during the next few months. Such an amount in such a place has an excellent chance of definitely ending deflation." This was not really inflation, Chase argued, or at most only "technical inflation." It was the use of the "people's credit" for the benefit of the people. If the government could go $20 billions in debt to wage a war, it could surely spend $5 billion to "create tangible wealth; and at the same time stimulate industry, strengthen banks, and...enormously reduce unemployment." This, however, was only adequate for the emergency: "Only a managed currency supplemented with a trenchant program of economic planning, can provide a permanent remedy." Yet Chase did not define his managed currency, and there is no indication that he had in mind the quantitative manipulation of the dollar envisaged by the Committee for the Nation. Chase concluded: "Whatever the technical method employed, bold and deliberate inflation is the way out of the immediate crisis. The only way out, in my opinion, unless God in his mercy swings us around the corner. I think that God is tired of the folly and shortsightedness of men."[6]

In a February, 1932 article for the *New Republic*, Edmund Wilson described Chase as "perhaps the vividest writer of the liberal camp; he has an unusual knack of making statistics take shape as things and people," while working "stubbornly to disillusion us with the blessing of the American 'prosperity' era." But Wilson criticized Chase, as well as columnist Walter Lippmann and historian Charles Beard for not following their criticism of capitalism to its logical conclusion, writing: "Who today in any camp on the left can have the optimism to believe that capitalism is capable of reforming itself? And who today can look forward with confidence to any outcome from the present chaos short of the establishment of a socialistic society...?" Yet liberals like Chase, Lippmann, and

Beard, "who presumably aim at socialism, still apparently pin great hopes on the capitalists" by drawing up "schemes for 'planned economies' which are designed to preserve the capitalist system while eliminating some of its worst features—though...they haven't the ghost of an idea of an agency to put even these into effect."[7]

Chase replied that Wilson, having "recently been converted to one of the forms of communism, and safe in the arms of Marx," now felt obliged to "take pot shots at those outside of the compound." He then described himself as follows:

> Chase is a man difficult to place. He is obviously not an orthodox liberal, for he supports the Russian dictatorship, and repeatedly hints at the benefits of an economic dictatorship in this country....He seldom mentions free speech, free press or political reform, while the majesties of political democracy and the ballot leave him cold. His criticism of the going economic system has been unremitting and severe. He has catalogued its appalling wastes with considerable industry; he has done his best to undermine the theory and the practice of commercial salesmanship; he has presented item by item the mismanagement of machine technology in the modern world; he has analyzed Coolidge prosperity quantitatively and found it largely myth; he has documented unemployment, overproduction, the lack of integrity in a pecuniary civilization....He has visited Russia, and returned enormously excited by the Gosplan....He has defended the Russian economic experiment consistently and on occasional belligerently.
>
> Since the market crash of 1929, he has made a number of reasonably drastic proposals for revamping the industrial structure, including mandatory national and regional planning, the social control of new investment, the breaking up of large incomes and large inheritances, regulation and profit limitation of all corporations affected with a public interest, compulsory unemployment insurance, a complete shift in the division of the national income to the end that workers receive far more, absentee owners far less. He obviously has no faith whatever in the profit motive as an automatic guide to economic well being.
>
> Such briefly, is Chase's official record. He has been attacking the whole American economic structure, until many are sick and tired of listening to him. Now why in the name of all the gods does he not announce himself, call that structure capitalism, identify his remedies as planks in the platform of socialism? Or better, why, in view of his analysis, does he not refuse to waste his time with palliatives and planks, but come out for communism and a clean sweep? Why all the hedging and crawling; the refusal to call a spade a spade?

The answer, Chase wrote, was that while Wilson had been busy "dissecting Proust and other literary gentlemen," Chase had been "dissecting the industrial structure" for almost twenty years, and the tidy syllogisms of the Marxists and other radicals were constantly "being punctured before my eyes by a new invention, a new financial move, a new industrial method, new findings by the anthropologists, a new hundred million horse power." He had tried, he said, "to make the facts fit the syllogisms and they would not fit." The canons of Marxist class struggle, in particular, were "blurred and unrecognizable over great portions of the American industrial front, sharp as they may be in Europe, and because a more dynamic conception is mandatory here." He continued:

> Some years ago I came to the conclusion that we were not going to resolve the problems of poverty, waste and human degradation in America by employing these standard dogmas. Somebody had to find out what was really going on, not what Karl Marx, seventy years ago, said might go on. He was a good guesser, but seventy years is a long time. Somebody had to find a new analysis to fit the American scene, the American temperament, molded by the frontier and a world of a billion horse power. I am looking for a synthesis a good way ahead of your orthodox communism, Mr. Wilson, and yet one which can begin to work.
> Now; here.

Implicit in Chase's response was the suggestion that Wilson should confine himself to literary studies, and leave economic thought to those who knew something of the subject.[8] Yet Wilson's article is a good example of the pressure being applied to non-Marxian liberals to embrace the *New Republic* and the *Nation* group of socialists/Marxists even before the New Deal began.

Responding to the agitation for more economy in government, Chase wrote that three items failed to follow the general deflation of the depression:

> (1) interest and long-term leases, (2) public utility rates, and (3) taxes. While raw materials, wholesale prices, security prices, profits, wages, retail prices, go over the precipice, one after another, the bondholder, the landlord with a long-term lease, the utility companies, and the government cling to the side of the cliff....Furthermore, as prices fall, the interest dollar and the tax dollar themselves grow heavier.

Yet the "best people" were complaining only about the tax bill, since they benefited from the maintenance of the other two! Such people had not grasped the significance of present conditions, when the excess of productive capacity over consumer purchasing power dictated that "government expenditures, so far as they can put purchasing power into circulation, may be vital not only to society at large but to business itself." Chase explained:

> It so happens that the government is the one employer in a time of tragic deflation which can carry its force; by means of public works it can even add to its payroll. No private business can afford to do so. The government is the one hope of maintaining purchasing power. It can, if it must, borrow and inflate; it can order a capital levy, it can step up tax rates upon incomes and inheritances in the higher brackets. That such action connotes a certain risk is manifest, but emergencies require drastic remedies.

On the other hand, to cut government spending "might so far shatter purchasing power and provoke unemployment that the dole, naked and wholesale, would be the only substitute for revolution."[9]

Just weeks before the banking crisis that brought the banks to the "holiday" of March, 1933, Chase predicted that "within the next few years America will be forced to revolutionize its medium of exchange," since the "money and credit system as we have known it is sinking rapidly." The dollar, he observed, had "lost all dignity as a useful medium of exchange by virtue of its wanton and scandalous disregard of common physical standards."

> Drunk and disorderly, it careens from a one-bushel-of-wheat value yesterday to a three-bushel value today. It suddenly pummels creditors through inflation, and as suddenly turns and crowns debtors through deflation. It has no fixed relationship with any stable human value, it turns securities into insecurities in one day's trading on the stock exchange, it is irresponsible, unmeasurable, flippant and defiant.

America needed to be "cured of the pathology of money." Some new basis of exchange needed to be found, perhaps the energy of Technocracy, but certainly not gold or silver.[10] For many, a world without money would become a reality within weeks after Chase's article appeared.

Gradually, Chase began to move more decidedly into the collectivist camp, although still rejecting Marxism. Weeks before Roosevelt's inauguration in 1932, he reviewed Adolf Berle and Gardiner Means, *The Modern Corporation and Private Property* for the *New Republic*, and proclaimed it the best book he had seen published in 1932. After quoting the following passage from the book:

> The rise of the modern corporation has brought a concentration of economic power which can compete on equal terms with the modern state—economic power versus political power. The state seeks in some aspects to regulate the corporations, while the corporation makes every effort to avoid such regulation. Where its own interests are concerned, it even attempts to dominate the state. The future may see the economic organism, now typified by the corporation, not only on an equal plane with the state, but possibly superseding it as the dominant form of social organization.

Chase agreed that this was "undoubtedly the trend," and "not quite the trend prophesied by Marx." Chase added:

> The bulbous capitalist is at the mercy of either a rapacious or an admirably professional inner group—often owning nothing but brains and a claim to high salaries. Unless the state forces its creature, the corporation, to serve community needs, we are faced with a new brand of feudalism, in which the owner suffers with the worker and the consumer. As the depression drags on, however, the blue chips lose their Olympian assuredness; the state is forced deeper and deeper into economic activity.

This increased the chances that the larger corporations would be brought under collective ownership and management," for "where owners refuse responsibility, and where control cannot be trusted, the community must sooner or later step in" to ensure that the corporations were operated to serve all of society.[11]

Means wrote Chase of his appreciation for the positive review, and added: "You have said what we have been trying to say, but you have said it very much more lucidly, so that I wish that you had written the book yourself." Chase's review, he wrote, had shown "a complete understanding of what we were talking about," and it would "insure a wider dissemination of the facts and theoretical material which it seems to me important the community should have in mind."[12]

The real choice, Chase wrote in a *New Republic* article that same month, was not between capitalism and Marxism, but between an acquisitive economy, of which capitalism as it presently existed was an example, and a functional economy, of which Marxism was only one example. An acquisitive economy was destined to fre-

quent booms and busts, such as was being experienced, with unemployment, poverty, and hunger, while a functional economy
would put its emphasis on service, a concept given lip service by
corporate managers, but utterly alien to their behavior.
Chase wrote:

> I have assumed all along that you have read Tawney and know what a
> functional economy is. Russia has one built on a state-socialism basis;
> Denmark has a less complete one built on a consumers' and producers'
> cooperative basis; every decent housewife has one in her own
> home....Functionalism is not necessarily socialism, bolshevism, consum-
> ers' cooperation or primitive village communism. It is any sustained and
> deliberate method for the direct utilization of an economic system to pro-
> vide human essentials and comforts with a minimum of lag, leak and fric-
> tion. Our acquisitive society, while interpenetrated with functionalism here
> and there, is basically at right angles to it. To expect functional attributes
> or behavior from it is naive. Worse, it confounds the issues.
>
> Let us keep the record and our thinking clear on this cardinal distinc-
> tion, and hear no more of paradoxes....At least not until we have elected to
> change the system.[13]

The bottom of the business cycle was reached in the summer of
1932, no less in the United States than the rest of the world, but it
was America's misfortune to suffer a presidential election at this
inopportune time. By fall the likelihood of Roosevelt's election,
and uncertainties over the policies he would follow, had erased the
summer gains, and by winter fear had begun to crowd out uncertainty, as the evidence began to accumulate that either Roosevelt or
a runaway Congress would force the nation down the path of devaluation of the dollar, raising the specter of inflation. As Roosevelt's
inauguration approached, the fear turned to panic. Runs on the
nation's banks in late February and early March caused bank "holi-
days" to be declared in a growing number of states. As the Federal
Reserve Board described the panic: "Between February 15 and
March 4 these demands amounted altogether to $1,630,000,000,
including demands for gold coin and gold certificates of
$300,000,000. Three fourths of these demands occurred during the
week beginning February 27, and more than half was concentrated
in the first 3 days of March." On March 4, Roosevelt was to be
inaugurated as president. That the frenzy of the withdrawals and
hoarding of gold grew in intensity the nearer Roosevelt's presidency approached is too obvious to be ignored.

Read again Chase's description of the origins of the wave of selling that brought the stock market to its knees in October, 1929:

> By October, the facts, though publicly unadmitted, penetrated to certain speculators on Wall Street—where stocks were still gaily selling for fifty times their earning power, instead of the normal twenty. The word was not passed around, it got through, by some strange telepathy. Suddenly men began to sell; suddenly the whole world began to sell; in a few days fifty billions of paper values went whistling out of Wall Street, and the depression became news.

The same phenomenon of panic clearly occurred in the weeks before Roosevelt's inauguration. At first confined principally to businessmen and other large depositors anxious to protect their assets against the devaluation of inflation by converting cash into goods and property, it quickly spread to smaller depositors, many of whom had no real understanding of the issues involved or why they were withdrawing their money. Thus, even before the Roosevelt presidency began, it had unleashed a wave of panic withdrawals from the banks that paralleled the wave of panic selling of stocks 3 1/2 years earlier.[14]

In the midst of the banking crash, Roosevelt delivered an inaugural speech that echoed many of the points argued in Chase's *A New Deal*. In a part of that speech, the new president told Americans:

> Plenty is at our doorstep, but a generous use of it languishes in the very sight of the supply. Primarily this is because rulers of the exchange of mankind's goods have failed through their own stubbornness and their own incompetence, have admitted their failure, and have abdicated. Practices of the unscrupulous money changers stand indicted in the court of public opinion, rejected by the hearts and minds of men.
>
> True, they have tried, but their efforts have been cast in the pattern of an outworn tradition. Faced by failure of credit they have proposed only the lending of more money. Stripped of the lure of profit by which to induce our people to follow their false leadership, they have resorted to exhortations, pleading tearfully for restored confidence. They know only the rules of a generation of self-seekers. They have no vision, and where there is no vision the people perish.
>
> The money changers have fled from their high seats in the temple of our civilization. We may now restore that temple to the ancient truths. The measure of the restoration lies in the extent to which we apply social values more noble than mere monetary profit. Happiness lies not in the mere

possession of money; it lies in the joy of achievement, in the thrill of creative effort. The joy and moral stimulation of work no longer must be forgotten in the mad chase of evanescent profits.[15]

Thus did the new president of the United States begin his administration with a speech more worthy of a backwoods rabble rouser, a speech that was both a gratuitous attack on the American economic system and an effort to inflame the kind of Marxian class conflict that the nation had heretofore avoided. Unfortunately, it was not simply a wild shot, but the opening gun in a prolonged assault that would prolong the tragedy of the depression for another eight years.

Nevertheless, the new administration began in a "honeymoon" atmosphere as even its opponents initially wished it well in producing recovery from the depression. And there began the famous "Hundred Days" that unleashed the famous New Deal that had been promised in FDR's speech accepting the Democratic nomination, a term apparently borrowed by his speechwriter from Stuart Chase. Chase was well known to collectivist liberals within the new administration. As noted earlier, he had traveled to the Soviet Union in a group that included Rexford Tugwell, and his acquaintance with Jerome Frank predated the New Deal by over a year.[16] In the first year of the New Deal, both Frank and Tugwell asked Chase to travel to Washington for consultations with them on matters of importance, but Chase replied that he was busy with other matters and could only get away if it were an emergency. He was, he told Tugwell, "keenly interested in the economic stuff I am working on now, and there is just the chance that it may help a little in the next turn to the left—a turn which I feel to be inevitable, sooner or later."[17]

But Chase did offer to visit Washington occasionally if his input was needed, and Tugwell responded that he would take advantage of the offer and "from time to time ask you to drop down for a day or two and let us have the benefit of your wisdom."[18] Chase did make several trips to Washington, and by 1934 he was at work on a research project for the National Planning Board.[19]

A few months after the inauguration of the New Deal, Chase took up the weakening connection between working and eating. That connection had long ago disappeared, he pointed out, for the two percent or so who comprised the upper class, or the "kept classes," as Veblen had described. By their ownership of property they were "totally exempt from its compulsions." It was the remaining 98 percent who could eat only by working. However, the machine was making the connection tenuous here, as well, as more and more workers were deprived of jobs by technology. On the other hand, the same machines required "millions and millions of the sturdiest sort of consumers; consumers with admirable digestive tracts and great powers for depreciating personal equipment." The result was that consumption was becoming, "as a matter of economic reality, more important than work; purchasing power more important than man hours." "Slowly," Chase wrote, the industrial nations were being driven "to the hitherto abhorrent notion that the consumer must be furnished with purchasing power whether he works or not."

It was touching, Coyle wrote,

> to watch the tortures of the moralists caught on the horns of this dilemma; one school of them seriously proposes that the output, rather than be allowed to fall into the hands of the consumer, should be destroyed. A billion pounds of coffee, millions of bushels of wheat, thousands of bales of cotton, uncounted gallons of milk have recently been subjected to holocaust and destruction, thus preserving the economic morality of the wayfaring citizen. He has not worked, so he must be prevented from consuming.

However, such an approach did not serve "economic realities, however much it may have served the cause of beautiful morals." On the contrary, the consumer must be permitted to consume, whether he worked or not. Chase acknowledged that it would take time to establish the right of the consumer to consume, might indeed take "a revolution or two," but it was inevitable.

The opposition, he concluded, would come principally from "the private banking system and the debt structure." Chase wrote:

> The creation of money, the allotment of purchasing power, is a social function of the first importance and should be restored to the federal government, in whose hands the Constitution placed it. It is forever impossible for the private banker, working for private gain, adequately to finance the consumer. It wounds his moral sensibilities, for one thing....If recent history does not demonstrate the incompatibility of private banking and effective consumption, mathematics can prove it readily. The consumer, therefore, cannot adequately consume until the private banker, as the chief

executor of the nation's credit is lifted gently but firmly out of the picture. It is unfortunate that Mr. Roosevelt did not seize the unparalleled opportunity to lift him out, to the applause of a grateful nation, on March 4 last.

Mass consumption, Chase insisted, must meet the requirements of mass production. As to the methods by which it could be done, Chase suggested:

minimum subsistence payments per capita or per family;...consumers' dividends, or a straight rationing of prime necessities, or an enormously shortened work week with undiminished wages—thus keeping all able-bodied consumers nominally employed; or a guaranteed job, more or less of a nominal character, in the public-works division; or a combination of these methods.[20]

Analyzing the position of property in the "Power Age," Chase wrote that "advancing technology had been responsible for the corporation, as railroads, steamships, quantity production, forced larger business units, opened wider markets."

Technical complexity and specialization inevitably divorced ownershipfrom operation. One set of men built and ran the industrial plant; some leighteen million stockholders...owned the plant. Their property came to mean chiefly a right to a conventional dividend, and a proxy which they forgot to mail. Owners, under power age conditions, normally know nothing about operating management.... Heaven and hell are not farther apart than the typical owner and typical operator. A hundred years ago they were one and the same person.

The "dispersed and unorganized owner" had become "the inevitable prey of a slick financial control." But the financial control derived its profits not from the operation of industry, but through disruptions that produced the buying and selling of its securities. "The control," Chase wrote, "did its bit to wreck the industrial system, but industry on half-time means no presumptive future earnings, and so the financial game has been wrecked in revenge." Chase wrote:

The Economy of Abundance promises presently to socialize the bulk of commercial and industrial property. If the owners have no use for it, the community has. Without its regular operation, the community must starve and freeze. The corporate owners have never been responsible for either its debts or its regular operation; finance capital even less so. The commu-

nity will have to become officially responsible if the community is to
survive, and I doubt if either workers or technicians will demur. Perhaps
even the Supreme Court will not demur....Finally, it is highly improbable
that the technical operation of the physical properties could be managed
worse by agents of the community, than by the agents of finance capital.
Indeed, it is difficult to conceive of a method more sinister from the standpoint of efficiency than that of managing industrial property with a view
single to a profitable turnover of imagined future earnings on the stock
market.[21]

In 1934 Chase published *The Economy of Abundance*, the basic
theme for which came from Thorstein Veblen's distinction between
servicibility and vendibility. Veblen had written in *The Theory of
Business Enterprise*:

> Industry is carried on for the sake of business, and not conversely; and the
> progress and activity of industry are conditioned by the outlook of the
> market, which means the presumptive chance of business
> profits....Serviceability, industrial advisability is not the decisive point.
> The decisive point is business expediency and business pressure....The
> vital factor is the vendibility of the output, its convertibility into money
> values, not its serviceability for the needs of mankind.

This was the reason, Chase argued, why the United States, with a
magnificent industrial plant and abundant natural resources existed
with half of its people nevertheless in "comparative want." But with
Roosevelt in the White House there were prospects this would
change. Chase wrote:

> The United States has not hitherto regarded itself as a social group com-
> posed of men, women and children who need food, clothing and other
> things. It has never had a national economy or, at least up to March, 1933,
> any but the most casual interest in the material welfare of the group.[22]

However, Chase lamented that as of February 1934 the Roosevelt
administration seemed unable to decide "whether it wants to restore vendibility—popularly known as Recovery—or inaugurate a
new economic system based on serviceability. Obviously, until this
choice is made, the conflict will be reflected in zig-zag administrative performance."[23]

A traditional recovery must depend on the revival of the capital
goods industries, and Chase saw only two methods by which this

could be accomplished: war or inflation. Both, however, would be but shots in the arm and would only postpone the day of reckoning. Far more surgery was required under the conditions that existed in the 1930s. These conditions included: declining population growth in industrial countries, including the United States, which would affect both land values and business markets; increasing competition from factories being built in hitherto undeveloped markets, and the rise of protectionism in all countries following the failure of the London Economic Conference; the overbuilding already of American industrial capacity, reducing the need or desirability of further expansion and investment; the end of the frontier for expansion; the absence of any "great new industries on the horizon to stir the capital goods sector'" and technological unemployment that was "steadily whittling away at purchasing power."

Chase quoted David Cushman Coyle that automated factories were likely to "be more productive than old-fashioned plants of equal cost and much larger size," thus offering the likelihood that "the total capital investment of the country will diminish as industry grows, instead of increasing as it did all through the machine age." This was likely to produce less demand for either labor or capital. Chase compared the situation to that of the parents of a growing boy.

> The boy is market expansion, the parents capitalism. For years father and mother have been adjusting their pocketbook to larger shoes, longer trousers, bigger hats, heavier meals. Some day the boy will grow up, and reach a replacement rate in his requirements. Such is the law of biology. Human parents know this. Capitalism does not know it, but expects the boy to grow forever....Gentlemen, the market has come to the end of its adolescent growth. The boy has reached maturity.

A typical example was the great expansion of the radio industry in 1928, as a result of the demand for plug-in electrical sets to listen to the presidential campaign that year. Great profits were made and reinvested by radio manufacturers, with the result that by 1929 productive capacity had reached 15 million sets per year, but in that year only 4 million were sold. Profits plummeted, and by 1931, when Chase toured "the deserted aisles of one of these great radio establishments" he found "the machines were cold and dead."[24]

Chase found Justice Brandeis a supporter of the serviceability philosophy in his opinion for the New State Ice Company case, in which Brandeis wrote:

> Increasingly doubt is expressed whether it is economically wise, or morally right, that men should be permitted to add to the producing facilities of an industry which is already suffering from over-capacity....Many insist there must be some form of economic control. And some thoughtful men of wide business experience insist that all projects for stabilization and proration must prove futile unless, in some way, the equivalent of a certificate of public convenience and necessity is made a prerequisite to embarking new capital in an industry in which the capacity already exceeds the production schedules.

The alternative to going through the whole "merry-go-round of bankers, capital goods sector, debt and compound interest" was for the federal government to make purchasing power available through such devices as Roosevelt's Civil Works Administration and Public Works Administration. This could take the form of either self-liquidating or non-self-liquidating projects. Unlike Coyle, Chase voiced no specific objections to self-liquidating projects. The important consideration was to increase purchasing power by circumventing the bankers. Chase also applauded the New Deal's intent to regulate electric power, radio, telephone, and telegraph.[25] He envisioned, also, the eventual federal incorporation of all interstate businesses. Much of this activity, Chase admitted, was outside the scope of the de jure, or constitutional government. He wrote:

> The de facto government, operating under the restrictions imposed by the de jure government, has sought desperately, if clumsily, to adjust itself to modern realities. It has been forced to centralize, to override states' rights, to take cognizance of the peculiar problems of Megalopolis—with the New York Port Authority—to hail scientists into government service, to regulate business, and lately...to circumvent the old doctrine of checks and balances, by setting up boards and commissions which, like the Federal Trade Commission, combine legislative, judicial and administrative powers.
>
> There is as yet no serious demand for bringing the de jure government into line with the de facto; in short, for a thoroughgoing revision of the constitution. But the old forms are visibly cracking. President Roosevelt has a battery of pile drivers at work as I write.

The growth of industry must hereafter be dependent upon the growth of consumer demand, as increased by more effective distribution of purchasing power. This would require, as some business-men already realized, the payment of higher wages. But few own-ers could be expected "voluntarily to forego interest, rents and divi-dends, in order that wages may be increased, and the national income redistributed in favor of mass purchasing power." The fact was that the national income could "be redistributed only by force—the force of blind circumstances or the force of government control. The depres-sion supplied a modicum of the former, and Mr. Roosevelt is now supplying a modicum of the latter. It is safe to conclude that the consumer can never be adequately financed under vendibility."[26]

Even as farmers were being paid to stop producing, the rest of society, too, should have a guaranteed minimum income so that it could fulfill the important role of consumption, for the absorption of production required not workers but consumers. The concept of the right to consume as depending upon work, was "a scarcity sur-vival from a time when man, not energy, performed the labor." Similarly "the strong habits of pecuniary thrift, saving and profit-able investment," only clogged the financial mechanism once tech-nology had brought production past a certain level.[27]

Americans harbored a curious combination of habits held over from the stagecoach age with those of the machine age, and the two sets could no longer work in tandem. The struggle was fero-cious.

> The stagecoach gentlemen are organizing for "sound" money—meaning, of course, scarce money; for a return to the gold standard; for less govern-ment in business; for judicial protection—especially by the Supreme Court—against federal control of hours, wages and competitive condi-tions. With their direction of high speed presses and broadcasting stations, they can fortify stagecoach vestiges in millions of humbler citizens.

Hoover's actions had revealed the conflict between the two, when he had tried "to preserve economic individualism by two billion dollars worth of socialism." As for Roosevelt, he had been

> moved—or perhaps forced—to a direct attack upon the institutions of vend-ibility. His policies have obscured party lines, by giving jobs to techni-cians rather than to deserving Democrats; they have overridden traditional political behavior. Power has flowed out of the states to the federal govern-ment in a tidal wave. The National Recovery Administration, the Agricul-tural Adjustment Administration, Public Works Administration, Civil Works

Administration, Civilian Conservation Corps, Tennessee Valley Authority, Alcohol Administration, railroad coordination policies, and the rest,
are one and all insults to stagecoach institutions.

These were useful steps in the direction of an "abundance
economy," which must include: capacity operations of its plants;
an unhampered flow of goods to consumers who would be guaranteed a minimum standard of living, regardless of work performed,
in order to keep the plants operating; "elimination of waste, restriction and private monopoly, as methods of maintaining prices"; conservation of natural resources; decreasing man-hours in industrial
production; encouragement of research and new inventions, with
no more corporate patent monopolies; restraint of capital goods
sector to only that growth consistent with new technology and consumer demand; a similar restraint on the growth of debt; "a sharp
distinction between use property and industrial fixed assets," with
the latter "socially controlled"; economic decentralization, "the end
of Megalopolis"; "industrialization of most agricultural staples, on
a quantity production basis, and a declining number of man-hours
in farming"; shorter working hours for all; "a wide extension of
social   services   and   public   works   to   absorb   those
inevitably...displaced from industry, agriculture and the parasitic
trades"; "continuation of industrial specialization;" and end to economic nationalism; "revised and simplified political forms," including the "scrapping of outworn political boundaries, and of constitutional checks and balances, where the issues involved are
technical"; "Centralization of government" with "the overhead planning and control of economic activity." Finally, there must be no
compromise on any of the above. It must all be accepted lest the
nation retreat to the economy of scarcity, though some of the imperatives might require modification and others might appear. Just
as the Nile had shaped the institutions of ancient Egypt, so the technological imperative, "impersonal, amoral and non-ethical," was
now setting the boundaries within which the American culture must
operate. Machines would not tolerate the "wastes and barriers of
vendibility."

The system required "an industrial general staff with dictatorial
powers covering the smooth technical operation of all the major
sources of raw material and supply." Political democracy could be

tolerated if it confined itself to non-economic matters. The standard of living would be leveled, with all guaranteed adequate living standards. The gap between the richest family and the poorest family, which had been 40,000 to one in 1929, would likely shrink to ten to one. Banking, credit, and the issue of money would be a government function, with no more private banks or stock exchanges. Work would "be carefully allocated, and what the general staff requires, citizens will have to perform." Alas, Roosevelt was working against the imperatives when he plowed up cotton, destroyed food, and bolstered "the debt edifice with loans from the Reconstruction Finance Corporation." These were "pure scarcity techniques."

In "The Age of Plenty," Chase pointed out that America's "very junk piles would have ransomed a king in the Middle Ages, with their stores of metal and findings," but the United States, he argued, was "a poor country to-day in terms of the human calculus." Why, Chase asked, "with such a magnificent increase in the technological apparatus have the tangible results been so meager? Primarily because the technological apparatus has not been built with human well-being in mind. It has been built not to make goods but to make money." This was in large part because of the financial system, which had worked well in previous centuries of scarcity and then in expanding markets, but was "unable to cope with Abundance in its maturer phases." It was geared to an economy of scarcity, but those "laws" had collapsed in an age of abundance. As Chase put it:

> Day by day the habits of the laity have shifted to conform to the technological pattern. These mass habits now form perhaps the strongest of all mandates imposed by the Economy of Abundance. The individual may protest that he abhors the machine, that the old days were happier, that science is a false messiah, that he is in the market for a patch of arable ground—but his acts belie the protestation. He must constantly watch clocks, consult timetables, ride on railroad tracks and in subways, thrust a forefinger in telephone dials, send telegrams; dodge if not use motor cars and busses; be hoisted in elevators, turn the cocks of water and gas faucets, twiddle with radio knobs, switch on electric lights, trust implicitly to the complicated equations back of suspension bridges.

As for work, all Americans had become "men on the belt, screwing one nut home" in return for the "figure on a piece of paper delivered Saturday night."

The vestiges of the economy of scarcity were at war with the new economy of plenty, as culture lagged behind the realities of the new age. The fact was that "energy has forced us into a collective mold." Chase wrote:

The cultural laggards are noisy; but tangible events since the impasse was reached show net gains for dynamo behavior and losses for stagecoach behavior; not only in the United States, but all over the world. Vendibility is definitely in retreat. Nation after nation has left the gold standard, to embark on managed currency policies in which the bankers correctly find no hope for maintaining a private monopoly of credit. The State has been forced to support millions of citizens without requiring the traditional quid pro quo of work, because there was no work for them to do. Autarchy has all but destroyed the world free market. Dictatorships, one after another, supersede voting, parliaments, checks, and balances. Centralization and government control of business proceed at a violent pace. The end no man can foresee, but the general direction is clear enough. All industrial nations are in the turmoil of a transition period, seeking more or less blindly for stabilities which accord with technological imperatives. History is at one of its most momentous passages.

The Abundance Economy, Chase told his readers, demanded:

1. Capacity operation of its plant, on the balanced load principle.
2. An unhampered flow of goods to consumers, involving the right to a minimum standard of living, regardless of work performed—if no work is available....
3. The elimination of waste, restriction, and monopoly, as methods of maintaining prices.
4. The conservation of natural resources to the degree which, consistent with existing technical knowledge, will maintain adequate supplies...for the calculable future....
5. The employment of a decreasing number of man hours in direct production.
6. The encouragement of research, new invention, and a fairly high obsolescence rate for plant and processes. No more suppressed inventions; no corporate patent monopolies.
7. The production of capital goods to grow only as technological improvement, mass purchasing power, or mass demand requires it....
8. A one-to-one relationship between the growth of physical production and the growth of debt....
9. A sharp distinction between use property and industrial fixed assets. The latter must be socially controlled in that the units are no longer independent enterprises, but interlock one with another.

10. Economic decentralization; the end of Megalopolis, because it is too wasteful a unit to support.

11. The industrialization of most agricultural staples...and a declining number of man hours in farming.

12. Shorter working hours for all.

13. A wide extension of social services and public works to absorb those inevitably to be displaced from industry, agriculture, and the parasitic trades.

14. The continuation of industrial specialization....

15. No narrow economic nationalism....

16. Revised and simplified political forms. The scrapping of outworn political boundaries and of constitutional checks and balances where the issues involved are technical.

17. Centralization of government; the overhead planning and control of economic activity....

18. Finally, and exceedingly important. Abundance demands no compromise. It will not operate at half speed. It will not allow retreat to an earlier level and stabilization there.

This was the bed, Chase wrote, that "we have made—it matters not how—and we must lie on it." It was a blueprint for a collectivist future.[28]

The Wirt affair (see chapter 3) was for Chase "the opening gun in a campaign which I expect to see grow in volume and intensity." Chase had, himself, been invited to the tea party that was the center of the controversy, but had elected to spend the day with Jerome Frank, instead.[29] The big news was not Wirt's charges, but "the enormous public interest" which they had stirred up. As Chase put it: "One does not have nation-wide hook-ups to congressional committee rooms unless the nation is eager to listen in." The campaign would likely grow by the addition of "hungry Republicans, by Wall Street boys who do not want to be regulated, and by certain big businessmen who are eager to get their feet in the trough again." But much as New Deal critics might yearn for bygone days, Chase was convinced that those days were gone forever, because "capitalism, to put it bluntly, has walked out on us," and without "instant and spirited government intervention" in March, 1933, "the nation would have toppled into an abyss of indescribable confusion."

Chase reviewed the reasons previously given for the inability of the capital goods industry to return to prosperity, and then wrote:

If we are to eat—millions of us—ways and means must be found to plug the hole left by the collapse of the capital goods sector; by the abdication of old-style capitalism. A year ago and more, President Roosevelt and his advisers rushed courageously into the breach. They distributed federal relief and rebates to farmers, raised wages through the NRA, got under the banks and insurance companies, devalued the dollar, and all the rest of it. A fine hodge-podge if you will, but they plugged the whole. Make no mistake about this; it was the government which kept the economic mechanism turning over, and it does not behoove us to be over-critical about how it was done. Anything is better than the pit we were headed for when the banks began to snap in February, 1933.

Moreover, the federal government was still "underwriting American industry to the rune of 7 or 8 billions a year."

What would happen if the federal government were to pull the plug on all of these band-aids?

Twelve million roaring unemployed; 30 million starving with relief cut off; 6 million raging farmers; out from the woods, 300,000 young CCC men with axes in their hands and fire in their eyes; banks and insurance companies falling like ten-pins; prices crashing into the basement; wages down to a dollar, 50 cents a day; the stock market trying to locate the center of the earth.

Roosevelt's methods might be criticized, but the result could not be. Now, however, the time for band-aids was over and the government needed a "long swing policy."

Chase concluded:

President Roosevelt still has the confidence of the masses of the people. They do not know where he is headed but they believe in him, and are grateful for his spirited leadership in the crisis of 1933. They would follow him, I believe, in a fairly rigorous program, if it promised economic security; if a tangible goal were held before them. It could be set up under Constitutional auspices, and could avoid many of the cruelties and absurdities of a fascist dictatorship. The program would have to be directed to certain group interests at the expense of other group interests. Only so would enough political pressure line up behind it to force it through.

Chase's program would include:

1. The nationalization of the banks.
2. The reduction of the debt burden.
3. The financing of public works, especially housing, on a vast scale by non-interest-bearing credit.

4. A reduction in working hours.
5. The control of new investment.
6. The control through government monopoly of foreign trade.
7. The resettlement of millions of displaced miners, farmers, city workers, in new communities where both wage work and home gardening may be practised.
8. The nationalization of energy—including coal, oil, and electric power.
9. The nationalization of transportation and communication.
10. The payment of minimum wages, by industries and locations, to provide an adequate standard of health and decency.
11. A redistribution of the national income, through stiff income and inheritance taxes.
12. Federal support of education, health, and scientific research.
13. The calling of a Constitutional Convention to simplify the present unwieldy political system.
14. A minimum standard of subsistence for every person, whether he works or not, provided he is willing to work.

Ironically, this program did not provide for old age security, which would be a New Deal concern the next year. Even more ironic, Chase's program was in some ways closer to that of anti-New Deal traditional progressives like Amos Pinchot than it was to the one that would be followed by the New Deal after 1934.[30]

In a review of James Rorty, *Our Master's Voice: Advertising*, Chase submitted advertising to a depression era autopsy. Chase wrote he, himself, had described how capitalism was "breaking down under the assaults of technology," and now Rorty had shown "page upon page, chapter upon chapter, how it is breaking down morally." For Chase, whose antipathy toward advertising had been aired again and again during the 1920s, Rorty's book was only confirmation of his charges against the profession. What could be done about it? Chase was pessimistic that anything could be done so long as the present economic system endured. He wrote: "Advertising is woven so tightly into the fabric of an acquisitive economy that it can no more be lifted out and disinfected, by itself, than the banking system can be lifted out. It stands or falls with the whole system."[31]

Marxist John Strachey took exception to much of Chase's *Economy of Abundance* in a review for the *Nation*, calling it "A Book That Scared Its Author." Chase's book went "a considerable way toward showing us the nature of the mess we are in," Strachey

wrote. "But it offers us nothing worth mentioning by way of guid-
ance in getting out of the mess." Essentially, Strachey meant that
Chase had shown all of the deficiencies of capitalism, but had failed
to embrace socialism as the solution. As Strachey put it:

> What seems to have happened is that Mr. Chase has been scared by his own
> argument. I do not know how else to account for the marked degeneration
> in realism and clarity of thought between the beginning and the end of the
> book. His main argument is, after all, a demonstration of the inherent con-
> tradictions of capitalism, a demonstration confused when compared with
> the Marxist analysis, but considerably in advance of the work of orthodox
> bourgeois economists of today. Mr. Chase does demonstrate empirically,
> though not theoretically, that an economy dependent on profit can, in
> modern technological conditions, no longer be maintained. He does show
> that Marx's great prophecy of the extant social system becoming an intol-
> erable fetter upon production has come to pass. Then he draws his socio-
> logical conclusions from this overwhelming fact. And all that he has to tell
> us is that many workers now wear white collars and are called technicians,
> and that somehow or other this has abolished the class struggle! Or, most
> pitiful of all, that all that is really the matter is that we do not print enough
> money (we starve "because of a shortage of pieces of engraved paper").
> Finally, when Mr. Chase comes to make a list of the eighteen points which
> he considers necessary to what he calls an "abundance economy," he says
> no word of the necessity for abolishing profit—and consequently the op-
> erations for profit of privately owned means of production. Yet this is
> surely the one thing which the corpus of his work has proved.[32]

Chase responded that Marxism was as irrelevant to the problems of the 1930s as was capitalism, since they were largely problems of distribution rather than production. The consumer rather
than the producer was "creeping to the center of the stage." Capitalism was being "liquidated under technological pressure," while
socialism was a kind of anti-capitalism, developed during the age
of scarcity, and thus as irrelevant as capitalism in age of abundance.
Chase then explained the evolution of his own views on economics, writing:

> For a long time I have been searching for a social philosophy which would
> fit the modern facts. Thorstein Veblen started me on this quest. I have tried
> to hold to the facts no matter whose toes were stepped on. I have not been
> able to find any hope in an enlightened or reformed capitalism. This is not
> because all capitalists are low fellows, but because of the inflexibility of
> their compounding formula. A production system cannot fit a distribution

age. I have been unable to find a realistic solution in the class-struggle tactics of socialism or communism, as popularly interpreted, because they too are production-age systems. Technocracy was an analysis with which in large part I agreed, but which carried no practical program of action. I have been unable to find any satisfying general solution in simple shotgun remedies....

This has thrown me back on the experimental method. Experimentation is a somewhat lonely business, lacking, as it does, the warm arms of faith and doctrine. Given the modern trend, however, what else can a fact follower do? There is no body of doctrine competent to deal with this trend.

"The Economy of Abundance" was an attempt objectively to describe the forces at work....But I built no complete program because I did not know enough. When a sufficiently large group succeeds in digesting the characteristics, trends, and imperatives of a surplus economy, a real program will be forthcoming, and not before....

The formulation of a clean-cut philosophy and a social program for the age of distribution is coming. It will contain many elements broadly called socialistic. It may win the allegiance of many socialists, now vaguely disturbed with their own lack of progress. It will be strongly collectivist; it will nationalize certain key industries; it will work out a method of non-interest-bearing public credit; it will largely displace the profit motive—not for ethical reasons but to move the goods. A vast extension in the public-works sector appears to be inevitable. The general objective will be the distribution of the surplus, rather than a wrangling over the ownership of a productive plant which has lost its scarcity position.[33]

Clearly, Chase's views and program rested largely on his subscription to the popular belief in the 1930s that American agriculture and industry had reached the point where they were capable of producing everything that consumers needed. This view, however, was challenged in 1934 by a Brookings Institution study that was, Chase wrote, "so well documented, so imposing, and so apparently impartial that the abundance men were put on the defensive. Had we entered an age of potential plenty or not?" Chase explained:

The question is more than academic. If the popular conception is now to be reversed, dooming the nation to an indefinite penury, the hope which inspires millions to keep going toward a better day, the programs for reform based on an expansion of popular purchasing power, the basic aim of the New Deal itself, will be bent backward into apathy and defeatism.

Fortunately for Chase and the other "abundance" men, a study by the federal government, prepared "by 60 technicians over a seven months' period," entitled the National Survey of Potential Product

Capacity, came to their rescue. Chase leapt to the attack on the Brookings survey, writing that its result was "all but meaningless. It amounts to an estimate of excess capacity which no survey based on engineering principles could accept, and yet one far in advance of what actual market conditions could accept."[34]

Chase could not be swayed by the Brookings Institution's genuine economists from his convictions.

6

Stuart Chase and the Second New Deal

When Chase published *Government in Business* in 1935, the New Deal was at high tide. All over the world, Chase found "the public interest and traditional rights of property" were locked "in gigantic combat of which no man can clearly see the end." The New Deal was "but a single engagement on a world-wide battle front." In Russia private property was "in disorderly retreat," but elsewhere the battle was "grim and unremitting." In the United States private property had been in an unassailable position, its superiority never challenged, until World War I, when it was found that private industry could not meet its demands and the federal government was forced to take over "the economic complex." The question arose: "If collective effort was an effective way to wage wars, why not to abolish poverty?"

But from 1920 to 1929, despite the continuation of some public services, private business "resumed its economic supremacy, and...touched heights both temporal and spiritual hitherto undreamed of." But the end came in 1929, and six years later there were still (in June 1935) some 22 million Americans on welfare. Would private business come back, or would the federal government have increasingly to take up the burden as it had during World War I? What was its function, and that "of collectivism generally, in respect to economic activity in the power age?"

Already there was "no important economic activitiy in America which the New Deal does not touch," and at least "70 percent of all Europeans are now living in the shadow of state controlled enterprise." That this "touching" of economic activity by the New Deal might account for the fact that after two years there were still 22 million Americans on welfare did not apparently occur to Chase. From his vantage point the march toward collectivism was a product of the march of "impersonal, historical forces."[1] Yet the task of those seeking to convince Americans of the efficacy of government enterprises was akin to "trying to prove to hardshell Baptists that hell is a pleasant place in which to live."[2] But the advance of technology had "driven in upon accepted institutions like a rotary plow upon a snow drift," leaving an array of new governmental responsibilities in its path.[3] In 1912 government operation of the Panama Canal Zone was virtually the only "camel's nose visible under the sturdy tent of private enterprise," but 1913 marked both the culmination of the rate of private industrial expansion in the United States, and the beginning of a new growth rate in public business.

It was also, perhaps not uncoincidentally, the year of the passage of the federal income tax. Taxes rose, and so did governmental expenditures after that year, with most of it going for highway construction and maintenance, education, regulation of interstate trade, and federal aid to the states. Even while private industry was reaching the pinnacle of its success under Harding and Coolidge, the growth of public business was also continuing. The onset of the Great Depression caused Hoover, against his principles, to expand the government's role even more. And after Hoover had "opened the tent door," the "camels came trooping in" under Roosevelt. The New Deal had

> released novel types of major regulation, new varieties of control-without-ownership, new publicly owned corporations of assorted types, a Tennessee Valley Authority, which acts like a corporation but has no capital stock, and an amazing dromedary known as a "partnership" between government and private business called the National Recovery Administration.

The Agricultural Adjustment Administration was an example of control-without-ownership, in the process of "collectivizing the largest private business in the nation, composed of 6 million farm units." By paying farmers to restrict their crops it had retreated to scarcity, passing the cost of the payments on to consumers, mainly the urban public, via a tax on food processors. The scheme had the virtue of bringing not only farmers, but food processors under collective control. Outright government ownership of farms was making progress, too, with the Federal Land Banks owning outright over 20,000 farms worth some $70 million. "The AAA has begun the task of socializing agriculture," Chase wrote, "and there is, for the discernible future, no turning back." Collectivism had thus spread to the 30 million Americans who were dependent on agriculture.

The National Recovery Administration, on the other hand, had begun as "an adventure in the collective control of industry, but became lost in the woods." After two years of great tumult and shouting, the Supreme Court had shot the Blue Eagle on May 27, 1935. Still, the NRA had "inaugurated three principles of great importance for social control—universal minimum wages, maximum hours, the abolition of child labor." By some method those standards "must be recaptured, and a constitutional amendment seems the most forthright way." Meanwhile, the federal government was "keeping more than 20 million Americans alive on a dole and on work relief, at a cost of about 2 billions a year." Work relief meant jobs for the unemployed, expanded purchasing power, and new physical assets for the community in the form of schools, roads, hospitals, water systems, and other projects. To which should be added the useful work being done by the 400,000 young men of the Civilian Conservation Corps. Chase estimated that a total of 51 million Americans, out of a population of 126 million, were receiving federal funds of one kind or another, with the number about to rise with the enactment by Congress of the Social Security Act. This was New Deal collectivism on a mighty scale.

But the above did not exhaust the "march of the camels" of collectivism into the tent. New ones were arriving so rapidly that Chase wished he could include a few blank pages in his page "for the reader to jot down new arrivals." Such a march would have been inconceivable just seven years earlier. The list was impressive, taking up six pages of small print. One remarkable feature was the fact that the Treasury Department

> appears to be turning into a vast investment trust, with portfolio already heavy with common stocks, preferred stocks, Class A stocks, Class B, debentures, and bonds of all varieties. We speak of the Treasury now, not the RFC which has its own amazing portfolio. Propriety interests of the United States in government corporations and credit agencies were $5,529,000,000 on March 1, 1935, according to official Treasury figures, of which $4,439,000,000 were in agencies wholly financed by the State, and $1,090,000,000 in agencies where private capital also participated.

At the same time, the nation's banks held over $7 billion of government securities, which made up almost 40 percent of their loans and investments.[4]

All of this was evidence that, in Chase's words, "economic power has been flowing from private business, from local governments, from the state government, from the courts to Washington," where it had flowed "from Congress to the President." Chase added: "It is probably not too much to say that the present time, and for the past two years, the executive arm, including Mr. Roosevelt and his administrative staff, has had direct responsibility for all business, whether nominally public or private."[5] The test of business had become whether its activities were consistent with general economic security or not. No such yardstick had appeared in America before, not even during the collectivism of World War I.

In a chapter entitled "Six Studies of Capitalist Decay," Chase looked at studies done by four engineers, an architect, and an economist. All but the study by the economist, Gardner Means, dealt primarily with debts and finance. Of the six, Chase found Means' study "the most alarming of all from the point of view of establishing our traditional economy." Means study compared prices with production between 1919 and 1933 and found one group of commodities has responded to the depression in a very different way from those in another group, "suggesting we have not economic system, but two." One group, which included agricultural implements and automobiles, showed "a drop in production far in excess of the reduction in price," while the other, which included textiles and agricultural products, "took the depression on the price end, and did not restrict production to any such degree." The difference could be accounted for by the existence of monopoly or "administrative competition," in the former group, and free competition in the second. The "controlled market" was roughly coincident with the 200 great corporations, while the free market was largely the province of the "small fry." Only in the latter did the laws of supply and demand continue to apply. In the controlled market, executives set prices by fiat and would reduce production rather than lower them. Means concluded: "The shift from free market to administrative prices is the development which has destroyed the effective functioning of the American economy and produced the pressures which culminated in the new economic agencies of the government." The net effect,

Chase added, was "to aggravate fluctuations in economic activity and to prevent necessary readjustments." The "inflexible prices" of the controlled market had "destroyed the effectiveness of the market as an overall coordinator." Chase argued that to leave industrial policy to the lords of big business would only lead to more administrative prices, more rigidities, and "less possibility of making essential readjustments." Pulverization was not the answer, but removing from them the power to make industrial decisions was absolutely necessary. In sum, the seven studies had shown that capitalism in America was no longer operable. It was passing, "and must continue to pass from the scene."

The intrusion of government into business had come initially as a response to the needs of producers, through such devices as the tariff, but now it was being driven by the needs of consumers, since the fundamental problem had become that of ensuring adequate consumption. Yet many inside and outside the Roosevelt administration continued to view a return to prosperity as a function of the revival of the capital goods industries, and billions had already been wasted in trying to prime that pump. As Chase put it:

> Neither the State nor the community at large has yet had the courage to face the critical problem of capital goods. Are we to admit that the zone must be relatively smaller in the future than it has been in the past, due to the deceleration of capitalism; or to expect that somehow the old proportions can be revived, and effort concentrated upon ways and means to restore the ratio? The function of the State will be very different depending upon the answer to these questions. Shall we prime the pump and then let her go under her own power, or make provision for a permanent area of public works to replace a shrinkage in flow which no priming can ever make good?

Chase agreed with David Cushman Coyle and others that pump priming was largely futile, and that the country should accept "the blunt fact of a capital goods sector different in kind and relatively smaller in size."[6]

Chase disagreed with Brandeis' negative view of bigness in industry, insisting that large units were a "technological imperative" in some industries, demanded by the power age. But their ability to make "wrong decisions" must be taken away from them by the imposition of government control. That control should include "excess profits taxes, complete publicity of accounts, prohibition against shut downs for the maintenance of prices, quality standards for the consumer, fair treatment of workers, veto power on new investment, the prompt distribution of corporate surpluses." The alternative was "outright ownership and operation" by the government.[7] "Big Business" was no longer as powerful as in 1928. Chase explained:

> High finance, which provided the glue that bound the whole structure together, has been weakened by frozen assets, Senate investigations, restrictive legislation like the SEC, and bitter public disapproval and suspicion. The whole banking system is moving into the control of the State, which is now furnishing the buying power—some sixteen billions to date—that enables Big Business to balance its books, where books are being balanced. If the RFC, the PWA, the AAA, the FERA, shut up shop, the several cartels would be in grave danger of shutting up shop, too. For the moment, Big Business must come to terms with the State, lest the mass income which feeds it be cut off.

In short, "Big Business" was not as impregnable as it might first appear.

The problem lay in selecting the method of control. There were numerous proponents of simple plans that they felt would accomplish that result. "Most of them," Chase wrote, "now turn on the control of money and credit; one little law, one little device, and the whole economic problem will be solved." One of these was the Social Credit plan, itself the product of a British engineer, which will be discussed later. Chase recalled talking to a member of the New Deal brain trust who "had no patience with Social Credit, but was nevertheless convinced that a wise federal control of money and credit was all that was needed to rescue us from the depression, and to maintain equilibrium thereafter." Another favorite solution lay in "the judicious application of the income tax" that would reapportion the national income. This was central to the theories of David Cushman Coyle, as we shall see, but Chase was not convinced that it was adequate, by itself. What was needed, he wrote, was not just a redistribution of income, but more income. Great Britain's "punishing income tax" since World War I had not saved her from the Depression.

While Chase agreed that "collective control of money and credit" was crucial, he did not believe that it would solve the entire problem. It was also important to establish the engineers and industrial administrators in control of planning. America had tried regulation and it was rife with abuses, including endless litigation in the courts. Control without ownership was the preferable method. As matters stood, stockholders exerted little, if any, control over the management of corporations. Under control without ownership, their role would not change, but the management of the corporation would be assumed by the government. Another alternative was, of course, public ownership, if control-without-ownership did not work out. The advantage of public ownership was that:

> When an economic activity is socialized, a grave source of conflict is automatically removed. The power lobby, or the railroad lobby, or the oil lobby, is liquidated, and with it friction, litigation, counter litigation, Supreme Court decisions, bribery, and a shifting balance of power from industry to the State. This gives the government administration a less storm-tossed area in which to operate, and an opportunity to concentrate on providing service rather than lawsuits.

Chase cited numerous example of government owned corporations in Germany and Canada, in addition to the semi-corporate state trusts in Russia. In most cases these public corporations operated under the same price system as a private corporation, but the government owned the stock and staffed the management. Chase wrote:

> In the great corporation, collectivism and capitalism meet. Administratively it is becoming increasingly difficult to tell one from the other. Old arguments dissolve in this new compound. Capitalism has been socializing its forms through the great corporation, collectivism has been adopting and adapting this most characteristic of capitalist institutions. Administratively there is little to choose; for years there have been no better run corporations in the world than German state utilities.

The large corporations were as "impersonal, cumbersome, bureaucratic, highly organized" under private control as they would be under public ownership, therefore "the tangible shock when the State acquires common stock control is theoretically no greater than when a Cyrus Eaton beats a Samuel Insull to a string of corporate beauties by fast work on the stock market."[8] Private investors might even be allowed to hold bonds, preferred stock, and a minority of common stock. Clearly, public corporations did not represent "such a sudden drop into cold, unknown depths as is generally supposed."[9] Clearly public business did not have to be done by dictatorship or a fascist State.

The New Deal had come in with "no philosophy, strategy, propaganda before its inauguration," but it had "changed more institutions in two years than all the reformers have been able to do in a generation." It had come by "default," and more collectivism could be expected to come by default so long as the capitalists saw only net losses before them, since "capitalists will not fight very hard for property which shows a net loss," although they could be expected to fight for those that were profitable. Chase wrote:

> The question of default or fight turns primarily on the outlook for losses and profits. When the economic mechanism sags, collectivism is likely to come precisely as it is coming in the New Deal. I look for more losses than profits in the next decade, and so a greater advance by default than by battle.

At a time when more and more New Deal critics were beginning to question the Roosevelt administration's commitment to recovery, here was a clear rationale by collectivists for delaying it—to provide the opportunity for further collectivization of the economy.[10]

For the next decade, however, the economic system must be kept afloat, while Congress legislated new economic controls:

> Extreme centralization we must try to avoid, but the unhampered right to lay down wage, working hour, child labor provisions, and to control natural resources, agriculture, coal, and such other industries as are primarily national in character, is a necessary legal tool of the modern community....Let the public make its demands explicit through a clean, open constitutional amendment of the interstate commerce cause, and if this is not enough, through a redrafting of the whole instrument.

At the same time, "the control of money and credit" must be transferred to the government. No real progress could be made without this step, which could be achieved either through "control-without-ownership, or outright ownership of the banking structure." Chase anticipated the latter. Income taxes should be raised, especially on the higher brackets, in order to finance public works without raising the public debt. This would also reduce the amount of savings seeking new investment. Yet another step would be "to hold models in readiness for the strategic moment to apply them." As one industry after another went under, the government would take them under according to the prearranged model.[11] Chase's book, he wrote, had been only an attempt to plot the situation as it existed, "and to follow the curve a little way into the future."

In a review of the book for the *Saturday Review of Literature*, Adolf Berle wrote that it revolved "around the axis of collectivism," in assembling an "impressive collection of data regarding the gradual emergence of the government as a dominant factor in business." For some, the evidence of "this driving progress towards state ownership and public operation seems a trifle frightening," but Chase had shown the movement had a long history behind it. Berle wrote:

> Conflict between groups which resist this process and groups which are prepared to recognize it is fundamental in American thinking today. It is fundamental because the one group usually conservative, emphasizes the possibility of enormous power for the individual if the government keeps out of business or limits itself to assistance. In emphasizing this the claims of a very large number of little people who are being handled with increasing roughness by the economic scheme of things are usually more or less ignored. The opposite group, paying less attention to the individual, insists that the claims of the little people come first; and believes, more realistically, that if they are not recognized, no individually is likely to get very far for any length of time....I can see no effective answer to Mr. Stuart Chase's presentation of the problem.

Chase, he wrote, was less an advocate of the collectivization process, than a marshaler of facts that showed how far the process had already progressed and was continuing to progress, that it was not the result of blueprint, "but...a matter of meeting situations; the combination of solutions falling into a more or less ordered pattern," yet allowing "a zone—and no small zone at that—for true private initiative—the initiative which tends to expand civilization rather than which tends merely to exploit it."[12]

When many opponents of the New Deal gathered together to form the Liberty League, Chase wrote an "Ode to the Liberty League" for the *Nation* late in the year, describing it as "the loudspeaker of what Veblen used to call the kept classes." Conservatives, he wrote, had never learned that "in an advanced technology, mass consumption and mass spending are the only guaranty of his income, that production of wealth is a dynamic process, and that the more goods there are for the many in the street, the more goods there may be for the many in the penthouse." While the Liberty League was demanding a balanced budget, a modicum of thought should make it apparent even to them that "balancing the federal budget in the middle of a major depression is about the last conceivable step which a well-kept gentleman who values his survival should advocate," since it would "not only crucify the unemployed but prostrate the whole financial mechanism." It was, after all, only spending that kept the financial system going, and if consumers lacked the money with which to buy the products of industry how were those products to be sold and wages paid? Chase wrote:

> What do you think reversed the tailspin, and turned a system deficit of thirteen billions in 1932 into a small surplus in 1934? What do you think opened the banks, stopped the farmers from shutting off the food supply of the cities...began to substitute black ink for red on business ledgers? Fairies? Elves? Mickey Mouse?...Spending. Spending reversed the trend of the national income, opened the banks, relieved the farmers....And saved your shirts, gentlemen.

When a Liberty Leaguer saw a WPA worker raking leaves in a park, he opened "his mouth like a seal in a long, horrified bark," since he saw only waste, inefficiency, and graft. But what he saw was irrelevant, since the man with the rake "was not there to do a job of production; he was there to do a job of consumption." The money he got from the government for raking the leaves would be spent in stores and then deposited in banks. So long as opportunities for profitable business investment were lacking, only government could fill the gap. There was, Chase wrote, "no moral issue here at all. There is a mathematical equation." The increase in the national income since 1932 approximated government spending during that time—about $8 billion in two and a half years. He told the businessmen of the Liberty League: "You were sinking. The government threw you a life line and hauled you aboard. And now you fill the front pages with agonized complaints that government has no right to throw out life preservers and haul citizens abroad."[13]

Federal Reserve Board chairman Marriner Eccles wrote Chase that his article was "superb," and added: "As a piece of writing and a penetrating and convincing analysis, I was so much impressed with it that I have sent copies to many of my close friends." Chase's article had expressed "with enviable force and clarity" Eccles's own viewpoint.[14] As if this were not enough of a pat on the back, a month later Thurman Arnold, soon to become Roosevelt's trust-buster, wrote Chase that his was "the best persuasive material now being written." It was important, he told Chase, "to attack the charge of superficiality which is the only weapon which a conservative can use against them. Of course all members of the church will attack heretics on the ground that they have not proved their conclusions. Remove this and there is no way to resist your arguments."[15]

The Brookings Institution having produced a study dealing with the "fundamental defects in the operation of the economic system," Chase submitted it to close scrutiny late in 1935. What it showed, Chase concluded, was "the extraordinary ineptitude of the prevailing profit system for maintaining the decencies of life." The study indicated that everything was present for an economy of abundance on the production side. "The great problem of American business men," it said, "is not how to produce more, but how to sell what they have already produced." It was America's capacity to consume that showed an "aching void," in Chase's words. The problem was, the Brookings study concluded, "that a substantial portion of the income was not expended for consumption goods but was diverted to savings channels, where much of it failed to be used productively." Vast sums went to the wealthiest class who could not use it all for consumption, and so put them into savings. Brookings concluded: "The greater the number of persons in the high income groups, the larger the percentage of the aggregate national income that will be set aside for investment purposes." And the number of such persons grew between 1900 and 1929. So great had the accumulation become in the 1920s that it far exceeded the demand for investment dollars. By 1929 only $5 billion of the $15 billion in savings could be invested in new physical equipment. Ten billion dollars had gone astray, into "foreign loans, into land speculation, and into the stock market for the sheer purpose of bidding up prices." None of these resulted in new capital goods that would have contributed to the economy. Why were there so few investment opportunities available for that $10 billion? Because it had been taken out of the hands of consumers who might have spent it on goods, thereby creating a need for greater production. In summary the Brookings report observed:

> Our diagnosis of the economic system has revealed that the way in which the income resulting from the nation's productive activities is divided among the various groups which comprise society, lies at the root of our difficulties. Inadequate buying power among the masses of the people appears to be fundamentally responsible for the persistent failure to call forth our productive powers.

The problem was to find a method for diverting the flow of the income stream so that more went into spending and less into savings.[16]

Late in December 1935, Chase surveyed the progress toward recovery after nearly 3 years of the New Deal and found the evidence mixed. Business was more active, prices and retail sales had improved, and the national income was increasing, but unemployment still gripped one-fifth of the employable population. "If recovery is to be measured in employment," Chase wrote, "there is none." Relief rolls were not markedly declining, and banks were not increasing their investments in private enterprise, but were instead expanding their holdings of government bonds. Nor did Chase foresee any imminent breakthrough in the absence of opportunities for profitable investment. And such opportunities could not occur without increased consumer demand. But consumers still lacked adequate purchasing power, and the higher incomes were "hoarding" their money in savings, just as they had in 1929, when it had triggered the Depression. In 1929, out of total savings of $15 billion, only $5 billion had been productively invested, the remainder had been "largely sterilized in stock-marked speculation. They might as well have been buried in the back yard for all the good they did the spending stream." There followed the parade of: "Deceit, depression, more hoarding, fewer opportunities for profitable investment, deeper depression...." Chase wrote:

> Short of taking over the whole economic complex as in Russia, two methods are apparently available to meet these conditions. They can be applied only by the government. The first is to reallocate savings into spendings through the mechanism of the income tax, and thus stop the creation of more interest-bearing debt. The second is to expand production in socially useful public works and services—including health, education, low-cost

housing, as well as the more orthodox varieties—through issues of non-interest-bearing credit. This operates to pump more dollars into the system in exchange for the production of more physical wealth, is not inflationary and does not stimulate the compounding [of interest] process.[17]

Chase's review of Tugwell's *The Battle for Democracy*, in early January 1936, was a celebration of pragmatism, both Tugwell's and Chase's. Of Tugwell's, Chase wrote that his "real objection is that the Old Order finally flunked its pragmatic test, and will no longer work." Democracy had been "betrayed by industrial anarchy. *Democracy and competition are not brothers but enemies*. The New Deal is far from a perfect instrument, but it offers the mass of the people the closest approach to democracy they have had since the frontier closed" (emphasis mine). As for Chase's pragmatism, he wrote that Tugwell's was "a reasonable and logical doctrine." He explained:

> Personally I do not bother much about high-order abstractions like "democracy," "liberty," and "regimentation." What interests me is the specific effect of a given policy on the tangible behavior of individuals or groups. This is the only way I can make "democracy" or "freedom" come alive. But many people seem to feel the need of getting their large generalizations in order, and if Tugwell cannot convince them that the New Deal is not an assault on democracy and on the best in the American tradition, nobody can.

The "thin red line" in Washington had "put integrity, courage, and intelligence back into a government sapped by a century of deference to the voracious exploiters and despoilers of a continent." Tugwell was "not primarily interested in attacking the profit system," but was "interested in driving foundations for a new system as capitalism relinquishes its responsibility." Chase concluded:

> Probably, within the next decade, at least a third to a half of all economic activity must become a collective enterprise, not because Tugwell wants it or the President wants it or the Communist Party wants it, but because the power age demands it....Perhaps Tugwell, like many of the Brain Trust, does not fit into the classification of radical versus conservative at all. He is an engineer of transition from automatic capitalism to some new system.[18]

In 1936 Chase took a different tack in arguing the necessity for central planning. In his book *Rich Land, Poor Land* (New York,

1936), Chase reviewed the historic rape and abuse of America's natural resources, their present precarious condition, and their tragic future if the present trends continued. Nothing was spared, from the pollution of waterways to the waste of mineral resources, as Chase made a convincing case for the need of national planning to preserve and restore the continent's natural resources. In its ruthless quest for profits the free enterprise system had made no provision for a limited supply of natural resources.[19] Upon learning of Chase's intent to write a book on conservation, Secretary of Interior Harold Ickes wrote him that such a book badly needed to be done, and that he did not know anyone more qualified to do it. He told Chase that he was the "one economist whose writings I not only can understand but can enjoy...."[20] *Time* magazine was less enthusiastic in its review, writing that he envisioned "a great campaign to protect U.S. resources that would create five million jobs, stop unemployment, and beautify the country as well." But it concluded that, while readers "may be dazzled by Stuart Chase's bold vision of a happier future for their country...they are more likely to close *Rich Land, Poor Land*, with an uneasy feeling that Author Chase has pulled some white rabbits out of his statistics, that there must be greater obstacles to his program than he admits."[21]

After Roosevelt was reelected in 1936, Chase wrote an "Elegy for the Elite" for the *Nation*. The election, he observed, had "put the economic royalists back on their haunches. If their old charms will not operate, they are in a sorry predicament, for their actual votes are few." The old order was breaking up. Chase explained:

This question of a slipping ideology and wavering public support for the religion of business is profoundly important. It explains the hysterical tone of the whole Republican press. The terror is eminently justified. The "American way of life" is indeed in jeopardy. The old gods are tumbling, the horse and buggy headed for the tomb. Private enterprise has demonstrated its inability to support the population. In the depression to date it has cost the American people one hundred billion man-hours of idleness through unemployment, and refuses to produce two hundred billion dollars worth of goods and service which the plant and the labor force were ready and eager to produce. This is failure on a cosmic scale. The people have turned to a new god—the government—led by Mr. Roosevelt. The new god works....

Mr. Roosevelt now commands the symbols and dominates the American economy. The only considerable barrier to any reasonable program on behalf of economic reform is the Supreme Court. This barrier will not be permanent; it cannot be, when a people speak so emphatically.

"Short of revolution," Roosevelt had "brought about reforms and breaches in the old order so colossal as to stagger the imagination." As for the radicals and progressives:

> If he continues on this road, there is no place for the radical movement except on the left flank urging him along....Mr. Roosevelt has blanketed the radical movement, except the simon-pure revolutionaries, since 1932, and it is about time the boys woke up to the fact. They are impotent while the New Deal proceeds on its massive, popular path. Often as rigid in their dogmatism on the left as is Wall Street on the right, they join with Wall Street in bewailing any increase in mass well-being because it has not been brought about on the correct principles. Both wings prefer bottomless depression to recovery on the wrong principles. The principles of neither Marx nor Adam Smith interest the American electorate. What it looks for is results.
>
> If Roosevelt succeeds in making a genuine liberal party out of the Democratic Party, there is nothing for the progressives to do but get aboard—of course, on the extreme left flank. If he tires of the New Deal, or if the Democratic Party reverts to its normal barrenness, it is manifestly up to the radicals and progressives to form a new farmer-labor party, pick up the torch, and appeal to that great mass who, in the election, showed their hunger for security, their willingness to accept change.[22]

When, early in 1937, Roosevelt unleashed his assault on the Supreme Court through his court-packing scheme, he aroused a storm of protest that eventually led to the defeat of his proposal. In an unpublished letter to the *New York Times*, Chase defended the proposal, writing that "hysterical appeals" to "Imperishable Traditions" did not help much in "the face of concrete situations." The fact was that the Supreme Court's decision on the AAA had left six million farmers "in a legal vacuum," and the NRA decision had stripped fifteen million workers of wage and hour protection, while a half million coal miners and many operators were "disgruntled and angry about the Guffey Coal Bill decision." Chase went on to list other problems that faced the Roosevelt administration and wrote that all attempts to solve them ran up against a stone wall in the form of a majority of the Supreme Court. While Chase preferred an amendment to the Constitution to the manner in which Roosevelt was approaching the problem, he recognized that the amendment process might take years, and the problems could not wait. "If we really cared about America," he wrote, "I think we should act. Now."[23]

In 1938, the engineer-turned-accountant-turned-economist, made a foray into semantics with *The Tyranny of Words*. *Time* magazine greeted it by writing:

> Primarily a popularizer of other men's ideas, Author Chase expresses each new enthusiasm in startling journalese. Without the authority of the learned or the wise, he has an indignant curiosity that is infectious. There are no satisfactory answers to be found in Stuart Chase. But at least he raises the Question. Five years ago he flung wide the question of "Technocracy." Last week he broached his biggest yet.[24]

His book was, perhaps, most noteworthy for revealing Chase's willingness to turn his considerable writing talents to anything that interested him, notwithstanding the absence of any qualifications for doing so.

In that same year Chase challenged an American icon—home ownership—in an article for *Survey Graphic*. Noting the high incidence of foreclosures in every part of the country, and the insecurity of unemployment, Chase questioned the intent of the National Housing Act's purpose of stimulating home building. Granting that there was a considerable need for more housing after 9 years of depressed construction, he found little evidence that those who needed them most could afford the mortgage payments on them, or possessed the economic or job security to lock themselves into long-term fixed mortgages even if they did. The machine age, after all, required mobility in employment. While the government should aid rural residents to own their own farms and homes, Chase wrote:

> Home ownership in cities today is an example of cultural lag. It is based more on sentiment and emotion than on facts. Home and mother, the misty eye, the silent tear, the couplet by Eddie Guest. It is one of those immortal "principles" which Thurman Arnold talks about, splendid for things in general but often disastrous for you and me and Adam. It fortifies the ego, rather than the family budget, which explains the strange fact that gadgets continue to sell more houses than sound construction.
>
> A lot of us feel better if we own, and that feeling demands respectful consideration. Let us try, however, to detach the desire from mere posses-

sion and transfer it to the sense of *living*. Will this projected house reduce
our worries, reduce our risks, reduce our headaches, and make a peaceful
homelike atmosphere really possible? If the chances look good, buy. If
they do not look good, rent. What one seeks, after all, is not a parchment
but peace.

Fortunately, the new housing act also made provision for the construction of rental units, and in the development of well-planned
rental communities lay "the best solution to the problem of American urban shelter at the present time," offering jobs during their
construction and a way to beat the Depression.[25]

By 1938 Chase's 1935 curve had not proceeded exactly as predicted. In that year he published *Idle Money, Idle Men*, and it ex-
hibited little of the earlier confidence in the inevitability of collectivism. Since *Government in Business* the Supreme Court had
voided the AAA early in 1936, the massive spending in that year to
ensure Roosevelt's reelection had triggered a wage-price spiral that
triggered a collapse of the economy in late 1937, and, despite FDR's
landslide reelection, his efforts to "pack" the Supreme Court with
New Deal supporters had failed, had triggered, instead, a rebellion
in Congress, and had left him with none of the political capital of 1933
to push any new reforms after 1937. It was difficult enough, now, for
the administration to even get Congress to appropriate the billions necessary to deal with the new emergency, with the billions already spent
having shown so little result. Thus Chase was more concerned in his
new book with arguing the necessity to put idle men to work than with
preaching a new economic system for the nation.

Chase first addressed concerns about the growing federal deficit, pointing out that federal debt bore no relationship to personal
debts, in that the national debt was simply money owned by American citizens to themselves. Moreover, the debt was deceptive in
that it did not adhere to the accounting principles of private businesses, where expenditures on capital improvements were classi-
fied as investments rather than as debts. Much of the federal spending, and resulting "debt," had been on dams, schools, highways,
and other capital improvements of benefit to the nation, and should
be considered in the nature of assets rather than debts. The money
spent on WPA and PWA and other such projects had put to work
idle men on projects that needed to be done, and so long as there
were idle men and useful projects remaining it made good eco-

nomic sense to continue them, especially since the wages paid contributed to consumer purchasing power and aided the rest of the economy as well.

Looking at a four-volume survey of the economy done by the Brookings Institution, Chase found support for his contention that the imbalance of income had produced "frozen" savings among the higher incomes that reduced consumer purchasing power. While Chase and David Cushman Coyle had long advocated confiscatory taxes that would redistribute those higher incomes among the consuming classes, the Brookings' study, while admitting some merit in such a course, preferred a return to free competition through a reduction in prices. The high prices maintained by monopolies, cartels, and trade associations in defiance of the free market, must be broken, said Brookings, so that prices could fall to their natural level. The problem of insufficient purchasing power would disappear if prices were no longer held unreasonably high.

Chase agreed that the restoration of free competition was a desirable objective, but he was skeptical that those who were guilty of maintaining high prices would be willing to reduce them. He wondered: "Is it possible to restore free competition to an economy which began to outlive those methods fifty years ago?" Clearly it would depend on how energetic the Roosevelt administration now proved to be in attempting to enforce the anti-trust laws, after ignoring those laws during the years of the NRA and after. That, in turn, would likely hinge on the results of the hearings of the Temporary National Economic Committee composed of three senators, three congressmen, and representatives from the Justice, Labor and Treasury departments, as well as the Federal Trade Commission and the Securities and Exchange Commission, under the chairmanship of Senator O'Mahoney.

The hearings, Chase wrote, had "established beyond reasonable dispute two outstanding economic trends." He explained:

> The first is that American business enterprises have little use for the savings of the public, and what use they have is declining. Going concerns increasingly find the money for capital improvements—plant and equipment—from their own savings, especially from the funds set aside each year for depreciation.
>
> Yet you and I and millions of others are saving in the aggregate from six to eight billions a year—about as much as business saves. The combined

amount is not far from 20 per cent of the national income....In the past a large portion has gone into industry for new plant and equipment. But now industry is rolling its own. Where shall our savings go? When they do not go somewhere promptly the economic machine must run on part time. The idle money breeds idle men.

The second major trend, in part a result of the first, was the decline of the investment banker. The investment banking business had "shrunk to a shadow of its former self," and the 'money trust' and the 'money power' were disappearing as a financial force. As Adolf Berle testified before the committee: "The alleged domination of Big Business by the banking system today is now largely sentimental." Investment money was going begging, and huge amounts of savings remained stagnant while purchasing power remained too low to stimulate the economy. Between 1929 and 1940 currency dollars had nearly doubled and demand deposits in banks had increased by $11 billion, but "these new dollars seem to be frozen; they do not move," whereas in 1929 they had been flowing busily around the circuit. In 1929 each dollar went around the circuit about 2.6 times, with a national income of $81 billion. In 1939 there were more dollars, but they had gone through the system only 1.5 times, produced only a national income of $68 billion. If they had flowed at the 1929 rate, Chase calculated that they would have produced a national income of $117 billion. "Idle money," he wrote, "is reflected in a declining rate of spending. It is luminously reflected in a falling interest rate. It is reflected in the unprecedentedly low rates for short term money.   It is reflected in a count of the unemployed."[26]

The federal government could reduce the savings rate by taxing idle funds, as Great Britain had been for a generation. The New Deal, he wrote, had not "greatly increased the kind of taxes which drain off idle funds."

Taxes on corporate savings (undistributed profits) were turned on for a while, and then turned off. The rate of investment has not been stimulated to the point of absorbing more than a third to a half of the 15 million unemployed who were on the streets when the New Deal took over in 1933. Control levers have been pulled, but not always the right ones, and not hard enough.

The way to improve consumer spending was "through a shift in the distribution of the national income, whereby idle funds are siphoned over to the lowest third, to employ them in public works, to give them unemployment insurance and old age pensions." When they spent the money the national income rose and eventually jobs were created. Until buying power was shifted in this way, the "great market will remain bolted and locked."

Chase now suggested:

1. A permanent PWA that would cease to be merely a pump-priming device, and would become, instead, a regular outlay, like defense spending. Its function would be to absorb stagnant savings and undertake needed projects.
2. Changing the federal budget to a business basis, like that of Sweden, in which capital expenditures would no longer be lumped with running expenses.
3. Amending the Social Security law to grant a flat sum pension to every citizen age sixty-five and over who was not working, and pay it from the operating budget. The present reserve fund was simply another device for tying up billions of stagnant forced savings.
4. For Social Security and other purposes increase personal income, inheritance, and corporation income taxes for the purpose of getting at idle dollars.
5. Providing a flexible WPA program for the remaining unemployed.
6. Creating a new bank for long-term capital loans that would take idle savings and lend them for business expansion, leaving to commercial banks the function of making short-term loans.

The program, Chase argued, would "not require any great uprooting of traditions," demanded "a minimum of new institutions," and it stepped on few toes, except perhaps those of investment bankers who were "on the way out in any event." He did not know, he said, of any other course that offered "so much for so little."[27] It was certainly a far cry from the proposals Chase had advocated earlier in the decade when collectivism was at its high tide in America. Paul Douglas hailed Chase's style as "muscular and red-blooded," and welcomed the book as one that deserved "to be widely read," since it would "lower the false heat which politics often engenders."[28]

Late in 1938 Chase wrote Jerome Frank of a new book he had just finished, the "central theme" of which he had "frankly stolen from your 'Save America First,' namely, the continental integration of the United States makes it a country different in kind from any other nation on earth, except Russia, and different from Russia because (a) we are so far ahead industrially, and (b) we have ocean barriers to east and west which Russia does not." He had touched on this thesis in previous books but never "as forcibly as you have done, and indeed, you gave me a new and exciting idea of its transcendent importance." The book also "leaned pretty heavily" on such other scholars as Charles Beard.[29]

In a 1939 article, "How to Stop Dictators," Chase noted that the Italians and Germans had turned to dictators because they were suffering from "terrible economic conditions." The same was likely to happen in the United States when the people were "fed up with being half-fed." Yet every time the administration tried to spend money to improve conditions there was a storm of protest. Ironically, now that the nation was being forced to spend more on defense, there were few objections. As Chase put it, "businessmen raise practically no objections about a budget unbalanced by submarines and raise merry hell about one unbalanced by soil conservation." Even more ironic was the fact that businessmen did not practice in their businesses the policy they preached for the federal government. As Chase put it:

> Business men often express horror at an unbalanced federal budget. They apparently forget that private enterprise as a whole has never balanced its budget, has never been on a pay-as-you-go basis. Net private debt—mostly corporate—has grown from forty billions in 1910 to almost two hundred billions today. By comparison the present federal debt of forty billions is chicken-feed. The 1922-29 boom was reared on private debt, just as the 1933-37 recovery was reared on public debt.

Chase was hopeful that the TNEC would find a method for eliminating administered prices. He reiterated the need to redistribute the national income, "through taxation or otherwise, so that more of it will be spent and less of it saved to rot in reserves." "Hoarding," he wrote could not be tolerated without disaster. The New Deal had laid the groundwork for a recovery, "but it is obviously not enough. Too many citizens are still unemployed." If the United States did nothing, it could probably not avoid its own variety of Mussolini or Hitler.[30]

In "If You Were President," published in the *New Republic* in mid-1940, Chase reiterated the six point program for recovery he had outlined in *Idle Money, Idle Men*.[31] Two weeks later he followed with an article, "Can We Afford the New Deal?" Pointing out the nation still suffered from nearly 20 percent unemployment, with about one-third of its factories idle, and billions of dollars idle in bank deposits, the economy he wrote, "sags like a partly filled balloon." He wrote:

> To bring the American economy to full capacity would require an increased annual expenditure of at least twenty billion dollars. The present defense program is far short of this figure, and even if Congress should appropriate the sum, it could not be spent in the next year....Nothing on the horizon indicates that more than five billions will actually be spent in 1941 unless we should go into a full-out war. Five billions will put more gas in the balloon but it will not fill it....If in 1942 ten billions should actually be spent for defense, by the end of the year full performance might be in sight. Then, some time in 1943, we could decide how much of the New Deal spending for relief could profitably be eliminated.

The United States could afford such a debt, but it didn't have to. Instead of borrowing the idle money in savings, the federal government should "slap a good, stiff income tax on those of us who save and have no outlets for investment—on both individual and corporations." Congress should "broaden the base of the income tax, stiffen the rates, go after corporate surpluses, excess profits, after every idle dollar in the economy. Take it and spend it for defense; make it perform the real function of modern money, which is to move." By thus stimulating the economy from part-time to full-time, the incomes of all Americans would be increased through the additional taxes. Coyle concluded:

> The New Deal is not the evil brain-child of Mr. Roosevelt and his advisers. It is the bow of our economic system to the power age and the compulsions of history. It is a safety valve which protects us against the explosion of totalitarianism. There is plenty of room in the nation for both private business and the measures called the New Deal. You can get along together....But if one or the other has to go in this critical period, it will not be the New Deal.[32]

With the world at war, and with both free enterprise and democracy either eliminated or under tight control in the rest of the world, Chase considered the likely results if Wendell Willkie were to win the White House in 1940, writing:

> One last stand we may have, on the line of free enterprise, "economy," and sound finance. I doubt if the line can be held for long. It will buckle because it cannot adequately move the goods, or substantially reduce the

number of the unemployed. With everything in its favor, including the blessing of Mr. Hoover, and the acclaim of the people, it buckled in 1929 right down to the edge of doom. If it could not hold then, how can it hold now, with our economy in a condition of chronic stagnation? This is a free country, and if the majority of the voters want it tried, it should be tried. Let Mr. Willkie see what he can do.

But:

> If after fair trial, it can be proved to the satisfaction of the voters that the old line cannot be maintained, then a program for genuine recovery becomes politically possible. Then we can do what needs to be done at home or abroad. The essence of such a program will be to use money to employ money and to move goods. If an interest rate of zero facilitates the movement, it will be used. If a heavy tax on idle money facilitates the movement, it will be used....We shall follow other nations in assuming that anything can be paid for if men and machines are unemployed and materials are available.

The United States should set an example for a world in chaos, but it could not do so with "economic models designed for the days of President McKinley," nor could such models do the American people any good. America needed "a program designed for the power age; for a time of great turmoil and transition," one that put "men first and money second."[33] That priority would come seventeen months later as a result of the attack on Pearl Harbor.

7

Coyle and the Irrepressible Conflict

The influence of David Cushman Coyle on the New Deal and on the new habits of thought during the 1930s has not received the attention both deserve. Noting that three of Coyle's books had sold over a million copies, *Scholastic* magazine wrote in 1936 that he was "credited with influencing more Americans than any other writer on phases of the New Deal."[1]

His influence on thought in the 1930s could be seen in the wistful letter of a woman on welfare when she wrote in *Scribner's* magazine:

> Thrift, industry, self-reliance, fortitude—these virtues have become vices and will destroy the individual who practises them. This is an unpleasant thought, but millions of us today are being forced to accept it. The farmer whose bumper crop is a sin, all those whose savings became hoardings— any one exposed to the economic conditions of today, if his character has been set in the old culture, will find himself hampered by ideas and attitudes which are no longer appropriate. At first this is only bewildering. But as the pressure increases, as adaptation to the new conditions becomes necessary, the bewilderment gives place to pain.[2]

She was expressing the bewilderment of a great many Americans at the changed nature of thought during the 1930s concerning the relative virtues of saving and spending, as expounded by Coyle and others.

Coyle was not alone, of course, in attributing the Depression to an excess of savings and investment over spending, nor in proposing governmental action to end this depression, and to prevent future ones. The so-called Progressive Era of the first two decades of the twentieth century had ushered in new ways of looking at almost everything. Under the influence of Darwinism and other intellectual influences of the late nineteenth century, the new philosophy of pragmatism, identified with Charles Peirce, William James, and John Dewey, challenged entrenched attitudes in every branch of learned activity from sociology to law. Economics was not immune to the new trends, and the "new economics" rejected the laissez faire attitude towards business cycles that had heretofore regarded them as inevitable and nearly akin to acts of God. The "new economists," instead, assumed that business cycles could be vitiated, if not eliminated altogether, through human action. For the more radical, the solution lay in eliminating the private enterprise system that was their source. For others, central governments could act in ways to smooth out the cycles of capitalistic boom and bust by intervening intelligently at strategic points in a nation's economy.

Some of the new economists saw the solution in federal monetary policy, by adjusting the nation's money supply. Others saw it in increasing consumption of the flow of goods emerging from the nation's factories, ensuring that consumer purchasing power remained as constant as possible. One device for doing this was through increased government spending on public works, preferably through deficit spending, when signs pointed to an impending slowdown in the economy, together with curbs on savings and investment that tended to reduce purchasing power and increase production. One of the most prominent of this group was William Trufant Foster, whose education was in English, rather than economics, and who had served as the first president of Reed College before embarking in 1920 on a career in economics as director of the Pollak Foundation for Economic Research, established by his frequent co-author, businessman Waddill Catchings, as a platform for their ideas. In their books, articles, and lectures, they preached that savings were harmful since they reduced consumer purchasing power even as they simultaneously fueled further production, expounded the virtues of contra-cyclical public works, and asked that government provide a constantly increasing flow of new money into the economy to encourage consumer spending.[3] The "new economics" made no great impression in the prosperous 1920s, when the prospect of a bust seemed more remote with each year of the boom.

The impact of Foster and Catchings on David Cushman Coyle is obvious, but whereas they had publicized their views in speeches, books, and magazine articles throughout the 1920s, it was Coyle who replaced them in hammering similar themes more persistently than anybody else in the 1930s through an even greater number of vehicles. In the 1930s it was difficult for a magazine reader to escape the Coyle message, so widely were his articles published in virtually every popular magazine from *Harper's* and *Scribner's* to *Survey Graphic* and *Atlantic*, not to mention a variety of professional, scholarly, and semi-scholarly journals. In addition, there were the numerous Coyle pamphlets and books, as well as his lectures. That Coyle was published so widely was proof that his theories were taken seriously, and indicated even to doubters that they could not ignore his ideas.

In arguing for consumer spending and against saving/investment, Coyle was reversing the traditional American virtue that had been preached at least since Benjamin Franklin's Poor Richard. For this reason, Coyle was sometimes referred to, ironically, as "the Poor Richard of the Roosevelt Revolution."[4] Yet in a broader sense, Coyle was also sometimes regarded as the nearest thing to an economic philosopher that the New Deal possessed, especially beginning with 1935. Others advocated individual policies that were a part of Coyle's program, but only he integrated them, with an engineer's precision, into a cogent and comprehensive whole in which each bore a relationship to the others, one, as will be seen, that synthesized the views of Foster and Catchings with those of Louis Brandeis.

Though Coyle presumed in many of his writings to speak for the New Deal, and while his views help to explain the rationale behind some of Roosevelt's actions that are otherwise inexplicable or have been interpreted wrongly, it is clear that the president did not totally embrace Coyle's views. Others were competing for Roosevelt's ear and scored their own victories in directing his thought and policies. Nevertheless, David Cushman Coyle was an important force in the 1930s, both for his influence on values in that decade, and for his role as "economic philosopher" of much of the "second New Deal."

Coyle claimed descent from arrivals on the Mayflower. Born in 1887, he was educated at Princeton (A.B., 1908) and as an engineer at Rensselaer Polytechnic Institute (C.E. 1910), where he lost his left foot as the result of a football accident, walking thereafter with a limp. After graduating he worked as a consulting engineer. During the 1920s a great many engineers were converted to a belief that economic problems were susceptible to engineering solutions, a view that led to the short-lived technocrat movement in the late 1920s and early 1930s. Coyle, too, managed to convince himself that he was an economist with the solution to the nation's economic ills. He published several articles and pamphlets that contained his analysis of the causes of the depression and his prescription for not only generating recovery and preventing any further such downturns in the business cycle, but for a Utopia that would result if his proposals were followed. He justified his intrusion into the field in a 1933 essay: "No one need apologize...for stating economic laws that fly in the face of what we thought were economic laws, nor for suggesting attitudes and policies that go directly contrary to the attitudes and policies of the past. Our old ideas of 'sound' economics failed to work; a new understanding is called for." Could any economic ideas be more outlandish than the reality of the "paradox of plenty" that people saw around them? "The more we make the less we have; the more we get the poorer we are; a good harvest is the ruin of farmers; and a first class earthquake brings prosperity to thousands."[5]

Coyle's articles and pamphlets, and the unorthodox ideas they contained, would probably have attracted little attention had it not been for the support he received initially from Felix Frankfurter. Indeed, Frankfurter's effort to promote Coyle's ideas even predated Roosevelt's inauguration, when the Harvard law professor sought to obtain publicity for Coyle's writings and to ensure that they received favorable reviews in the media. These two amateur economists - the one a consulting engineer whose letterhead listed the specialties of "Buildings," "Foundations," and "Wind Vibration Tests," and the other a law professor - shared in common a lack of appreciation for economic orthodoxy and a willingness to undertake "liberal" experiments in economic affairs.

Coyle first attracted Frankfurter's attention with an article on "Business and Finance" that he published in *Corporate Practice Review* in mid-1932. After reading the article, Frankfurter told its author he had "the feeling that one has when clear air and sunshine break into a dank room." Coyle had "shown more shrewdly and comprehensively than I have seen in any single piece of writing how anachronistic are the economic assumptions which underlie the essential efforts of Washington and Wall Street to deal with the depression from any long-range point of view."[6] Coyle responded:

> This article was a trial, to see how people of the upper middle class would take new doctrine. Our theory is that if action of this kind can start in the higher business levels perhaps it can go through without developing a war between business and the unemployed that would tear the country all to pieces. We have had a good reception from people like [Senator James] Couzens, Bernard Flexner, Flinn of the Engineering Foundation, [Ralph] Flanders of the Engineering Council, and many others.

Then Coyle sought Frankfurter's help, writing:

> Now we want to publish an enlarged form of the same as a pamphlet, to sell for about 75 cents, but the financial end of the C.P. Review is scared of the initial cost of $750. None of us have any money that we can risk. I should like your advice. Would people like you buy this? Would you be inclined to get a number of copies at a reduced price for distribution? Do you know anybody who would be willing to risk any money on it?[7]

Frankfurter then busied himself with promoting Coyle's views and distributing reprints of the article.[8]

Shortly after the article was published, Coyle expanded it into a self-published 45-page pamphlet entitled: *The Irrepressible Conflict: Business and Finance.* In the preface, Coyle explained that his article had "received so many favorable comments that it has been considered desirable to reprint the material, with revisions to meet changed conditions, and with explanations and illustrations of points that were not clear in its more condensed form." His intention, Coyle wrote, was not to present "a detailed plan for a new social order," but to promote "a new orientation of thought." In the early years of the Republic, he observed, "frugality and hard work held the only hope of survival." Money had to be diverted from spending by consumers and into the hands of financiers who could "use it to build factories, and later to develop railroads and great cities." Quite naturally, Americans had continued to cling to those traditional virtues, and were now dismayed that they seemed powerless against the depression. The problem, Coyle observed, was that America was a different place from that in 1790, and the "insistent demand" now was "not for labor, not for capital, but for buyers to carry away the goods."[9]

Coyle explained that in "the power age" there were two new mechanical factors. The first was that the new age required less labor, due to automation; the second was that the same amount of investment could now produce a more productive plant. These factors reduced the need for both investment and labor. What the economy needed now was markets. And since the "mountain of foreign credit" from World War I had reduced the ability of foreign markets to absorb American goods, those goods would have to be bought by American consumers. Another factor was "the slackening of the growth of population," which meant that "if the market for goods is to grow up to the present capacity of productive plant, it can do so only by the increase of average buying power, not by the arrival of more buyers." Also, a larger part of the product of industry was now made up of "durable goods like automobiles, electric refrigerators, and houses," the market for which collapsed in bad times. Recovery and a healthy economy depended on renewed spending for such durable goods. "The central economic law of the power age," Coyle wrote, "is that business cannot stand too much capital.... It is evident that the moral precepts of Benjamin Franklin do not fit the necessities of times like these. From now on, the intolerable sin is not extravagance, but avarice." What was needed was the power to direct money "away from any form of investment whatever." Planning was obviously necessary, but "simply planning the first thing that comes to hand is not the answer."[10]

In his pamphlet, Coyle examined and rejected the various proposals for planning the United States out of the Depression. One proposal, popular with some businessmen and politicians, involved various degrees of cartelization, with or without governmental involvement. Written before Roosevelt's election and inauguration, Coyle's views on cartelization are interesting in light of the National Industrial Recovery Act that was pushed through Congress during the Hundred Days. Of cartelization, Coyle wrote that "controlling the volume of production and preventing a fall of price" was "a positive plan that goes directly at the instability of prices which is so injurious to any business." However, the negative effects were injurious to the "uncartelized" segment of the economy, shifting deflation to "consumers' incomes, i.e., in the only source of business, with the result that the last state of industry is worse than the first." Such a system could operate effectively only if it could "fix prices, wages, and incomes to keep consumption up to production, which makes it technically indistinguishable from the communist state," and it was "questionable whether the American people are temperamentally suited to militarized planning, and whether we could easily find rulers with enough vitality to stand up to us."[11]

Coyle then proposed his own solution. The problem was that too much money was going into investments, many of them worthless, rather than into consumer purchases, or, as Coyle put it, to Wall Street rather than to Main Street. The solution was to divert money from investment and into consumer purchasing power. As Coyle put it: "The traditional method of directing the flow of money from one part of the economic system to another is by use of the tax system. Taxes are the most powerful pump we know of."[12] He explained:

> The present problem is how to divert money from investment in commercial equipment to the consumption of the goods which business is trying to sell....The taxes which draw from money headed toward investment are the higher brackets of the personal income and inheritance taxes. The effect of these taxes is passed on not to the consumer, but to the promoter and the bond house. The heavier these taxes are made, the less money there will be for investment in the overequipment of industry....Above this ceiling [on income] the supertax would take practically all the surplus income, except as the taxpayer could show that he had contributed it to some project of a non-commercial kind.[13]

Coyle then explained why business and finance were in an "irrepressible conflict."

> It is evident that in attempting to free itself of the poison of overbuilding business is pulling the beard of that man-eating ogre Finance. It is only beginning to be dimly recognized that in a plenty economy there is and must be between the interests of business and those of finance an irrepressible conflict. The normal processes of finance are poisonous to business....Business needs stability to prosper; finance get its profits from instability. To be more specific: the income tax makes for stability and hurts finance; the sales tax makes for instability and hurts business. Over this conflict of interest there must be a battle, because so long as finance dominates business both are headed for the precipice, and finance will not loosen its grip without a fight.... The crossroads of history will be the place where we do or do not develop means for keeping money out of Wall Street and making it travel up and down Wall Street where it belongs.[14]

Coyle discarded any consideration of a collectivist solution to the nation's problems, writing: "Among our people dynamic emotion attaches to the idea of freedom of initiative. . . . the communist solution, while mathematically sound, is fatally handicapped, for us, by our temperamental distaste for discipline." Sounding very Brandeisian, Coyle argued that it was vital to promote the interests of "middle-sized concerns" in order to provide "openings for individual initiative and leadership." [15] All other issues, however, were subordinate to the "essential" one of "the distribution of income and the allocation of income between equipment and consumption....The master plan of the economic system for a power age will necessarily be a plan for directing the flow of money. All other plans are either supplementary to their central objective or else inconsequential." Money must be diverted "from investment in commercial equipment to the consumption of the goods that business is trying to sell."[16]

George Soule of the *New Republic* was doubtless referring to Frankfurter when he wrote in his review for *Books* that Coyle's "pamphlet" had "been favorably received in influential places." Coyle, he observed, had expounded "what is in almost every respect the exact opposite of ex-Secretary [of the Treasury] Mellon's view of taxation and public finance." Soule explained:

> Mr. Mellon argued for reduced rates on large incomes, profits and inheritances, because he believed that money left in the hands of the rich would be used for new investment and would thus stimulate prosperity....Mr. Coyle argues for the highest possible rates on large incomes, profits and inheritances because he believes this will severely limit new investment by the rich and will thus prevent overproduction and depression.

Soule, a collectivist, doubted that Coyle's approach would work, but he revealed the attraction of Coyle for the "planners" when he wrote that if Coyle's advice were followed "we should find ourselves on the high road to broader planning. We cannot make the economic complex behave by taking hold of a single part of it alone."[17] A reviewer in *Commonweal* found his argument "realistic and unanswerable," and suggested all businessmen and members of Congress should read it."[18]

Looking at the paralysis that seemed to exist in the early 1930s, Coyle argued in an article for the *American Scholar* that two "unnoticed appendages" had "upset the smooth course of history," so that the "tail has become the dog, and the whole animal has to proceed from this point in the opposite direction."

> During the post-War period the disposal of excess savings by investment and bankruptcy has become an increasingly important function of finance. The War left the country with a building shortage and large profits were made in the building industry and its speculative adjuncts. The interest on our investment balance abroad was also a kind of cream we had never before tasted. Added to this, our income tax was cut down, freeing considerable sums and making them available for investment. The total volume of savings thus grew beyond the needs of industry, and the excess savings naturally took the form of investments destined to subsequent loss. A good many billions went into foreign bonds, now either in default or selling at a loss. About 5 per cent of the country's income was currently dissipated by bankruptcy. But the major part of the savings of this period were expended for machinery that was to stand idle, and "rentable area" that was to prove unrentable....Either people will have to be persuaded not to set aside very much money for investment, or else the money that has been set aside for investment will need to be reconsidered and spent after all. The standard method of investing it regardless, and losing it afterward, can be worked only so long as the bankruptcy is kept hidden from the investor by a decent veil. The effect of the new technological processes is to make it increasingly hard to keep even the most simple investor from realizing what happens to those who think it is smart to be thrifty.

Coyle then looked at the future:

> There are apparently two divergent directions we might take. They may be called the democratic and the technocratic roads. It is best to admit that, so far as now appears, Technocracy is the apparent heir, if democratic adjustments are not effected adequately and rather soon. The democratic alternative has been already implied in the earlier part of this paper. Specifically it consists in the abandonment of the idea that accumulated money has to be invested, whatever the consequences, and the use of income taxes either to collect such accumulations and spend them or to divert them into contributions for cultural purposes....There is no mathematical reason why capitalism cannot operate, at any rate of productivity the engineers can make possible, and with large differences in individual incomes, provided those who get the larger incomes are persuaded, forced, or otherwise led to devote their surplus to public or semipublic services. The only thing that has become obsolete and that cannot any longer exist in this new age of productivity is the reinvestment of large incomes....The question is this: whether to plan only the flow of money and preserve our freedom to experiment in production, or to plan production and sacrifice freedom to

efficiency under a Technocratic dictatorship....There is no logical necessity for cutting down our freedom of initiative because we can produce more with less labor. Such a situation requires planning, but not detailed planning of individual schedules and activities. It needs social control to prevent a jamming of its distribution system; but outside a few measures like these, it is our world to enjoy. Because there is plenty for everybody it is less rather than more necessary to be careful about small matters. Restricting our freedom because we have solved the problem of production is the last absurdity. Rather have we been made more free to waste time and money in experimentation and exploration, and in art and sport, and in adventures in all the arts of life.[19]

By November 1932, Coyle had attracted enough notice to be invited to address the American Academy of Political and Social Science on "New Aspects of the Distribution Problem." In his speech, Coyle argued that "the reason the United States ran into the ditch was that the road along which we had been driving for three hundred years took a sharp turn, and we failed to notice it in time." Events of the past twenty years, especially, had transformed the situation. As a creditor nation, the United States could no longer rely on "a so-called favorable balance of trade," and with population growth flattening out, there would no longer be "a rapid growth of the home market" unless there was a rapid rise in the standard of living. On top of these, "the new developments of technology appear as the portent of another industrial revolution like the one which followed the invention of the steam engine."

The use of the "continuous process machine," he pointed out, was spreading throughout industry, with the result that in one after another "human labor is being almost entirely eliminated as a factor in production." But, Coyle argued:

> Somehow, the vast majority who cannot be employed in making or distributing goods must be given the means to purchase those goods or else business is hopelessly paralyzed. This is the new form of the problem of the distribution of income, and in this new form it has become the central toothache of the whole economic body.

Unemployment had become not cyclical, as in past depressions, but permanent. Thus, measures to promote cyclical recovery were not enough to solve the problem. The "widening divergence between a small demand for labor and a large demand for free-spending customers has thrown the common theories of economics per-

manently out of step with the realities of the economic process."
Increasing production would not increase purchasing power, so long
as the increased production was being achieved through the use of
machines rather than by hiring workers. Other ways of creating
purchasing power must be found than merely the traditional ones.
Employment in the services was one "answer to the problem of
how to distribute buying power without subjecting any one to the
disintegrating effects of permanent idleness....The new industries
which are to absorb the surplus labor discharged by manufacture
must be industries which make not goods but services." Public
policy must "encourage or require those who might invest to re-
frain and to divert a large part of their savings into the market for
service."

This would require "for some years to come...a large program of
public and semi-public projects, supported by income taxes or by
large contributions stimulated by the tax laws." This type of "artificial encouragement" would be necessary "until the public has become educated to a sufficient scale of private expenditure to keep
the new plenty economy in fairly permanent balance," and they
must be in sufficient amount to do the job. "Small quantities of
Federal expenditure," Coyle argued, "such as those that have been
tried so far, serve only to use up Government credit without curing
the situation." Once the pump had been primed, "the prosperity
can be continued indefinitely so long as the market for services is
kept continuously supplied with money diverted from unnecessary
investment in new plant."

Looking at the presidential election of a week earlier, Coyle concluded that the American people had "given a clear indication" of
their desire "to keep the capitalist system if it can be made to come
out of its coma and get to work....They have called in a new man
and given him a mandate to find out what it was that ought to have
been done and do it now." The Hoover administration had failed to
come to grips with the problem of distribution of purchasing power.
All the system needed to make it run was a "means of distributing
buying power without loading industry with more capital than it
can carry."[20]

In December, Edward Rumely of the Committee for the Nation
sent Coyle $5 in payment for copies of *The Irrepressible Conflict*
which he asked be sent to a number of people, including New Deal

braintruster Rexford Tugwell and several people affiliated with the Committee, including Frank Vanderlip. In a letter later in the month, Rumely told Coyle he found his logic "compelling."[21] On December 23rd, Coyle sent Rumely half of his remaining copies of the *Annals* article and told him:

> Your paper on the farm problem interests me very much, and I can see that for anyone interested in selling anything to farmers the problem comes pretty close home. There is of course still a lot of resistance in this part of the country [New York City] to inflation of any kind, and some of us feel that we still have a long fight on our hands before that resistance will be broken down. All the pressure you folks can exert is to the good. Ultimately, I guess we all agree, the farmer's problem can only be solved as an incident to a broad general rise in the standard of living that will draw enough farmers into other occupations to leave the others in a good position to make a living.

The *Annals* article, he told Rumely, was also being published in the *Federal Employee* and in *Pencil Points*, an architectural magazine. He was also hoping that it would be taken up by *Reader's Digest* and he asked Rumely to recommend it to them. In a p.s., Coyle added: "I hear that Vanderlip is all sewed up with Technocracy. If that is so you wasted my book on him—the Technocrats consider me as one of the lowest forms of animal life."[22]

A fourth edition of *The Irrepressible Conflict*, published in 1934, took note of the New Deal legislation of the Hundred Days and offered advice. Coyle found Roosevelt a kindred soul in his awareness of the danger of encouraging enterprise as an easy road to recovery, quoting FDR's fireside chat of May 7, 1933, in which the president had said:

> I do not want the people of this country to take the foolish course of letting the improvement come back on another speculative wave...the ruinous practice of increasing our crop output and our factory output in the hope that a kind Providence will find buyers at high prices. Such a course may bring us immediate and false prosperity, but it is the kind of prosperity that will lead us into another tailspin.[23]

For Coyle, however, the imperative need was to not only dampen investment, but also to increase consumer purchasing power, and both goals could be reached "by the use of the income and inheritance taxes if they are made sufficiently drastic. The primary effect will be to transfer money directly from the investment market to the market for goods and services." And another "primary effect," Coyle added, would be to permit "a vast increase in public and semi-public expenditure for services, utilizing the labor that is no longer required in industry."[24]

Meanwhile, new investment, and the corporate debt that it represented, could be "obstructed" by "taxes on new security issues, the new law requiring full disclosure of the facts about new issues of stocks and bonds, stock transfer taxes, perhaps even a graduated corporation tax on gross capitalization." Of assistance, also, would be "a generous and all-embracing old age pension," since it would "not only render unnecessary the pathetic and hopeless effort to save up for old age," but would also "encourage people of all ages to spend as they go." Despite the influence of finance, anything was possible so long as the White House was "occupied by a man who is determined to bring before the public whatever measures may be required to make the economic system work."[25]

Frankfurter offered to use his "intimate friends" to promote Coyle's ideas, including Bruce Bliven, editor of the *New Republic*. He told Coyle he was writing to Bliven to suggest "that he and the other editors of the *New Republic* get hold of you to enable you to canvass with them your ideas and the appropriate channels for their promotion."[26] Coyle, however, was hesitant that his ideas should be identified with that liberal organ, writing Frankfurter:

> Last Thursday the editor and I lunched with Mr. Flexner and Bruce Bliven, and we all agreed that it would be good tactics not to notice my stuff in the New Republic at present, as we might as well get the benefit of my extreme respectability while it lasts....By the same token I have persuaded Paul Kellogg not to put me in the Survey for the present, and, if you will pardon me, I am not mentioning your name except to people whom I know to be either liberal or intelligent or both.

Frankfurter had also provided an opening to Louis Brandeis and others in Washington, and Coyle reported that a meeting with Justice Brandeis had "pepped up my vitality immensely."[27]

Frankfurter responded a few weeks later that he fully appreciated "the importance of capturing minds that are not obsessed by foolish Red-phobias," but he thought that Coyle was worried unduly, for the depression had caused "the breaking down to no small degree...the humorless inhospitality to people with different views which characterized the prosperity decade." The *New Republic*, for example, was "now being quoted in respectable quarters." It seemed to Frankfurter a waste of Coyle's energy "to be hedging yourself about with the simulated appearance of a 'conservative,'" when he ought, instead, to avail himself "of every opportunity to saturate the atmosphere with your ideas" in whatever journal was available."[28]

Coyle finally relented and agreed to meet with Bliven and Paul Kellogg (editor of *Survey*), but added that he would be "damned if I associate with socialists, as such," a recognition of the collectivist bent the *New Republic* had taken.[29] Indeed, it is difficult to imagine Coyle's work in a journal by now so committed to collectivism and showing such "humorless inhospitality" to other views as the *New Republic*. And there is no correspondence between the two in the Frankfurter Papers after 1932, suggesting a deeper alienation over Frankfurter's attempt to identify Coyle with his collectivist friends. Thereafter it would be Coyle who would be more representative of Brandeis' unrelenting hostility to the collectivists whom Frankfurter had begun to find so congenial.

The Irrepressible Conflict was well known in the White House, however. The president's uncle, Frederic A. Delano, a former member of the Federal Reserve Board, sent him a copy, and Roosevelt forwarded it on to Treasury Secretary Henry Morgenthau with a note: "You might read this over for it is entitled to some weight coming from a former member of the Federal Reserve Board. Please let me have it back." FDR also sent along another pamphlet by Coyle, *High Productivity and the Distribution Problem*.[30]

Parts of Roosevelt's inaugural speech echoed Coyle's position, particularly the new President's excoriation of "the unscrupulous money changers." Those "money changers," Roosevelt told America, had "fled from their high seats in the temple of our civilization. We can now restore that temple to the ancient truths." But Roosevelt also went beyond Coyle to attack the pursuit of profit, and implicitly business as well as finance. The nation, Roosevelt said, needed to "apply social values more noble than mere monetary profit."[31] In short, the new President had lumped both business and finance together as the enemy, while Coyle saw between the two an irrepressible conflict that business must win.

The legislation of the "Hundred Days" also was of mixed value in Coyle's vision of reform. Certainly the Emergency Banking Bill, by increasing federal control over money, was consistent with Coyle's position. It gave the president authority over gold movements, made "hoarding" of the metal illegal, and gave him the power to reopen "solvent" banks while reorganizing the rest. But Coyle was an advocate neither of restricting production, nor of sales taxes, and thus the Agricultural Adjustment Act (AAA) was totally at odds with his program. By imposing taxes on processors of agricultural products, the legislation virtually guaranteed that these processing taxes would be passed on to consumers, thus amounting to the equivalent of a sales tax on food and clothing and reducing the consumer purchasing power that was so important to Coyle.

Nor could Coyle have objected strongly when Roosevelt "torpedoed" the London Economic Conference in the summer of 1933, turning the United States towards an isolationist recovery policy, although from different motives than those behind Coyle's advocacy of a a similar approach. As will be seen, Coyle was opposed to any reliance on foreign trade for American prosperity since, like historian Charles Beard, he saw in it dangers of possible war.

Although certainly not one of Frankfurter's "red hots" - that group of young lawyers who regarded themselves as his disciples and whom he placed at strategic positions in the White House and in New Deal agencies, Coyle clearly benefited from their support. Early in the New Deal he was tapped by Interior Secretary and Public Works Administrator Harold Ickes to serve on the Technical Board of Review of the Public Works Administration, the first of several such appointments he held in the New Deal during the 1930s.[32] By 1936 he had also served as a technical adviser to the Rural Electrification Administration, the Resettlement Administration, and the Federal Reserve Board.[33]

Coinciding with Roosevelt's inauguration in March 1933, Coyle published an article in *Scribner's* magazine on "The Road to Prosperity," which outlined his major points. During the 1920s, he pointed out, the number of workers in manufacturing had actually declined even while production increased, yet unemployment had remained low. This apparent anomaly was explained by the growth in service industries during the same decade, when the market for services had increased by fifty percent. "Census figures," he wrote, "also show that an increasing percentage of the gainfully employed were in the service industries," making that segment of the economy "the answer to the problem of technological unemployment." There was, he asserted, "no limit to the field for employment in improving the conditions of civilization, of health, knowledge, religion, and art, in the provision of modern treatment for criminals and defectives, and in a host of other cultural or quasi-cultural developments with all the various grades of labor and management required." The problem was that as a result of the depression, the service industries had slumped in the 1930s and were not providing the employment opportunities they had in the 1920s.[34]

The slump had occurred because many services were in "the luxury class, so that when depression came they were quickly cut off as each family began reducing its expenditures." Another factor had been "the increasing volume of saving and investment" during the boom period, which had taken income away from expenditures on services and wasted it, instead, on such things as excess commercial construction. Returning to his essential point, Coyle wrote: "If the poisonous effects of overbuilding are to be avoided, it can only be by government action that will divert large amounts of surplus income from possible investment into private or public spending on a grand scale."[35]

In doing so, the government would simultaneously solve another problem—eliminating from investment use the savings that triggered overexpansion of business and produced the booms and busts of the orthodox business cycle. A number of more desirable avenues were available for distributing "surplus income" to "wage earners without forcing it to pass through the orthodox saving-investment-loss process." Coyle explained:

> Surplus income is now in part distributed by way of contributions to semi-public organizations in cultural and philanthropic fields, and by way of income taxes which are spent by the government on the public services. This type of distribution mechanism transforms accumulated money into buying power among lower income groups, without producing salable goods to compete with private business and without adding to the total of business debt....The graduated income tax, suitably sugar-coated with exemptions for contributions, will do the trick provided it is made sufficiently drastic....The buying power available for purchase of manufactured goods can be kept at any desired quantity by deliberately enlarging the

volume of income taxes in the higher brackets, and of the contributions stimulated by tax exemptions.[36]

Large expenditures on relief and public works would increase consumer purchasing power, and "very heavily graduated income and inheritance taxes" would "supply funds for paying off Federal bonds and retiring the Federal Reserve notes on which they were floated, and also to draw off surplus income and prevent it from flowing in large quantities into new investment." Coyle continued:

> The key to stable prosperity is the continuous distribution of buying power; the key to distribution is the diversion of money from unnecessary capital investment into the market for services; the key to an immediate enlargement of the market for services is the education of public opinion toward an expanded program of public expenditure.[37]

Late in 1933, Coyle returned to a familiar theme in an article for the *National Conference of Social Work*, on "Necessary Changes of Public Opinion in the New Social Order," writing that: "Our environment has changed with a vengeance." The main cause of unemployment, he repeated, was the collapse of the service industries, which had prospered in the 1920s. The service industries were primarily "luxuries," and expenditures on luxuries were the first casualty in hard times. "Society," he wrote, "will have to develop means for stabilizing the market for services. Old values, old judgments, and old maxims that interfere with the necessary stabilizing of the market for services cannot survive the coming of the age of plenty." What was required was that the "distribution of income through overinvestment and the building of debt. . . become a small item, and the distribution of income through income taxes and through contributions to the social services stimulated by tax exemptions. . . become a very large item." In short, surplus income would have to be diverted from investment and circulated through spending.

In order to stimulate such spending, consumers must be relieved of the sales taxes, tariffs, and public-service charges that drained away their purchasing power. Their place would be taken by "heavy income taxes on the upper brackets, with large exemptions for contributions to semipublic institutions. . . [and] heavy taxation of undistributed corporate surpluses, to force corporation income into dividends and wages." "Communism," Coyle conceded, "is one way of providing for the necessary distribution and allocation of income. The control of the flow of money by the tax system is the other way. . . . At the present time the American people are not willing to try communism. Whether communism is adapted to the American temperament is very doubtful."

The successful "passage into the new age of plenty will depend on whether the public can be led to agree to the necessary measures for distributing purchasing power and for allocating surplus to spending for services." An essential measure would be "old age pensions," which must "come to be regarded not as a dole to the destitute, but as a universal right." Such pensions would create "a class of buyers who have nothing to sell . . ., encourage retirement and make more room for the younger workers, and above all . . . will remove the necessity of the pathetic and hopeless efforts to lay by investments for old age." Other plans for "guaranteeing personal security" would also have a place, such as "accident and sickness insurance," to remove the "desperate pressure to save and invest and lose money." Since too much investment was a "poison," the provision of economic security was "not only a moral obligation resting on society, but it is a technical necessity for the operation of the age of plenty. Basic security is the prerequisite for that habit of spending and not saving that the age of plenty demands."

Industries that, by virtue of being natural monopolies, did not lend themselves to decentralization, would have to be absorbed by "full public control." Modern technology was leading others in the direction of decentralization. Government might impose control over "working hours and a moderate minimum wage," without destroying the freedom of business, but control of production and prices destroyed business elasticity and "restrictions on freedom tend to become very severe." The "genius" of the American people "for not obeying superfluous laws is immense," he pointed out, and there was "no widespread desire in America for any neatly organized society" at the expense of "freedom of individual action."

Coyle then addressed the collectivist mood of the new liberals, writing that:

> public opinion, and especially liberal opinion, has by the existing preponderance of the economic crisis been led into a false perspective. We have temporarily overlooked the fact that in the new social order manufacturing

will be a minor activity; that the service industries will be the dominant half of the economic system; and that the growth of our culture demands freedom of experimentation in the field of services. In the long run a planned economic order is not the central focus of an adequately planned society for an age of plenty. . . . If a satisfactory adjustment to the age of plenty is to be attained, it is vitally important to plan for the preservation of the largest possible freedom of variation, of experimentation, and of adventure. . . . The civilization now beginning will not be invented and imposed by a dictator; it will develop out of the reactions of all the people to the conditions of their life and to the sporadic contributions of genius.

Coyle told social workers:

You have struggled for years to establish the decencies of life for their own sake. The time has now come when you can demand the means for an expanded social-work program in the name of economic law. The fates have taken your side. The heavy artillery has come up—in fact it is parked in the White House.[38]

In early December, Coyle delivered the annual Henry Robinson Towns lecture before the American Society of Mechanical Engineers and told the assembled engineers that "only inflation, controlled by the Federal Government, could lead the nation into a stabilized prosperity." According to the *New York Times*, Coyle "urged higher income taxes in the upper brackets, non-self-liquidating public works, government control of transportation and power and decentralization of private industries as necessary steps in bringing about a new economic order." As for inflation, it should be done through the sale of federal bonds to the Federal Reserve System in return for paper money which it could then use to increase consumer purchasing power either by investment or by direct expenditure. The federal government must also assume greater control over concentrated industries. The two actions were necessary, Coyle told the engineers, because "business cannot operate in a system of high productivity unless the surplus income can be continuously distributed to non-producers," and because the government's intervention was required to provide stability to business. The creation and preservation of a market for business was the key to prosperity, although the full implication of this was not yet thoroughly grasped in America.

Criticizing the consolidation of business that had taken place during the 1920s, Coyle argued that the effect of such mergers was "to increase the disastrous consequences of wrong judgment, to increase sales costs and to encourage the growth of stuffed shirts. Moreover, there is a tendency to attempt to control output and prices, which, if it is attempted in part of an economic system only, causes the system to become more unstable. For these and related reasons, the downswing of 1929 might have been expected to extend to depths previously unplumbed." Coyle went on:

> A body vibrating on a spring hanger can move up and down with increasing amplitude so long as the spring does not break on the down-swing. In the business cycle the spring was bankruptcy. Bankruptcy was the means by which debt was eliminated from business. But if the time ever came when we dared not face the cold bath of bankruptcy, then the business cycle would be ended. Without bankruptcy the spring would be broken, the famous "corner" could not be turned.
>
> The moment came when we dared not let the swing go to the bottom of its path in 1932 and the R[econstruction] F[inance] C[orporation] was called upon to stop the wave of bankruptcy.
>
> That was the end of the strictly self-acting harmonic vibration of the business cycle. From that time on the recovery of business depended on artificial hoisting mechanisms, to be applied by the government. Nineteen hundred and thirty-three is being devoted to the constructions of those mechanisms.

The government, he said, must force "all stagnant accumulations of unspent money" into spending. "By suitable provision for insurance and old-age pension the government will have to guarantee the basic economic security of all members of the economic system, so that the people can freely spend their income without fear."[39]

In December 1933, Coyle published an article in the *Atlantic Monthly* in which he examined the promise he saw for the economy in an expanded public works program. Prosperity had always been driven by some new industry, most recently by the automobile. That industry had furnished employment for many people, both directly and indirectly. "Where," Coyle asked, "did all the money come from to pay the wages in all of these new jobs?" He answered:

> Out of the pockets of people who were spending more money on the car than they used to spend on the family bicycles. Surplus income, instead of being saved, was being spent on worldly pleasure. Benjamin Franklin's bones rolled over in his grave, but the national income rose by leaps and bounds. The new toy was making the American spend more money, so the American people were getting—ore money to spend—for every time one person spent a dollar someone else got it.

But in the late twenties, Coyle observed, Americans had begun to pay more attention to bond salesmen than to automobile salesmen, with the result that money was drained away from spending and into savings. Far from being a period of extravagance, as was frequently charged, the "boom" years were a period of "unprecedented thrift. Never in history did any people 'save' such a lot of money or 'invest' their savings in such a magnificent array of cats and dogs." Business had collapsed under the burden of the colossal amount of debt thus accumulated.

If America were now to recover from the depression, it needed "a new industry that will make us start spending again, and one that will not lead us into the fatal paths of 'investment.'" Contrary to the cries of orthodox economists, bankers, and businessmen, the last thing the nation needed was a revival of the capital goods industry, which would only recreate the conditions that had produced the crash and Depression. Public works offered the promise of being the new "industry" that could furnish employment and create the buying power that would not be diverted into savings and investment. "The real function of federal spending," Coyle wrote, "is not to furnish extra buying power out of hat, but to turn surplus income back into buying power while preventing surplus income from getting into excessive investment." Its effectiveness, therefore, depended upon taxation of surplus income." In the Age of Plenty, "a large part of the surplus income will be spent by the people themselves on their own personal activities." This could only be done, however, after a "universal guarantee of basic economic security for all members of the social body, quite regardless of age, color, or previous condition of economic ineptitude." This would include "free education, free public health services, accident and unemployment insurance, and, above all, a generous old-age pension system. With such a system in place, the people would "dare to spend their incomes, and when the people dare to spend their incomes the Age of Plenty will really be at hand."

In supporting federal control of concentrated industries, Coyle was close to the position of the "planners" within the Roosevelt administration, and he initially supported the National Industrial Recovery Act. It would, he wrote, be a start on the road to recovery, but after it had "done all that can be done with shorter hours and higher wages, the public works program must take hold and carry on from that point." But he also viewed the NRA as the blueprint for a new industrial policy that would "turn surplus income into buying power without forcing it to pass through the classic sequence of hope, investment, bankruptcy and disgust." Coyle would not always be so complimentary of the NRA.[40]

Coyle conceded that there were not enough potential public works projects in America to generate recovery. Moreover, they would eventually have to be built anyway, and were, therefore, "just a part of the ordinary market that business counts upon." The United States, he wrote, would "have to think in larger terms than these." [41]

Meanwhile, Coyle expanded on his vision of an "Age of Plenty" in an article for *Survey Graphic*. Technology, he pointed out, was rapidly replacing the monotony of factory labor, which had never been well suited to human nature. Workers would be shifted to other pursuits, including the service industries. Coyle wrote:

> When society becomes adjusted to plenty, there will necessarily be a large expenditure for goods and services, and workers will find themselves in a situation similar to that of 1917-18. Armed with power to change their jobs, they will ask either shorter hours or higher wages, whichever they want most. The net result will be that a large number of people who are unaccustomed to leisure and money will have a good deal of both to spend....
>
> The central thread of the pattern of a new Age of Plenty is the fact that a large expenditure will have to be devoted to services. There will be a definite pressure of money into service-expenditure, in contrast to the condition with which we are familiar, where the service-organizations have to raise money against discouraging odds. It is the difference between a "buyer's" and a "seller's" market. The consequent expansion of even the types of service that we have already invented will produce far-reaching effects on the nature of our people....
>
> Like it or not, the necessary adjustments to technological productivity will set the stage for a Homeric drama. People will be different when they are economically secure. They will gaily seek insecurity in adventures of all kinds. Our moral code, as it has always done in other golden ages, will adapt itself to the heroic mode. Avarice and parsimony (i.e., thrift) will again be the meanest of sins; magnificence will be a virtue as it was in the days of the Medici....

Coyle then drew a line between himself and many other New Dealers:

Not by reforming politics, by revising the educational system, by establishing collective bargaining, by legally imposing shorter hours and the minimum wage, or by "controlling" production, will we pass the gate of the Promised Land. The key of the gate is the pouring out of surplus income for cultural plant and services on a scale more vast than we have yet comprehended. With that key we can enter, and all the rest will be added unto us. Without that key we cannot enter, and all the rest is futile. For the present, we may dream on Sundays of the joys of the Golden Age, but on weekdays we had better fight for our lives against all the power of economy and paralysis, to win the chance to build our dreams into reality.[42]

In a later article for the *American Scholar*, Coyle added this utopian vision of the Age of Plenty:

The imminent age of plenty will no doubt have new and previously untried kinds of art—such as the art of human adjustments to life and to society. We shall devote our science and our effort, as no social order has yet done, to a conscious attempt to bring the "good life" within reach of all people. We dream of a time when the great majority will be free from lifelong fear or humiliation or pain, when everyone shall have a fair chance at the essentials of health and happiness and pleasant surroundings.[43]

By the end of 1933 Coyle had clearly become something of a New Deal "insider," held in high esteem by those who continued to adhere to Brandeisian views of the economy. As Arthur Schlesinger, Jr. has written: "[Thomas] Corcoran and [Benjamin] Cohen, like Brandeis and Frankfurter, were working mainly behind the scenes. Moreover, all four men, as lawyers, were more inclined to respond to specific cases than to develop a general rationale. Accordingly, the most rounded presentation of the Brandeis position in 1935 came from a nonlawyer outside government, David Cushman Coyle."[44] Of course, Coyle was not "outside government," nor did his "presentation of the Brandeis position" begin in 1935. It had begun in 1932.

Thus, when a Marxist, Mary van Kleeck, attacked the New Deal in a speech before the National Conference of Social Work to an enthusiastic response, it was Coyle, says Schlesinger, who "was quickly summoned to reply," which he did with a "powerful piece" for *Survey* magazine.[45] In his article, Coyle drew a contrast between what he described as "engineering planning" and "policy planning." The former, he wrote, was appropriate for projects like the Panama Canal, where a blueprint was followed and full regimentation was required without provision for personal liberty.

"Policy planning," on the other hand, had a long and successful tradition in the United States, dating back to the imposition of high tariff policies at the insistence of Alexander Hamilton. Their purpose had been to "cause money to flow from the consumer and farmer into the hands of the financier," in order "to cause the building of factories to free us from dependence on England." Policy planning had also made possible the acquisition of the western territories, and the land given to railroads, homesteaders, and schools. "There is," Coyle wrote:

always danger that we may adopt measures that will require too strict a discipline of too large a number of citizens. Prohibition was an example and NRA shows signs of being another. These were national plans of the engineering or operational type, and in the absence of an enforceable death penalty, they had small chance of success. The people have a technique for throwing off discipline of this kind. The lesson is plain that national planning of the operation of industry, while practicable and necessary in certain limited centralized activities such as power and oil, is not technically suitable for general application to the nation as a whole.

Absent the consent of the governed, engineering planning could be achieved only through revolution. But Coyle warned:

Violent revolution, like all forms of violence, with its prospect of emotional release and its illusion of easy victory, is a tempting prospect for those who are weary of the long struggle against inertia and stupidity. But after the first elation of bloodshed, the long struggle settles down again with new wrongs, new intolerance of reason, new horrors. There is value, therefore, in considering with all the intelligence we can muster, how the new social order may be established without forcing a trial by blood.

The conflict in America for the foreseeable future, Coyle argued, was between, on the one side, "all those who get their living by producing, distributing and selling goods and services: farmers, miners, laborers, the professions and the owners and operators of business and industry." The other side, a decided minority, consisted of "those who get their living by producing, distributing and selling securities, so called, and the paper that stands for speculation in commodities, capital goods and land." He explained: " High Finance must be reduced to a humble servant of production before this nation can have stable prosperity. That is the irrepressible conflict on the outcome of which lies the fate of our social order."

Finance possessed money, but the people had votes, and if "the people decide to tax away the power of Finance, there is no effective way of resistance." It was vital to define the issue in such a way as to win the support of the middle class rather than to drive them into the arms of the enemy. Coyle wrote: "If we fail, the financial powers will sweep back in a fascist revolution. They will attempt to run the economic system by the same principles that wrecked it in 1929 but with every avenue of criticism blocked and every safety valve wired down....We had better win this fight now while we have a chance."[46]

Meanwhile, Coyle had already begun to attempt to influence a new and important figure in Washington, Federal Reserve Chairman Marriner Eccles. Early in February he even declined a dinner invitation from Justice Brandeis, himself, explaining that he had "a previous engagement with Mr. Eccles of the Treasury, whom I've never met and who may be an important help to our side." He added:

> I thought perhaps you would forgive me for violating all the etiquette, just I am afraid of losing my chance at Eccles if I put him off....I don't know but what I'll do a little good with this new man. Excuse me, please, - war is war, and in my simple way I'm taking this war seriously.[47]

The extent of Coyle's influence on the new assistant secretary of the treasury, and later chairman of the Federal Reserve Board, is not clear, but it is apparent that he found in Eccles a kindred soul. A "credo" that Eccles penned in 1939 for a volume of his public papers enunciated an economic doctrine that, in virtually every particular, could have come from the pen of David Cushman Coyle.[48] Yet there was a subtle difference between the two. While both men subscribed to the underconsumption theories of heretical economists like William Trufant Foster (who supplemented his works on economics with books on public speaking), Eccles was not a Brandeisian. Thus, while they could agree that the key to recovery lay in programs that would increase consumer spending, Eccles occupied in other respects a middle ground in the division between the collectivists and Brandeisians on other issues.

In a *Scribner's* article in July, 1934, Coyle addressed the question on many minds since the inauguration of the New Deal - "Recovery, Reform—or Both?" Past recoveries, he repeated, had always come with a revival of investment in the capital goods industries, and conventional wisdom was insisting that such would be the course of a recovery from this one if only the New Deal would begin to give precedence to recovery over reform, thereby stimulating business and investor confidence. But in this depression the business cycle had not been allowed to run its course, business had retained a burden of debt that made new investment (debt) unlikely and unwise since it could only lead to another smash-up like that of the 1930s. And the next might be even worse than this one, with a consequent threat to the social order. Thus, not only recovery, but stable prosperity and preservation of the social order, required reform of the system in the midst of the present depression. What was needed, in short, was what Coyle called a "boom-proof recovery." He explained again:

> The Government must start the wheels by a spending program so large as to destroy unemployment; the money must be truly spent, not lent; the temporary financing must be by credit inflation not by borrowing from the public; the graduated income taxes must be powerful enough to balance the budget in prosperity; and the people must be given a guarantee of security so that they can spend without fear.

Coyle concluded:

> The fact is, the only kind of recovery that will stay by us is one that is rooted and grounded in reform. Perhaps it is impossible for us to get any other kind, or perhaps we must have one more gorgeous smashup before we are satisfied. Either way, some day those who survive will learn that recovery without reform is an airplane without a rudder.[49]

A few months later Coyle repeated many of these same points in an essay for the *Virginia Quarterly Review*. He admitted that "the New Deal has not presented a complete picture of a road to recovery and beyond recovery into a stable prosperity," but this was because Roosevelt was "a skipper who knows what direction he wants to pursue, but who sails day by day according to the weather." The result was that the parts of the recovery program, "like paths in a cow pasture, may be found leading almost anywhere," but in Coyle's view "the most significant path so far is that along which the nation has been slowly bumping toward an understanding of the problem of new investment." Initially, the New Deal had in large part conformed to orthodox thinking that any recovery would have to occur, as those in the past, through the revival of long-term capital investment in the capital goods industries. Herein lay an unwillingness or inability to face the reality that deflation in this depression had not been carried through "to the bitter end." The RFC, by shoring up the nation's credit structure had interfered with the business cycle, thereby perhaps preventing a collapse of the political system, but also rendering impossible a recovery along orthodox lines.

Absent a clear understanding of this reality, the New Deal had followed a number of dead ends, including the National Industrial Recovery Act, "a sort of omnibus wish-dream, collecting into one dramatic picture the incompatible desires of various conflicting groups whose conception of the crisis was as yet inadequately generalized." This "Share-The Misery Movement" had been "partly rationalized by adding a minimum wage clause, to satisfy those who had hastily concluded that technological unemployment could be met by shorter hours, and those who had the notion that high wage rates were the simple answer to the problem of purchasing power." Both assumptions were only half-truths, according to Coyle.[50]

After a year and a half of the New Deal Coyle found events shaping that would "blow away the fog from the minds of the experts and of the people, leaving the New Deal face to face with public enemy number one, the power of high finance."

> The New Deal is the quest of the American people for a way to free themselves from the octopus of finance that has been strangling their free business for several generations. The essence of the New Deal is that some day the lines shall be drawn for a battle between the American people and the Lords of Finance. Everything that interferes with the coming of the Day and the drawing of that battle line is an obstacle to the New Deal.

The alternative to the orthodox recovery and the inevitable crash that followed was "to force surplus income into expenditure that does not create excess capital plant and does not form new debts," which in simple form meant expenditures on public works that would be paid for out of income and inheritance taxes. But a more practicable "line of attack" was through "measures of economic security—old-age pensions and various kinds of insurance." This would simultaneously reduce savings and relieve the problem of redistribution of income. Another line was through "heavy taxation of the upper brackets" that would turn money away from investment and send it into public works and services that did not involve increased debt.

Coyle continued:

> Along these lines the New Deal will have to fight its way toward a new social order capable of handling high productivity. Much progress has already been made. The Gold Standard, sacred calf of Finance, has been violated and the heavens did not fall. The parts of N.R.A. that were supposed to increase buying power are no longer regarded as the solution to the problem of distribution. The parts of N.R.A. that lead to monopoly and irrational forms of planning are already well tangled and losing popular approval....The banks have been closed and opened by order, and if they try to hop aboard recovery and run a private inflation, the means of control are easily available. The Securities Market Bill was passed with enough teeth to make a bull market hard to run....The idea that economic security will have to be guaranteed is growing rapidly, and the income tax is making converts among the middle classes. The more desperate parts of the journey are still to come, but the tide of destiny is setting strongly in toward the new land of plenty. If the country can keep its nerve...and if the leaders of the New Deal can think fast enough, the chance of arriving successfully appears to be good.[51]

As 1934 drew to a close, Coyle attacked what he called "The Capital Goods Fallacy" in *Harper's*. Noting that the "preponderance of expert opinion...is now well agreed that the road to recovery lies through a rapid stimulation of the capital goods industries" where the "bulk of the remaining unemployment" was to be found, Coyle argued that the experts were as wrong in 1934 as they had been "in the good old days of 1926." To do so, he insisted, would be to simply resume the boom and bust experience of the business cycle, which those same "experts" accepted "without indulging in unprofitable speculations as to its morals, its necessity, or its permanence." In the usual scenario:

> Each man did what was right in his own eyes, and it happened that the sum of their activities was the business cycle, by which the voluntary and involuntary savings of the poor ended up in the hands of the rich. There was a sort of unplanned innocence in the process that was a real obstacle to the growth of moral indignation and of radicalism. It was also a means of misleading the students of economics. Observing that the alleged conspiracy of capital was largely imaginary, the experts were inclined to jump

to the conclusion that the business cycle was a natural phenomenon, tied to the immutable laws of nature and bound to continue...without end. Thus they came to look with insufficient seriousness upon other economic influences of a non-cyclical character, that were gradually undermining the whole foundation of cyclic or laissez-faire capitalism, especially in America.

These included a drop in the rate of population growth, as a result of restrictions on immigration and falling birthrates, disruptions in world trade caused by World War I and America's creditor status, improvements in mechanical productivity, and the rise of service industries, all of which were "undermining the market value of our ancestral virtues—thrift and hard work," and making "the world in which the business cycle ran...unsuited to a further continuance of the cycle and of laissez-faire capitalism."

The Roosevelt administration, he noted, had received no mandate in 1932 for trying out a "new theory," and the voters had emphatically rejected the radical candidates. They wanted a president who would "find out from the economic experts what had to be done and to go ahead and do it." The experts, alas, had been wrong, but their doctrine that recovery could only come through the revival of long-term investment had subtly influenced and frustrated the New Deal. Only the Civil Works Administration (CWA) had been helpful, largely because it was initially in the hands of "amateurs, in such a hurry that it was months before the experts were able to emasculate it."[52]

A sound recovery would require federal control of credit, provision for "basic economic security" for all, and eliminating "the surplus of the larger incomes." These, Coyle argued, would "necessarily be the main framework of the New Deal when the moment comes for the New Deal to attack the depression with intent to kill." But first "the orthodox economic theory that thrift is always a virtue, that there is no such thing as oversaving, and that any possible accumulation of capital is economically sound," would have to be overcome.[53]

8

Coyle and the Second New Deal

A couple of months later Coyle was in *Harper's* again, this time examining the effects of Roosevelt's public works program on recovery. Its advocates, he admitted, were disappointed, for "the program has reached its peak and the depression is still flourishing. The big gun that was to blast the depression out of the landscape finally went off with a pop that was not heard round the world." Still, the combination of the Public Works Administration, the CWA, and the Federal Emergency Relief Administration (FERA) had "kept the country alive and...given the people time to prepare...for more effective action."

Not surprisingly, Coyle found the "most vital error" in the PWA was the emphasis on self-liquidating public works as an instrument of recovery when, in fact, by reducing consumer purchasing power, they had the opposite effect:

> One of the most serious obstacles to any adequate program of direct expenditure is the belief that spending is "extravagance." The truth is that from the national point of view a flood control project or a bridge built with the labor of men who would otherwise be doing nothing whatever costs the country just nothing. Wealth made by salvaging what would otherwise be wasted is pure profit....Those whose idle money is the cause and symbol of the idleness of men naturally call public spending extravagant; but to the country at large there is no extravagance in turning idleness into public wealth....An effective public works program would be like a pump that forces the circulation of water by sucking the water out of one place and driving it into another....Everybody knows that there is a short-circuit somewhere in the New Deal, but not everybody, even among the New Dealers themselves, knows where it is. The short-circuit in the New Deal is the Capital Goods Fallacy, the belief that money should not be pumped out

into business except with formation of a debt that will turn it back again through the same hole where it went out. The Self-Liquidation Fallacy is merely a special form of the Capital Goods Fallacy, the inability to think of anything but lending more money.

Another cause of the PWA's failure was that the effort was too small. As Coyle put it: "The United States has been losing some forty billion dollars a year by staying in this depression, and three billion dollars, spread over a couple of years, was an attempt to feed an elephant with a teaspoon." Coyle continued:

The public works that form a legitimate part of a recovery program are those that produce free services for the people outside of the commercial services now being provided by private business. Just as the automobile made the country prosperous for a time by supplying a new avenue for spending surplus income, and just as air-conditioning may help to create prosperity by luring wealthy people into a new luxury spending, so a sound public works program is one that adds to the existing fields of spending for the national surplus income. The CWA was a crude and hasty attempt in the right direction. "Raking leaves" failed to win general approval; but a well planned program for extending and improving the national parks and forests may be approved by the public. The CCC has been generally successful and should be extended. Flood control and sewage disposal are definitely Federal interests and ought to be done largely or wholly with Federal money. Roads and grade crossings can be more extensively built with Federal grants.[1]

In May 1935, the reign of the collectivists within the New Deal came to an end, with the 9-0 Supreme Court decision against the constitutionality of the National Industrial Recovery Act in the Schechter case. Brandeis summoned his disciples Tom Corcoran and Ben Cohen immediately after the verdict was handed down, and "visibly excited and deeply agitated," told them they must explain to Roosevelt that the decisions that day "change everything. The President has been living in a fools' paradise." Apparently as yet unaware of the great gap that had developed between his philosophy and the ideas of Frankfurter, he insisted they bring Frankfurter down from Harvard to counsel Roosevelt.[2]

With collectivism in retreat, Roosevelt sent to Congress a number of bills in 1935 that could have been influenced by Coyle's recommendations, and the president sounded two notes dear to Coyle in his annual message for Congress, calling for better use of national resources and for enactment of social security. Coyle greeted Roosevelt's proposal for social security legislation enthusiastically, since he had advocated it for some time as a key element in his program for reform of the economy. However, he foresaw difficulties if the act were not fashioned properly, particularly in the use to which funds collected for the social security trust were put. If they were invested, they could aggravate "the instability of business with one hand while preparing to relieve the casualties with the other." Funds invested would "serve only to blow up the bubble and make unemployment at a later date," in which case "they might as well not have been collected at all. On the other hand, if the funds are withdrawn from circulation and hoarded in a box, the effect is to deflate the market and perhaps to create unemployment immediately," while a third approach would be to do a little of both and thereby to "avoid interference with the business cycle." "But, Coyle wrote, "the main object of the New Deal Administration is to interfere with the business cycle," making the second of the three courses the more desirable.

Not only was it necessary for the government to withdraw all funds collected for unemployment insurance "from circulation in either the goods or the capital market," but the Administration also needed passage of

> a law that will eliminate loose corporate surplus funds and will prevent their investment. The law should provide a prohibitive tax on all corporate profits, exempting such monies as are distributed in dividends or bonuses, and funds deposited in a custodial account without interest and with privilege of withdrawal on demand. Such a law would prevent "ploughing in" with all its attendant dislocations, and it would prevent playing the market with surplus funds to the detriment of business.[3]

The growing influence of the Brandeis philosophy was obvious in Roosevelt's 1935 legislative program. The 1935 session of Congress passed a number of bills consistent with Coyle's recommendations. The Wagner-Doughton-Lewis bill provided for federal grants to the states for old-age assistance, aid for dependent children, and child welfare and health services, and also established a system of old age and unemployment insurance. The Revenue Act of 1935 embodied many of Coyle's recommendations at various stages in its transit through the House and Senate, although his direct influence on the bill is not clear. The new law boosted taxes on higher incomes to 75 percent on those over $500,000, instead of the 59 percent over $1,000,000 under the previous law. It also established a graduated tax on the net income of corporations that increased from 12.5 percent on incomes of $2,000 or less, rising to 15 percent over $40,000. For the first time corporations were allowed to deduct gifts to charitable organizations up to 5 percent of their net income. An inheritance tax did not survive the Congressional debates, but the estate tax was increased, and the amount of exemption reduced.[4] Particularly dear to Coyle in its objective, but not in its details, was the Social Security Act. While convinced that unemployment insurance and old age pensions were indispensable to the shift from saving to consumption that he advocated, Coyle would express much opposition to the provisions for a trust fund and to those for contributions by workers and employers that would result in reduced consumer spending at a time when it was vitally needed for recovery. The $4.8 billion work relief bill similarly missed Coyle's mark in that the money was to be spent primarily on work relief rather than on public works.

The Brandeis/Coyle philosophy was also evident in the Wheeler-Rayburn Public Utility Holding Bill introduced in Congress in 1935. The bill was intended to break up the large holding companies that dominated many public utilities in the United States. While many observers regarded it as a Brandeisian attack on bigness in American business, it could more realistically be described as an effort to free the public utilities from the control of Big Finance, as Coyle had long advocated. *Business Week* magazine accurately noted that the bill was not "regulatory," but "purely punitive and destructive."[5] The Brandeisians were exhilarated over the bill, two of their number, Corcoran and Cohen, having written it. Brandeis wrote that if Roosevelt were successful in getting the bill passed "we shall have achieved considerable toward curbing Bigness—in addition to recent advances."[6]

Equally close to the Coyle philosophy was the Eccles Banking Bill, introduced in the same session, which was designed to give the president direct control over the entire Federal Reserve System. Opposition to the prospect that the Federal Reserve might be used for political purposes led Eccles to compromise over the provisions and an amended bill was finally passed into law in July. The new law was far from what Eccles had proposed. Even *Business Week* magazine found that it had been "so greatly modified that the good in it possibly outweighs the bad," and a University of Iowa econo-mist concluded that it had made the "Federal Reserve Board, in effect the whole banking system, less responsible to, and less un-der the influence of the administration than it was before the pas-sage of the act."[7]

When Coyle wrote an essay on "the Fallacy of Mass Produc-tion," it was not mass-production that he attacked, but the bigness of those industries that adopted it. The principal economies that resulted from such uses of mass production were, he wrote, "merely more or less polite forms of holdup." Such economies were only gained at the expense of somebody else - the miner, the farmer, the smaller shipper, etc. "Much of the value of mass production is the value of being strong enough to operate a racket."

Then Coyle disposed of the claim that mass-production indus-tries were more stable, and more likely to offer better wages and working conditions, so that the more of them there were the better off the economy would be. By concentrating production in fewer companies, the effect was actually to make the economy less stable. Large companies became more stable, but all others became less so producing a net effect on the economy that was negative. He ex-plained:

> The law of capitalism is that, when the buying power of the people is diminished, prices must fall. If some prices fail to fall, others must fall farther to compensate. Consequently, if any large fraction of a capitalist system is able to organize and fix prices, the remaining fraction is forced to take all the brunt of price fluctuations....The extraordinary demoralization of small-scale industry in many fields, which we have seen since 1929, is in part the result of the ability of large-scale industry to rig the market.

Communism was being seriously suggested as an alternative to capitalism by those frustrated over the behavior of big business. In Coyle's view: "small-scale industry may be operated as a capitalist system; large scale industry is practical only in a socialist system." Where large operations were essential in a capitalist economy, they should be owned by the government. The line dividing those that should be operated as smaller units, and those better placed under government control, was not always an obvious one. In the latter category, however, should be included the railways, oil and natural gas, and probably electric power. Public ownership brought with it numerous disadvantages, which could make them only slightly preferable to private monopolies. Coyle cited the case of the post office department as an example. When the depression hit, it "should have cut the letter rate to one cent as an aid to business. Instead it acted like a private monopoly and raised the rate to three cents in an effort to make a profit at the expense of business."

Coyle then wrote:

> Instead of attempting to make lists of industries and of their allowable sizes, a more practical way of approach is through the tax system. The most important contribution of the New Deal before 1936 was the taxation of corporations in proportion to their size, When the differential can be made severe enough, there will be results. Within any given industry, the concern that tries to grow beyond the point of maximum efficiency will be penalized, giving the advantage to smaller concerns....The justification lies in the fact that small industries are harmless in themselves; large industries have power to corrupt government, obstruct justice, and oppress the people. For that reason the consumer should pay an extra tax when he buys the product - however harmless - of a large industry which constitutes a danger to the State.

One advantage of smaller size in industry would be its "geographic decentralization." Large industries had tended to be concentrated in and around large cities, leading to a "progressive degeneration of the rural economic life." Coyle wrote: "The debtor sections want moratoriums or inflation, the creditors want 'sound money' and protection of the sanctity of contracts. The conflict interferes with the overall efficiency of the economic system." Small, decentralized industry would contribute to regional self-sufficiency, which would reduce the strains between sections. "The efficiency of the nation as a whole, and the peaceful relation of its parts, will be improved by spreading as many industries as possible among the agricultural areas."

This was, of course, an attempt to turn the nation back to the pre-railroad era that was so dear to Brandeis. Acknowledging this, Coyle wrote: "The saying is that we cannot turn back the hands of the clock, although there are few machines, even clocks, that cannot be turned backward as well as forward." He saw "spontaneous trends" toward decentralization already taking place, largely as a consequence of cheaper electrical rates that made it preferable to steam power. One result was that "many functions are going back again into the home. With electric machines the housekeeper can do many jobs that were for a while more efficiently done in the factory." Travel had become decentralized, with more people traveling about independently in their automobiles instead of being "centralized" in railroad cars. The trend was inevitably against big business.[8]

In a July 1935 article for the *Virginia Quarterly Review*, Coyle espoused again the very Brandeisian position in appealing for the decentralization of industry. "The illness of capitalism," he wrote, "from which our radical friends derive such keen satisfaction, is closely connected with the tendency of capitalism to run to extreme centralization....If the American people want to avoid communism, they will have to tackle capitalism and force it to decentralize." Centralization led to control of big business by Big Finance, with all its attendant abuses, and also to the price-fixing that was inimical to a free economy. Some businesses, by their nature, were inevitably centralized and fixed prices, and must eventually be taken over by the government. Railroads, he wrote, were "already far along" toward that state, while electric power was moving rapidly toward it.

Historically, Coyle pointed out, the American people had tired of the tyrannical use of the rate-making power by railroads to "crush little business," had rebelled, had "seized the rate-making power and will ultimately swallow the railroads themselves." The time had come, however, when "new rackets" in "raw materials and marketing and credit...must in turn be seized and emasculated." The "war" was already on, and Coyle described the progress so far achieved under the New Deal:

The major offensive against overcentralization is a part of the general war of the people against high finance, in the early stages of which we are now engaged. The present lines of attack are several. Already the first securities acts are in effect, after bitter fighting. The power holding companies, citadel of High Finance, are being heavily attacked, with the President fighting in the front rank....One line of attack is through social security, especially the old-age pension, that will reduce the hopeless and pathetic effort to save against a rainy day, and thus cut off from the financiers their customary supply of lambs. Another will be heavy income and inheritance taxation, to destroy the financial group itself. Federal control of bank credit is already on its way, under the leadership of Marriner Eccles. Some help may also be found in taxation of undivided corporation surplus and in graduated taxation of corporations according to size. . . . [H]owever it is done, there will be no peace till high finance is destroyed. If the financial cancer can be extirpated before the system dies and turns to disorder, business will be able to decentralize itself into a healthy growth of small and widely distributed industries. The race is between reform and revolution, and history will tell us afterward about the result.[9]

The month after the article appeared, Norman Hapgood wrote to Louis Brandeis: "In a letter to me about the Virginia Quarterly article Coyle writes: 'Rex Tugwell read the article and told me he had never read anything with which he disagreed so completely. Jerry [Jerome] Frank, who was present, said, "for gosh sake, Dave, you haven't gone Brandeis, have you?" and I told him, "hell, I've always been Brandeis...." The big battle is coming on, and them that is here will have the fun.."[1]

While not identified as a planner, Coyle clearly envisaged a form of management of the economy, albeit one that took a very different course from that advocated by the Tugwellians. Instead of direct supervision of industries by such devices as the NRA, Coyle would impose "order" on business through government control of taxation and investment. In a *Harper's* article on "The Twilight of National Planning" in October 1935, Coyle was candid in his views on the now defunct NRA, writing:

For two years Washington has been full of sincere and intelligent men and women trying to plan, and there is not much sign of utopia yet. The advocates of national planning, which was to be the road out of chaos, have some explaining to do.

If you ask one of the original national planning enthusiasts what is wrong with the New Deal *he* usually answers that it hasn't been doing what he would call planning. That answer is too simple. The fact is that Americans who had hopes of promoting one kind or another of national planning were themselves in a confusion what planning is and what it can do. The New Deal administration, in tackling its various emergency jobs, was subject to the pressure of various groups who thought somewhat prematurely that they had plans that were plans....Order, we were taught in Sunday School, is Heaven's first law; and with timbrel and harp the people marched singing into the heaven of the NRA, while tailors by their companies and the stockbrokers by their companies strode down Fifth Avenue behind the Ark of God. Well, after all the singing and dancingthe NRA turned out not to be Heaven.

Coyle recalled that planning of one sort or another had been a characteristic of the federal government from the days of Alexander Hamilton, when he had sought by tariff and other legislation to stimulate the growth of industry in the United States. Echoing the Brandeis philosophy, Coyle wrote:

> The job now has to be tackled on a more fundamental plane, by putting brakes on high finance and by making the environment unhealthy for private monopolies.... Taxation is usually a plan not only for raising money, but also for changing the distribution of income or effecting some other social purpose. Sales taxes are plans for soaking the poor, income taxes for soaking the well-to-do, and liquor taxes for soaking the soaks.

Formal planning through agencies like the NRA must inevitably fail, because "Social-economic planning is too big a problem for that kind of a framework. The United States is too large and complicated to be put down in lists and arranged in schedules." Instead, planning by the federal government should, Coyle wrote:

> promote a more practical allocation of the national income between spending and saving. It would accomplish this not by drawing up precise and infuriating rules as to what people should do with their money, but by using the going powers of the government to bring about the desired result with as little dictation and engineering planning as possible—by shifting the relative emphasis in our established system of taxation and appropriation. In order to cut down savings among the larger incomes we need income and inheritance taxes, or similar measures, that will draw off surplus income and surplus wealth, and convert the money to spending for private reasons and without any general control or plan, by manipulating stock prices and bank credit....We shall need a practical plan to control the volume of money, the first stage of which is the Federal Reserve System, and the second the Eccles banking bill in its present form....We need plans for cutting down the amount of price and production control to the proportion that a capitalistic system can stand without getting out of gear. Some big businesses which are inevitably monopolies or near-monopolies by nature will probably have to be taken out of the system entirely and turned over to the Government. Others have no necessary technical reason for being big, but were consolidated by bankers and promoters merely for milking purposes. They will need to be gradually eliminated, by the effect of income taxes and by measures such as graduated taxation in proportion to size, and their places taken by smaller concerns....The idea that we could handle price-fixing merely by code-making turned out to be too simple. We need to go at it indirectly...with a more general recognition that the price of free initiative is free prices....Plans of the type which I have mentioned are less

definite in detail but more potent in effect. They call for a minimum of daily discipline. Most of them the ordinary citizen would never feel or know about; the effect upon him would be merely that he would have a good job at good wages.

The kind of planning he advocated, Coyle wrote, was "like hormones in the blood." He explained:

> The thyroid gland does not attempt to crawl around the body, poking and patting the cells into their places. It controls by a subtle chemical added to the fluid in which the cells are bathed. Influenced by this factor the cells develop in one way more freely than in another and the whole body is formed or deformed accordingly. The New Deal, after passing through its first emergency stages, is now struggling with the beginnings of the environmental or hormone type of plan. Several of this year's measures are of this type. The full development of a body of liberal national plans is a long job, with many years of national discussion ahead of it.

"The great plans," Coyle wrote, "are not plans for regimenting the people....They are policy plans that will make it easier to work in ways that are good for the national prosperity. They are not plans for fencing us in, but for making roads to where we want to go."[11]

In an October 1935 article published in the *NEA Journal*, Coyle continued to sound a Brandeisian note, writing:

> If I were President and when I believed the hour had come I would force the circulation of money by heavy public spending and income taxation, priming the circulation in the early stages with moderate inflation and preventing the usual runaway in Wall Street. I would work for decentralization and a free price system for little business and public ownership for big business. I would work for national self-containment in the necessities and international intercourse in the luxuries at the same time. Above all I would use the radio to override the conservative organs of propaganda and lead the people in the overwhelming attack on Public Enemy No. 1, the power of High Finance.[12]

In sounding the call for "national self-containment in the necessities," Coyle was espousing the economic nationalism that had been followed by the Roosevelt administration since the president "torpedoed" the London Economic Conference in 1933. It was an issue that he would return to in greater detail later in the 1930s.

It is clear from Monica Niznik's dissertation on Thomas Corcoran, that he had become a devotee of Coyle by 1936.[13] The importance of this can only be appreciated when one understands the influence that Corcoran and Ben Cohen exerted with Roosevelt. Felix Frankfurter was only slightly exaggerating that influence when he wrote them in mid-1934 that they had "wormed" their way "not only into the heart but even into the mind and will of the President of the United States, so that he says what you tell him to say and he does what you tell him to do, that he lets you think for him and even act for him."[14]

The influence of Corcoran, in particular, grew even greater after Frankfurter persuaded Roosevelt to make Corcoran, in effect, a kind of "assistant president" in 1935.[15] Roosevelt quickly adopted Frankfurter's suggestion, and thereafter it would be Corcoran who would furnish "the intellectual traffic directions" and who would "sift" materials before they reached the president.[16]

Thus, for Corcoran to adopt Coyle as the "economic philosopher" of the New Deal was significant, indeed, after 1935. "Tommy the Cork" described Coyle as "an engineer who has expressed in Maine fisherman language how the New Deal wants to resolve the struggle for economic power—if a court will let it."[17] This description of Coyle's "language" was literally true. When he rewrote his book *Brass Tacks* for a wider audience as *Uncommon Sense* while vacationing in Maine (with Tom Corcoran and Ben Cohen as neighbors), he tried it out on a Maine fisherman and his wife, rewriting those parts they found difficult to understand.[18]

Injecting Coyle's work into FDR's 1936 reelection campaign, Corcoran sought to popularize his book *Waste*. Corcoran also arranged for 150,000 postcards to be printed and mailed with the *New York Times'* review of *Waste* on one side, and Roosevelt's comments about it in a press conference on the other. The *New York Times* had written of *Waste* that "every sentence in it counts," and that it "should be read by every man and woman in the United States. Indeed, the children might well read it, too. It is so clear, so definite, so practical." The *Nation* described it as a "brilliantly written little book" that provided "superb examples of the art of popularizing technical engineering problems." No American, it added could "read the book and remain indifferent to such problems as soil erosion, flood control, and the conservation of our natural resources."[19] Recipients were urged to send fifty cents to the publisher for the purchase of the book. The book was also endorsed by the Democratic National Chairman, James Farley, who urged "every Democrat and Friend" to read it, and who included it on his list of recommended campaign readings.[20]

In *Waste*, Coyle examined the "waste" of wealth in the United States, which included soil, water, forest, animals, power, metals, and humans. Under the latter category he included waste through diseases, human erosion, lost morale, lost youth, and other forms. Relief, he concluded "is a confession that we don't know how to use our resources in a sensible way." The only sensible way to attack unemployment was to provide jobs. Coyle explained that there was plenty needing to be done which could furnish men with jobs that would provide them with self-respect. Money spent on public works was not money thrown "down a rat hole," for the nation was "getting something in return." But public works spending until now had been too severely limited by public opinion, with the result that in 1935 "only four billion dollars could be appropriated for a job that required eight or ten billion." If adequate appropriations were made, public works could be "done in a normal business way either by the government or by private contractors," and the purchase of materials would stimulate private industry and create jobs in that sector, as well. The CCC had, through the expenditure of just a few hundred million dollars, "turned the tide of disintegration that for twenty years had been sweeping away the young men of the nation in war, in corruption and finally in idleness."[21]

The nation faced two great problems, but the two problems solved each other. Coyle explained:

> What are these unemployed? They are the manpower to do the extra work that we need for saving our land and our people. With no drain on the manpower that is now employed in private business, we can call millions of workers to protect our forests and terrace our hillsides. We can call millions more to guard the public health and provide the services of education, science, religion and art, that make a strong and successful people and a great civilization.
>
> What shall we do with the idle men? Where shall we find the power to save our soil and our people? There are the men. There is the job. That is the answer.

The problem was where to find the money.[22]

Clearly Coyle was calling for a reorientation of the New Deal away from spending on relief and toward "investments" by the federal government in the nation's resources that would create jobs, and by his support for *Waste*, Corcoran seemed to indicate that he favored such a reorientation.

In addition to *Waste*, Corcoran busily circulated other Coyle books, including *Brass Tacks*, which he described to its recipients as "the most effectively irritating writing on economics the enemy has yet seen. I think it deserves recommendation."[23] "It ought," he told another recipient, "to be circulated among all our campaign workers and forced on the newsstands (which are all enemy controlled and don't want to sell it) by concerted demand." It could be sold for twenty-five cents on the newsstands, and was "only fifteen cents in quantity from the Democratic Committee."[24]

The director of the speakers bureau of the Democratic National Campaign Committee thanked Corcoran for copies of *Uncommon Sense* and *Waste*, and told him that "if we can get them at no cost to the Committee we will be glad to send them to all speakers."[25] In mid-September, Roosevelt praised the book at a press conference, prompting Coyle to exaggerate his importance by writing:

> Of course, this means that I am placed in the front line of the battle, as sort of powder-boy to the Chief, where I'm quite likely to get shot. Also, if the people don't like my stuff, we may lose the election by this shift of policy. But meanwhile all my Irish is having a damn good time. Also we should be able to sell books.

Circulars promoting *Brass Tacks* and *Uncommon Sense* were, at Corcoran's suggestion, included in each copy of *Waste*.[26] In early September, Corcoran wrote that he was trying "to get angels to present the Speaker's Bureau with copies of 'Uncommon Sense' and "Waste.'" and asked how many were needed "adequately to equip the speakers?"[27] Corcoran also succeeded in getting selections from Coyle's *Uncommon Sense* published in pro-New Deal newspapers like the *New York Post*, which wrote:

> One of the best [books] for those who would like to understand the issues before the country is David Cushman Coyle's "Uncommon Sense." We reprint on this page a section from the book—his explanation of a balanced budget—as an example of the simplicity and clarity with which Mr. Coyle handles complicated problems.
> Mr. Coyle's "Uncommon Sense" is an encyclopedia in miniature for the voter, covering old-age pensions, inflation, public debt,

technologicalunemployment, housing, hours and wages, taxation, monopoly, foreign trade, economic planning, the farm problem, the Constitution and the Supreme Court.

Though we may not agree with all the views he expresses, we have no hesitation in recommending Mr. Coyle's work—and others in this series—to the intelligent voter who wants a clear and swift summation of the problems facing America in 1936.[28]

In late August, Corcoran wrote Coyle that he was looking forward to good reviews of *Waste* in the *New York Times Sunday Book Supplement* and in *Time* magazine. He told Coyle that the two books were "being run together in advertising with a flyer in each referring to the other. We'll get circulation all right."[29] A few days later Corcoran wrote Frankfurter: "If we could get the Filene store [Boston] interested in showing UNCOMMON SENSE and WASTE, it would mean a display in White's in Boston, Bamberger's in Newark and Abram and Strauss in New York."[30] Coyle was also contributing material to be used in Roosevelt's campaign speeches.[31]

Alas, despite all of the publicity and the president's own endorsement of the book, sales of *Waste* were disappointing in 1936, far below what had been expected. *Brass Tacks* had sold over 200,000 copies, and *Uncommon Sense* about 70,000 by this time, but *Waste* turned out to be a losing proposition for Bobbs-Merrill.[32]

In a short "discussion" piece for the *American Scholar*, Coyle wrote that the Renaissance princes were essentially "a Public Works Program, collecting the surplus income of   the country and distributing it to masons and sculptors and painters and goldsmiths." Coyle described the new age as the "Power Age," and in it "the new industrial organism will not work unless fed with the required proportion of spending money and investment money," just as a gasoline engine required the proper proportion of gasoline and air. There was no longer a place for the "king of finance who can collect millions of his own and other people's dollars and build with them great financial structures with which to astonish the world." He explained:

There was a time when the king of finance had his work to do. By whatever strange methods he may have collected his millions they were capital for a country that needed capital, but now the country needs its capital in small doses. The new machinery is so productive that small quantities of it will junk large quantities of existingindustry. Meanwhile the people can easily save, under normal conditions, enough money to build ten times as much machinery as industry can use. The right to invest savings will have to be rationed to those who need it.

In the new Power Age, wealth could survive only if it were spent, not invested, spent for purposes that were "approved and tolerated by the people at large." Coyle wrote:

Not wealth as such, but money-lending as a way of life, is obsolete, and if money-lending fights too strongly against destiny, there is danger that wealth itself may be abolished in the heat of battle. America would be unfortunate if in freeing itself of the incubus of large-scale money-lending it were to be forced to abolish large-scale incomes, for all the signals are set for the early beginning of a great cultural advance.

The Power Age, by freeing people from labor, would lay the basis for a social order based on plenty - like those of "the South Seas, in Periclean Athens, in Renaissance Italy, in Elizabethan England." It would, "as no social order has yet done," make a conscious effort "to bring the 'good life' within reach of all people." Coyle concluded:

In times like these, when a great tide runs in the affairs of men, there is an advantage in taking the tide at its flood. If men must struggle to preserve the privileges of high finance, that is their hard fate, because the tide will wash them away. But if they can struggle to survive as the collectors and distributors of part of the cultural surplus of an age of surplus, then they may live to take a noble part in the great adventure of our new world.[33]

After the AAA was found unconstitutional by the Supreme Court early in 1936, Roosevelt asked Congress for additional revenue, ostensibly to replace that lost as a result of the court's decision and also to meet additional expenses that it had caused. In particular, the president asked for a new tax particularly dear to Coyle's heart, and advocated in nearly all of his writings—a tax on undistributed corporate profits. Typically, the arguments framed in support of the bill by the president and the Treasury Department were not identical to those advanced by Coyle, but they were often similar. The new tax, says Blakey, "was imposed on corporations with the intent of inducing them to distribute their profits," with rates graduated from a minimum of 7 percent if the "undistributed net income" was 10 percent or less, to a maximum of 27 percent if it was in excess of 60 percent of adjusted net income. A penalty tax for improperly accumulated surpluses could range as high as 35 percent for corporations not subject to the surtax on undistributed profits, and 25 percent on those that were.[34]

The new law was fraught with possible consequences, some unanticipated by its advocates. The First National Bank of Boston concluded that it would favor strong corporations at the expense of young and weak ones. The latter generally financed their early expansion largely from profits retained for that purpose, an option that would now be denied them, thus perpetuating the existing stratification of business by keeping the large large and the small small.[35] Even Brandeis, himself, worried that there might be "dangers in the tax bill," and wondered if it should not "be gently shelved for further study & as a 'compromise' get [an] increase of corporation taxes in the highest brackets & high estate taxes—'temporarily?'"[36]

In an article for *Survey Graphic* magazine, Coyle worried again about the prospect of fascism for America if the power of big finance could not be controlled. In order to cope with the power of big finance, he wrote, farmers and workers had organized themselves, and the nation was now "divided into contending factions, each one trying to restrict production so as to get a larger share of a small national income. Fighting fire with fire, they burn up the house." He explained:

> Out of this system of competitive scarcity there seem to be only two ways of escape. One is the way of dictatorship. Some one of the private powers may grow so strong as to take over the government, as high finance has done in Italy and Germany, and as labor has done in Russia. It might happen here. The other way is for the national government to strengthen itself, as it is doing in the other democracies of the world, until perhaps it may control the power of high finance and make it unnecessary for other organizations to grow dangerous. The survival of democratic processes depends on the effective control of democratic government.

The depression had overthrown the power of "Big Business in government," and had made it possible now for the federal government to use "taxes as economic instruments." "The New Deal," Coyle wrote, had "begun to use taxation for purposes of economic adjustments, but the principle has not been fully recognized in Congress nor fully accepted by the people. Most of the work is still to be done." Income taxes must be raised on higher incomes so as to "take money from the taxpayer in proportion to his power to save and invest." In this way, "more money will be taken from savers and turned into spending," which was the "first requirement of a well planned tax system." The second requirement was "a series of taxes for the control of business practices." These would include taxation of capital gains to reduce "gambling in securities and land," and a graduated tax on corporate incomes." A third tax, related to the others, was "the new tax on undivided corporate profits," which Coyle supported based on three premises:

> First, a corporation should not be allowed to reinvest the income of its stockholders for them, so as to protect the rich stockholders from the income tax . . . . Second, no corporation should be allowed to invest the income of any stockholder without first sending him the money and then asking him if he wants to invest it in additional stock. This is to cut down the arbitrary power of managers to play games with the stockholders' money. . . . Third, no corporation that wants to set up a surplus of cash against a rainy day should be allowed to do anything with the money except hold it in cash. This is to prevent using the cash to help blow up the stock market at the top of a boom, or investing it in various things that have no value when hard times come.

A fourth regulatory tax was one on dividends paid by one corporation to another, in order "to put a penalty on complicated interlocked companies." Coyle explained:

> The real purpose back of all these varied tax measures, from income taxes to corporation taxes, is the restoration and protection of capitalism, believe it or not. Capitalism is another name for small business competing, either on price or on quality, in a free market. Big business, controlling prices and production, abolishing by force the law of supply and demand, and crushing competition, is a disease of capitalism. The job of government is to cure or control that disease. . . . Taxes are a main instrument in the building of a wall of protection within which capitalism can survive.

Coyle conceded what many of the new collectivist "liberals" denied, that "the capitalist profit system has an important place as the breeding ground of free men and the guarantee of free speech. With all its faults and wastes, an area of economic action where a man can make a living without being subject to centralized planning is a necessary organ of democracy." Therefore:

In these times, when immense social forces have to be socially controlled, the power of taxation stands out as the main road to freedom. For the alternative is control by centralized planning of production and distribution, that is, by dictatorship. And dictatorship cannot permit freedom.[37]

So popular had Coyle become by 1936 with the young Brandeis-Frankfurter group around Roosevelt that ex-braintruster Raymond Moley wrote:

> the youngsters in Washington (and I know this personally) look upon Coyle as the economic philosopher that Roosevelt had been looking for all these years, and that they call him the Poor Richard of the Roosevelt Revolution. The reason the young Brandeis proteges like [Tom] Corcoran and [Ben] Cohen and others, like him, is that he takes the Brandeis position that so far as capital expenditures are concerned in this country, they will have to be made through public money.

Moley also noted that "some of the Brandeis boys have been energetically promoting the sales of Coyle's books."[38]

As noted, Coyle also published *Brass Tacks* in 1936 through the National Home Library Foundation, a book which he told his readers was "not for radicals who believe in the abolition of capitalism," but for "ordinary Americans" who were looking for a solution to the nation's economic problem that was consistent with their "ancestral liberties." Coyle repeated many of the themes familiar with his earlier articles and books, including the need to increase spending and to reduce savings. This could be accomplished, he wrote, by two methods: old age pensions and income taxation. Of the former, he explained:

> The legitimate purpose of old age pensions is not merely to relieve cases of destitution, but to help the prosperity of business. The old age pension, provided the costs are collected by income taxation, is a means to prevent saving and to force the rapid circulation of money. It will prevent savings by relieving fear, and it will force the circulation of money by taking money from those who won't spend it and giving it to those who will.[39]

But Coyle did not approve of the social security system established the previous year, since it "frustrated" both of these purposes through the "reserve system" it had created. "Instead of forcing the circulation of money, it withdraws the money from circulation and forces the money into the investment market." It would be preferable to put the system on a pay-as-you-go basis, funding it from taxes on the higher incomes. Moreover, by making the social security system contributory, it also added to the burden of taxes on the poor, which only increased "the present wrong distribution of income. Any old age pension that is based on anything except income taxes will be ineffective as a help to business."[40]

Coyle was not opposed to profit, but he did seek higher taxes on the wealthy, "not to make the poor richer by making the rich poorer, but to increase the income of the American people by improving the ratio between spending and saving. The issue was not the "justice or injustice of inequality of wealth," but simply one of "making the system operate." Public works would be ineffective as a recovery device "until the people are sufficiently tired of the depression to be willing to go after it seriously. . . . These little programs increase the national debt without killing the depression." Public works during a depression cost nothing, because they made use of idle labor and productive capacity. It was this "idleness" that the nation could not afford.

Sounding a Keynesian note, Coyle wrote:

Who is going to start the spending? Each of us is personally afraid to start spending because we are not sure of getting any more. Only the Government has power to spend money which it does not yet have and force its revenues up to the point where it can get the money back. Only the Government can possibly dare to spend enough to get us out of the depression. . . . Now we need a   new industry that will make us start spending again, and one that will not lead us into the fatal paths of "investment". . . . The principal field for new expenditure is   in public, semi-public and private services—in a general increase of the standard of living.[41]

Yet Coyle's advocacy of federal spending differed significantly from Keynes. Keynes expected federal deficit spending to trigger an orthodox recovery, by eventually stimulating investment in an expansion of productive capacity. For Coyle, that was a step to be avoided.

But the profit system could not work "without the law of supply and demand," and the operation of a free price structure was stifled by the fact that "a large section of the industrial system has freed itself from the law of supply and demand" because they were so large that they controlled the market, reversing the law of supply and demand. "If the American people can be led to adopt policies that will first of all encourage small business rather than big business, and that will reluctantly but firmly drive the remaining big business into public ownership, they will be able to maintain and protect a system of free prices." World trade was not the answer, for such trade "disorganizes business in several ways" and any country that could free itself of a dependence on foreign markets and could "distribute incomes so as to find a market at home," would be "less tempted to go to war."[42]

What Coyle envisioned for an America in his Age of Plenty was, as earlier noted, something like that of Polynesia before the intrusion of Western influences. He wrote:

> When the economic environment will furnish to everyone a chance to make at least a bare living without much labor or trouble, the whole color of human nature is different. In the South Sea Islands, as Melville describes them, the natives have adapted themselves during many centuries to a constant condition of plenty. A little work provided all the material goods that could be made out of the available resources; after that there was nothing to do but play. The people spent their surplus energy in art and ceremonies and in dancing and swimming. The idea of poverty was incomprehensible to them. The natural human desire for danger, not being used up in worrying about the rent, was directed into tribal warfare carried on rather for sport than for gain. The people were gay and youthful at all ages, always laughing like children. They were generous and hospitable, without ever thinking of generosity as the mark of a noble character. Economic determinism meant nothing to them because their economic situation never entered their minds.[43]

Shortly thereafter, Coyle published *Uncommon Sense*, explaining on the title page: "Some people thought "Brass Tacks" was too technical, so I have written it in 'plain American.' The choice I leave to the reader." While the book added little to the points made in the earlier work, the language was somewhat more comfortable. "Saving for a rainy day," he wrote, "only makes it rain." Sounding the same note of concern as some anti-capitalist "liberals," Coyle wrote:

> There is danger that the financiers who own the monopolies, in an effort to protect their interests, may organize a "Liberty League" and try to take over the Government and abolish freedom altogether. That is what is called a "Fascist revolution." Economic fascism, or "private socialism," is a condition where centralized national planning is done by rich men in their own interest.

It will go into political fascism unless we can stop it. Either we drive back the advance of monopoly, or we fall into fascism and lose our freedom entirely.[44]

Coyle's position on Roosevelt's 1937 court-packing proposal is not clear, but he could hardly have been enthusiastic about it. It was, for one thing, an affront to Brandeis, who sat on the court. For another, it was a challenge taken from Rooseveltian pique that harked back to what was, for Coyle, the mistaken early period of the New Deal that had no relevance to the new direction it was pursuing, one more in line with Brandeisian goals and tactics. It was for that reason that the president's plan was so vociferously supported by collectivist liberals like those of the *New Republic*, who recognized the impossibility of resuming the nose-in-the-tent march to collectivism so long as the Supreme Court blocked the first steps in that march by a 9-0 vote. For the same reason, they opposed any compromise that would give Roosevelt the simple majority necessary to approve most of his legislation. What was needed for their collectivist agenda was enough new members of the court to overrule the nine who had voted down the NIRA.

Thus, Coyle was as concerned with the motives behind the court packing plan as he was with the plan itself. It was not the Brandeis/ Coyle New Deal that was encountering difficulties with the Court, nor was there any real prospect that it would. But in 1937 Roosevelt had begun to push a program that bore resemblances to the early New Deal in, for example, his desire for the government to take control of the wages and hours of industry through a board or commission. Coyle wrote Corcoran:

> Personally, I'm worried lest the Skipper commit himself to the idea that wages and hours are the main object of this whole move [the court fight]. I'm sure there will be trouble if he goes strong for heavy restrictions in that field, vide Marriner Eccles, etc. That is not the road to distrib[ution] of income nor to reduction of unemployment, and he is going to get bumped again if he tries it again. Only the CWA saved us from a bad accident last time! I wish you could get him to mind his eye here, and at least not stick his neck out in the course of the present battle.[45]

Corcoran and Frederick Delano certainly had not lost interest in popularizing Coyle's ideas after the 1936 election was over. For 1937, Corcoran was primarily interested in a book by Coyle on taxation, designed to encourage Americans to shoulder the necessary burden of taxes to accomplish the goals of his other books.[46] The deficit for the taxation book soon exceeded the expectations of those who had supported its release. Corcoran busied himself with the attempt to raise money for the deficit, but with limited success as the second Roosevelt Depression was underway in late 1937.[47] Corcoran thanked those who contributed, writing that the "ripples should go far."[48]

To help achieve this ripple effect, Corcoran arranged for Coyle's book, *Why Pay Taxes?*, to be serialized in newspapers that supported the New Deal, including the *Newark Ledger*, the *New York Post*, and the *Philadelphia Record*. Corcoran wrote them:

> If you want to help the New Deal I think you can do nothing better than reprint this illuminating serial on its principal problem—taxes—at this time. It means public education on a subject of which the public knows practically nothing. And if the New Deal means anything to me it means an informed public. With that, I'll take any kind of chances.[49]

Proofs also went from Corcoran to Congressman Jerry Voorhees, of California, for serialization in a Los Angeles newspaper.[50]

The book that Corcoran was so avidly publicizing to help the New Deal was one that Coyle had written to educate the American people for the higher taxes that he advocated. In *Why Pay Taxes?* Coyle wrote:

> As modern life becomes more and more complicated, the need for planned adjustment grows more pressing. But the task of arranging all the multitudinous details into a rational system seems each year farther beyond the capacity of the human mind. Realistic people are coming to the belief that a well designed use of economic forces, such as taxation, is the way of escape from the over-complexity of economic problems. By such means it may be possible to reduce the area of detailed planning and detailed regulation to somewhere within the bounds of human capacity.

The federal budget, Coyle wrote, was what economists called an "open-market operation." He explained:

> That is, the Government buys more or less goods and services from the people, which has an effect on business, whether the effect is planned or accidental. We can get better results by recognizing this fact, and planning this operation to give us the effects we want. In some ways this great open

market operation acts like a movable weight inside a ship. If the weight is moved by an automatic gyroscope device, so as to climb up to starboard when the vessels rolls to port and vice versa, it will reduce the rolling of the vessel....So with the budget. Whatever we do or don't do, the budget is going to have an influence, good or bad. We had better manage it so as to have a good influence....[W]e may make up our minds to work for a heavy surplus in good times and a heavy deficit in hard times. If we do that, on a large enough scale, there is a chance to calm the capitalist system and stop it from hitting the ceiling and the floor and perhaps breaking its venerable bones.

But the economic budget included more than just money. There were also the nation's renewable resources, "such as oil and forest," which "should not be destroyed faster than they are renewed," and "our mineral resources," which "should not be destroyed faster than science finds abundant and acceptable substitutes." There were also America's human resources, who "should be given enough education, public health services and security to be improved in their skill and productive power from generation to generation instead of being allowed to degenerate." Budget balancing that ignored these realities was not real balancing of the budget at all, since "True budget balancing is first to provide for the maintenance of our national wealth and then to tax heavily enough to pay the bill."[51]

Sounding more like Tugwell than Brandeis, Coyle wrote that land ownership encouraged speculation as bad and disastrous as that in the stock market. "And yet," he wrote: "We cannot suddenly do away with the ownership of land, honestly bought out of savings. But the government is always acquiring land in one way or another; it should hold on to it and get more." Coyle did not believe that any large percentage of American real estate would go to public ownership in his generation, but wise tax policies could "take the gambling feature out of land ownership, and make it an investment for productive use rather than a means of speculation."[52]

Coyle then turned his attention to local governments, which "should be consolidated and simplified so as to waste as little of the taxpayers' money as possible." Local governments should be "relieved by State and Federal services of some of the expense for highways, education, and public welfare. Further increases in real estate tax burdens could in this way be prevented or kept at a minimum." Communities should also have "a well organized planning authority to plan the most desirable use of land and there should be effective zoning laws to prevent wrong uses. The tax system should be made to fit the zoning law, penalizing the least desirable uses and relieving the taxpayers who use their land in ways that will be best for the community."[53]

The graduated income tax, he wrote, incorporated two features. The first was to tax middle-class incomes to meet the government's revenue needs "with as little disturbance to business, as possible." The second was to tax

> the mammoth incomes, that swell like a great tidal wave, washing away the little men who stand in their path and threatening the safety of the nation. The taxes on mammoth incomes are not so much for revenue as for police purposes - to control those floods of money, and to direct them into harmless paths.

This, Coyle noted, was different from the original motives of the graduated income tax, which had been primarily "a way of making the taxpayers carry the load in proportion to their ability to pay." Now the purpose was to keep America from being "ruled by unseen powers, responsible to no voters, caring for no interest but the increase of their own power, pushing their control farther and farther into the business of our country." "The top brackets," he wrote, "are not cows to be milked and protected, but wolves to be controlled and reduced in number."[54]

Taxes on consumers, whether direct or indirect, should be eliminated in favor of higher income taxes, Coyle insisted:

> The higher the income tax, the larger will be the middle class incomes. Business is like a farm where more fertilizer gives more yield. Income taxation fertilizes business. For when the poor man is relieved of sales taxes, he has more to spend, and the customer's spending is the business man's income. Moreover, when the Government spends the revenues from income taxation, it increases the business man's income, because it is pumping money from Wall Street to Main Street....Finally, anything that restricts the power of high finance naturally increases the opportunity for ordinary free business men. Altogether, if you have a middle-sized income, you may expect that in the long run higher income taxes will net you a profit.[55]

Coyle advocated a constitutional amendment, if necessary, that would "do away with tax exempt bonds," and also make it possible to tax the incomes of government employees. "The salaries of public officials are not large enough to yield any tremendous tax revenue," he admitted, "but their freedom from income tax is an unnecessary discrimination against the ordinary private citizen."[56] In 1938 President Roosevelt did seek to remove the income tax immunity of government salaries, but Congress did not include it in the tax bill that passed. A decision of the Supreme Court in the case of employees of the Port of New York Authority opened the way, however, and the Public Salary Tax Act of 1939 empowered the Internal Revenue Service to tax both federal and state employees.[57]

Coyle also argued the need for much larger inheritance taxes, because " a $10,000,000 inheritance is just as much a hereditary lordship over other people's lives as a dukedom in an old fashioned monarchy."[58] The revenues from the higher income and "death" taxes should be used to "reduce the taxes that rest on consumers, or to increase needed public services, or to reduce the public debt, according to the particular conditions at any time."[59]

Coyle decried the fact that Americans living in small communities were receiving so few of needed public health and other services. The solution, he wrote, was to combine the governments of neighboring counties so that those services could be afforded. There were, he noted, more than 175,000 governments in the United States competing for the money with which to do their jobs and creating anarchy in taxation. "Local self-government is a fine thing for any country," he wrote, but it would be possible to "get even more self-government out of one local government than you do out of five or six overlapping ones."[60]

In April 1937, Coyle devoted a lengthy article in the *Virginia Quarterly Review* to "The South's Unbalanced Budget." He began by noting the conclusion of a southern newspaper editor that the southern states were losing roughly a billion dollars per year, which it was making up by "selling its property to investors in other parts of the country, by borrowing money and going bankrupt, by destroying land and forest to make products for sale." It was also losing its human resources to the Northern states. The condition of the South could not "be cured by the automatic action of economic forces." It, and similar conditions elsewhere, could only be addressed by an enlightened federal government.

Coyle reversed his usual position on spending and saving where the south was concerned:

I am an advocate of spending as a way to prosperity. For the United States, suffering from too many factories and too few customers, less saving and more spending would make better business and more jobs. But the excessive saving is not taking place in the South. It is in the North that the great masses of capital pile up, with which the resources of the agricultural areas are bought in and controlled. The South is still in the scarcity condition that was universal in earlier days all over the country. Therefore it is proper to preach spending in the North, and in Washington, and to preach thrift in the South.

Coyle concluded:

The economic deficit of the South is one part of the great national maladjustment that comes from a wrong distribution of income. Until that national income in general can be redistributed by government action, no local remedy will cure what ails the South. First of all, then, must come a national policy of income taxation and subsidy that will work powerfully against the unbalancing forces of a commercial system that is controlled by high finance....If we Americans can break the deadening power of high finance in our country, as Americans we shall breach the power that has held the South confined. Then if Southerners have not lost their vitality, they can get up and capture their own land of plenty.[61]

In September 1937, Coyle wrote Morris Cooke that he was pleased to see Roosevelt "taking conservation and power as his lines—they look good for a basis for long time policies, now that the emergency has ceased to service."[62] In October, 1937 *Harper's* published Coyle's article "Balance What Budget?" It made familiar Coyle points in arguing that the nation's budget included not just the bookkeeping entries in Washington, but all the assets of the country - including the health and training of its people, its raw materials, minerals, and other natural resources. The nation's forests and other natural resources Coyle found disappearing at an alarming rate, many times faster than they could be replaced or than substitutes could be found. He admitted that there was as yet "no emergency in the sense that would require immediate public intervention on the grand scale. But," he added:

neither is our position sound. For the wastes go on, the day of diminishing

returns is approaching, and looming in the background is the great unsat-
isfied mass of Americans who will not forever be denied the comforts of
life. Sooner or later the question will stare us in the face: When are we
going to look to our economic budget? When shall we make sure that our
irreplaceable minerals are not to be wantonly dissipated faster than science
can find abundant and acceptable substitutes?"

It would cost money, as would tackling the "economic budget" in
all its other aspects, including adequate public health and education for all Americans, and there was strong resistance to "spending" money that Coyle insisted was an investment. The reports accumulated by the National Resources Committee and other public
agencies showed, Coyle wrote, that Americans were "living by
wasting the patrimony handed down by the Fathers," as they had
been doing for 300 years.[63]

When the economy collapsed late in 1937 creating the "Roosevelt
Depression," Coyle submitted the situation to careful analysis. The
downturn, he concluded, demonstrated the importance now of the
Federal budget for business. While he did not question Roosevelt's
decision to balance the budget, he did argue that it should have
been done by raising income taxes rather than by cutting back on
government expenditures. There were, he decided, three ways by
which money could be put back into circulation and the march
toward recovery resumed. One was to "call off the New Deal and
try normalcy again." This might produce prosperity for a year or
two, but would inevitably lead to another crash. Another was to put
the nation on a wartime footing as the fascist nations were doing in
Europe, as well as those democracies that felt threatened by the
fascist powers. The course Coyle clearly preferred was what he
described as "a peaceful form of patriotism that will make us willing to spend money in improving our own country."[64]

As a proponent of increased consumer spending even in normal
times, Coyle was not impressed with arguments to "stop the spending spree," though he recognized that economy in government was
appealing "to all prudent men and women." However, Coyle reiterated his point that all history taught "that 'economy' is destructive
and 'extravagance' is constructive." The federal budget was like a
pump that caused money to circulate: "When it runs slowly—that
is, when the budget is small—some people are idle, some businesses are without orders. When it runs fast, with a large budget,

more people work, more business is done." According to Coyle's analysis, "Already, by a little economy in Washington we have lost several billion dollars of national income." Expenditures by the federal government were unavoidable, he insisted.

> When will we learn that it is not economy to neglect the great underlying resources of our country—the soil and forest, the strength and skill of our people? Stop the spending spree? Yes, it is high time. We have gone too long spending our resources to comfort our pocketbooks. It is time to stop, but it will cost money. The instinct is right, but we have attached it to the wrong object.[65]

9

Coyle and the Decline of the New Deal

In 1937, Coyle devoted an entire book, *Age Without Fear*, to his misgivings about the social security system. There was a difference, he pointed out, between economic security and social security. The former meant "protection against the hazards that threaten your personal income," whereas the latter could only be achieved when "your economic security is assured in ways that help to make the nation itself more secure." In dealing with the former, Americans must "keep always in mind that we want not only economic security but social security too."

> In our discussion of the old age pension in particular, we cannot be contented with merely trying to get as much as possible for ourselves. The old age pension is too large a matter to be handled safely on the principle of the devil take the hindmost. There are more than ten million people over sixty in the United States, and the number will increase steadily for many years to come. Whatever may be done to give security to ten or fifteen million old people will mean the handling of money on such a scale that it will affect the prosperity of the nation for good or ill. No old age pension, however generous, can free us from fear unless it is planned and established in such a form as to add security to the whole American system of life.[1]

Alas, the existing law did not meet that test for several reasons. The first was the method by which the money was collected:

> Taking it all together the tax on payrolls, like the ordinary sales tax, is a burden on industry and has a depressing effect. Being a tax on labor costs, it offers a small but visible reward for not raising wage rates. Being partly

a tax on consumers, it reduces the market and keeps business from growing as fast as it otherwise might.

So far as the workers are concerned, the tax which they pay themselves comes out of their own pockets; the employer's share comes out of everybody's pocket, including the workers but also including the rest of the population. To offset the depressing effect of taking money away from the workers and from industry is the fact that the annuities paid to old people will be added to the market for goods and services and will help to make new jobs and new wages. The two effects balance in the long run, though it is rather a long run.[2]

Coyle advocated moving the cost of the program to the graduated income tax, since putting the burden on the "upper income levels would bring the whole tax system nearer a just balance" and "would also improve the general distribution of income. The market for industry would be better, and both wages and profits would increase." He explained:

In 1935 the contributory plan was an excellent device for warding off the extremes of Townsendism and for making the voters realize that whatever comes out of the Treasury has to come from the taxpayers sooner or later. As a long run proposition, however, the workers' tax is probably not a strong bulwark against foolish legislation. As a form of income tax, it suffers from the fact that it rests on only a part of the smaller incomes and does not give any exemption from sales and other taxes that are imposed on the lower incomes generally. The employer's contribution has the usual disadvantage of indirect taxation, of falling no one knows where, probably most on the poorest....If you accept the general principle of social engineering, the conclusion appears to be that the contributory system is not quite so perfectly suited to the United States as to the smaller and poorer countries of Europe. But it should be changed slowly and with due regard to the progress of public knowledge.[3]

Coyle's other principal objection to the existing social security system was, as noted previously, the reserve feature and the enormous amount of money that would be accumulated in that reserve. The enormous fund in the reserve would presumably have to be invested somewhere, and the effect would be to "pump money out of Main Street into Wall Street," which was exactly the opposite of what the nation needed:

The fact is that the Government cannot go out and buy up large quantities of bonds of any kind without disorganizing the economic system. If a large new reserve fund is to be created, a new debt has to be created to invest it in.

One way or another the Government will have to go in debt enough to create the new bonds required for the reserve....The present program, if it were carried out, would gradually deflate business and inflate business debt for a long time to come.

Instead, Coyle advocated simply paying "out the contributions for current annuities as fast as they come in, with whatever subsidy from general taxes may be desirable, as it is done in England. In that case no new debts will be built up, and no blanket of fog will conceal the revenue and the spending of each year."[4]

Another omnipresent requirement for the federal government was that it act to stave off another boom that would produce yet another collapse, while simultaneously proceeding with necessary reforms:

The National Administration, having been reelected by a large majority [in 1936], was exposed to serious consequences if it should be found unable to protect the country against another collapse. The first duty of the Government, therefore, was to take such action as would effectively prevent the crash which various economists were predicting for some time between 1938 and 1940.

In addition to this immediate requirement, the Administration had also a popular mandate to continue and improve upon various reforms, such as the control of financial operations in Wall Street, and the gradual reduction of overgrown monopolistic power in business. The general New Deal theory that taxation and spending ought to be managed for the benefit of the people had been openly discussed in the campaign, and had been approved by the voters.

The second term of the New Deal, therefore, started with a general, long run program of reform, together with the emergency problem of preventing a repetition of the Hoover era....

In general, what the country needs is more buying power among the masses and less money in Wall Street. It is true that we need new machinery and more modern factories, but only after the market has grown up to them, not before. The tax on undistributed profits has had a good effect so far, in forcing up wages and dividends, and in keeping some companies from building additions to their plants too soon. But the tax system in general is unbalanced on the wrong side. There are too many taxes on the consumer and on business, and not enough taxes on the investor. That is why business is still not strong enough to give jobs to the unemployed, while the investment markets are full of money....The only way to prevent any boom in the speculative markets and at the same time keep the ordinary business market growing is to take money from investors and pass it to consumers. That brings us back to the redistribution of income, which is one of the jobs which the people have given to the New Deal....If we could find a large and simple program for redistributing income, that was not limited by the number of useful public works projects, nor by the danger of damage to morale and skill, it would fit well into the needs of the emergency. By revising the method of providing old age pensions we can make it a good redistribution system, without hurting its usefulness as a method for protecting the old folks.[6]

This method was better than "redistribution by income taxes and spending," since "we may need more redistribution than we need public spending." There was a limit to how many new roads and post offices the nation needed. The advantage of the old age pensions was that they were not "public spending" at all, but spending by private persons who would derive far more fun from spending it "than watching the Government spend it." The people would typically spend the money on themselves, which meant it would "appear in the stores on Main Street," contributing to business prosperity and new jobs. Thus:

One of the first improvements needed [in the social security system] is that old people turning sixty-five within the next few years should get full-sized annuities. There is no necessity for penalizing them because we have been so slow to start the national security system....The old age annuities should be transferred as far as practicable to the general budget in 1937 or 1938 so as to provide a channel by which additional income-tax money can be distributed to the business markets. This Administration naturally wants to deflate Wall Street, but it does not want to hurt business and industry. On the contrary it hopes for further growth of prosperity and of employment. Deflating Wall Street is fairly simple: a heavy income tax, combined with suitable policies in the Federal Reserve, the Treasury, and the SEC, will do it. But keeping industry on the upgrade at the same time is another matter. For that we need a means of pumping money into Main Street as fast as we pump it out of Wall Street. The old age pensions can be made one of the most powerful of pumps for this purpose. It should be brought into action as soon as possible. The social security plan has more in it than we have yet realized. It is more than a rescue squad to save those who are crushed by the onrushing juggernaut of modern industry. As a part of a well designed body of public policies it may be made into an effective instrument for steering and controlling the juggernaut itself. That is the ideal of social security—that the people shall be made secure and the nation shall be given stability and strength.[7]

Coyle's longest book, *Road to a New America*, was published in 1937, and was an attempt, as he put it in the preface, to "bring together in a single chart my...previous explorations in this field, starting with *The Irrepressible Conflict, Business vs. Finance*, which was published in the spring of 1932." The momentum of the New Deal, he acknowledged, had been lost, and America needed "a new vision of the needs and purposes of our national life." Simply focusing on recovery from the depression was not enough to meet that need. That vision must be built around a strong and active federal government which, far from being a danger to American liberties, was their guarantor so long as the American people kept "a watchful eye on it." The collapse of the economy in 1929 had been the result of wrong, but mostly legal, actions by men in government and business and finance who were unaware that the world had changed. It was sad, Coyle wrote, "that millions of innocent people should suffer as a result, but if they look for vengeance there is no human culprit to be found." It was an accident, and it was now up to the American people to ensure that no such accidents happened again.

Coyle repeated his familiar arguments for conservation of natural resources, pointing out again that the "close connection between mineral resources and national defense provides a broad constitutional foundation for extensive Federal interest in mineral conservation." In a similar plea for federal regulation of forestry, Coyle noted that the governments of Norway, Sweden, "and other well-managed nations" were regulating private lumbering and it would "undoubtedly have to be adopted here." It was the only way, he argued, to avoid depleting the nation's timber resources and it would also involve the federal government in a massive program of planting trees on the estimated "138 million acres of idle land that should be planted to forest."[8] The destruction of forest reserves had left thousands of people destitute, and putting those people to work on reforestation projects that would bring back their jobs was clearly preferable to supporting them on relief payments that would leave them no better off after five years than when they began.[9]

A better distribution of buying power would "raise the standard of living, reduce the birth-rate, and give those children who are born a better chance to grow up into first class citizens." Coyle added:

> The importance of national policies for improving the population would be hard to exaggerate. The dictators have no hesitation in spending great sums of money to promote the birth and training of healthy cannon-fodder.

If our democracy is to hold its own, we cannot afford to neglect the quality of our people.

Indispensable to improving the population was better public health. "The success of modern medical science has been spectacular," Coyle wrote, "and yet millions of Americans are almost completely cut off from its benefits." In New Zealand, which had higher income taxes than the United States, life expectancy was six years longer. Half of American infant deaths could be eliminated "if the best American practice were applied over the whole country." One of the great killers of Americans, syphilis, could be eliminated by the expenditure of but $50 million per year, or 39 cents per American. Yet 2,000 American counties were without a full-time public health officer.[10] A healthy population could more easily pay taxes for public health than a sick one could afford to pay hospital bills. Yet the depression had caused cities to cut their appropriations for health services. Coyle concluded:

> Public health is an investment that has already been tried in so many places that its profits are proved. Only ignorance allows the money that might still be profitably invested in public health to lie idle while people die who might have lived.

Also indispensable was quality education for the greater challenges that faced Americans in the twentieth century than during the nation's farming days. However, quality education was beyond the means of many poor school districts. At least a quarter of America's schoolchildren in 1935-36 were "in places where school funds are seriously inadequate," and more than 800,000 children under 13 years of age were not in schools at all. For the country, the average spent per pupil was $74.30, but in Mississippi it was less than $30, but Mississippi was actually spending a higher percentage of its resources on education than the average for the nation as a whole. Clearly, the federal government must increase its subsidies to public education in order to ensure a quality education for all. Even taxpayers in the cities had a vested interest in the education of rural youth, lest they turn up in the cities with skills inadequate for urban employment.

To accomplish these things required that Americans adjust their views of thrift. Thrift, in a simpler America, had involved saving spare time and putting it to use in improving one's property. The earlier thrift had involved little use of money and no distinction between saving and investment. The contrast with the present was obvious:

> In the direct relation of saving, investing, producing, and consuming, all inside the family, there was a reality and a positive assurance of real values that is of course impossible in a market where savers, investors, producers, and consumers are separated and are forced to guess at one another's wants and future actions.

Saving money and investing it for monetary profit was not the only kind of thrift. Investments in public health, education, conservation of resources, and the other causes Coyle had discussed earlier, were "a sound form of national thrift." "We can," Coyle wrote, "well afford to pay income taxes for conservation, education, public health, scientific research, and all the services that improve our future security and wealth." Such "intangible investments" by the federal government were commonly lumped as spending, when in actuality they were investments in building up the strength of America.[11]

Such a rethinking of government spending was essential if capitalism were to survive, and in Coyle's view democratic society could not exist without a free economy. He warned his readers that there were three possible scenarios for the future. First were the orthodox economists, who hoped for a "natural" recovery through the liquidation of "obsolete investments" and a wave of new saving and investment. Such economists believed that the only obstacle to such a recovery was the government interference with the "normal" process by Presidents Hoover and Roosevelt. Second was the extreme left, which harbored the Marxist theory that "capitalism must necessarily explode." Coyle's own approach was "the common theory of capitalism is not an iron law, but that capitalism is flexible enough to escape and go on, in a new kind of dynamic balance."

Economists, he wrote, offered three approaches. Coyle explained:

> One is to inflate the money system, so as to drive down the rate of interest. This was done under Mr. Hoover and Mr. Roosevelt. It is a temporary medicine, since it does not touch the problem of where to find profitable investments. The second suggestion, offered by Mr. [John Maynard] Keynes, is a policy of "socially controlled investment," which in America works

out to a program of public works and public lending in fields such as railroads and housing. In essence, this is a policy of using government credit to push money into investments that private investors will not enter because of high risk and low return. The government solves the conflict between low interest and high risk by guaranteeing the loans or by investing money on its own account.

Coyle then drew the line between himself and Keynes by describing his own approach.

> The third suggestion goes to the root of the matter. It is "policies to stimulate consumption." If we can change our feeling about consumption so as to consume a larger percentage of the amount produced, we raise the ceiling that limits our possible national income....How can our feelings about consumption be changed?[12]

"The real way to increase consumption," Coyle argued, was "to increase the incomes of consumers and to increase their feeling of security." The poor had the greatest "propensity to consume," and so consumption was increased with every dollar that was "transferred from a rich person to a poor one," especially if they had social insurance to provide them with security. Therefore: "To change our average feelings about consumption...it is necessary to increase our security, and to distribute more money to the people who are naturally mostly in need of articles that are for sale in the stores."[13]

Stability of business required that more be spent on the products of business. One way to do this was by "heavy income taxation and the use of public money for investment in building up the economic strength of the country," such as Coyle had advocated earlier in the book. "Intangible" investments of the kind he had advocated would not compete with business investment, but would rather promote spending on business products. Another was to provide insurance of the social security type which, by reducing the necessity for saving, freed consumer income for spending. Another solution was war:

> If we fail to adopt the less painful ways of dissipating our excess capital, the pressure of necessity is bound to drive us, as it has driven Italy and Germany, and other nations, to military expenditures as a way out....Patriotism in its military form can make the people use up their money, and to give property and employment, though at the cost of limitless waste and possibly of final destruction.

It would be tragic if the American people could only be induced by war to consent to the taxes and other sacrifices that could in peacetime simultaneously produce recovery and a stronger nation. Coyle continued:

> The fact is beginning to be clear that business as a whole has become so delicate and precarious that it must be carried on, like the manufacture of rayon, in an airconditioned atmosphere. Although it may not be necessary for the Government to plan and control each item of industry and business, it is apparently necessary for the Government to put a roof over the economic system and provide a guaranteed climate in which business will not be subject to wind and rain, or heat and cold.
>
> Airconditioning a whole economic environment will be expensive but may be found to be extremely profitable....A liberal platform may be built of policies designed to increase the amount of capitalist or free business in this country. Finance-capitalism is not so well regarded; it may be reduced in importance by restrictions on big business, causing some industries to go back to free competition, and others to drift into Government or public ownership, depending on the type of business and the technical necessity of large size.

Fascist countries, on the other hand, had inclined toward the encouragement of finance capitalism at the expense of free business. "If our democracy is to succeed," Coyle wrote, "its success will be measured by the eating away of finance capitalism and by the gradual growth of small business under Government protection."[14]

Conversely, as freedom shrank, capitalism was "changed into the massive but aged dinosaur of 'finance capitalism,' with hardened arteries and feeble resistance to paralytic strokes." Coyle warned: "Capitalism, in its early competitive form, with all its faults, worked better than this present system, and we had better get back to as much capitalism as possible." Several options were available, including restrictive and regulatory legislation, and taxation that favored small business at the expense of large.[15] Sounding more Brandeisian than in 1932, Coyle wrote: "Big business has some resemblance to a cancer in the body of capitalism. It grows because it has lost its normal self-limitations," and in the end it devoured the normal cells of the body and replaced them with "the regimented, one-purpose cells of the cancer, whose only purpose is meaningless and limitless growth."

Among the powers required by the federal government to provide "air-conditioning" for the economy, was greater control over
the monetary system:

> In our country, as in all civilized nations, it is becoming clear that business
> cannot afford to depend on a haphazard money system. If the banks are
> allowed to create and withdraw money as they please, and if the Govern-
> ment borrows and repays according to its own convenience regardless of
> the consequences, the medium of exchange becomes a mere accidental
> result of unrelated actions. But prices depend on the quantity and the
> circulation of money. Business and employment are vitally affected by the
> general price level. The interests at stake are too important to be left en-
> tirely to chance. That is the reason for the fact that in every civilized nation
> the money and credit system is being seriously studied with a view to
> bringing it more effectively under public control.[16]

There were two reasons for this, Coyle explained: First, "Heavy
fluctuations of prices and markets inevitably wreck our modern
mass production system." Second, "the more desperately we have
needed a money with a stable value in terms of goods, the more
unstable our actual money has come to be," since it had become
divorced from any connection with a standard and had "floated off
into a cloud-world of credit instruments founded on beliefs and
legal fictions where its behavior is more and more irrational and
undependable."

The federal government must also have a consistent policy where
business profits were concerned:

> The Government should forget any lingering moral objections to profits,
> and take a general position favoring profits in all legitimate industry, sub-
> ject to necessary rules of fair trade practices.
>   As a result of this policy, the Government should try to avoid taxes that
> prevent profits, such as payroll taxes, sales taxes, and complicated taxes that
> add wastefully to the cost of bookkeeping.
>   The Government should offer tax reductions to corporations for certain
> virtues considered to be in the public interest.

Among these virtues would be "small-scale initiative," which could
be encouraged by exempting small businesses from as many taxes
as possible that were required of large business, taxing profits going to wealthy stockholders more than those going to less wealthy
ones, making impossible the reinvestment of the profits of large

corporations without the consent of their stockholders through such devices as the undistributed profits tax, and the elimination of the holding of stock by corporations in other corporations by a special tax on dividends paid by one corporation to another. Taxation for revenue by the federal government ought to rest on personal incomes, not on corporate profits, and taxes on corporations ought not to be for revenue but as a device for regulating business. Coyle explained:

> Initiative can be encouraged...only by keeping the tax load as much as possible from interfering with the making of profits; nothing can be done by trying to relieve the tax load on high-bracket incomes. The march of events is the other way. Small savings are more than enough to supply all the venture capital that business can ever use. The big capitalist is no longer needed, and the big corporation as a direct saver of profits for investment is on the way out.[17]

"The wholesome growth of capitalism," Coyle wrote, "depends on favoring small investors."[18]

That "wholesome growth" also depended on improving the geographic balance of the American economy. Historically the agricultural areas had grown poorer as the industrial sections of the country had grown richer. Such areas had become debtors to the richer areas, and there was a stream of population from the impoverished rural areas to the towns and cities. The "drift of money and ownership toward the metropolis" could not be eliminated by any "automatic economic adjustment," but could only be done by government in seeking to create a balance between poor areas and rich ones, in the same way that it could curb the saving power of the rich and increase the consuming power of the poor. One method would be by government subsidies to improve "education, public health, or any other definite national purpose that can win public support" —a process of "equalization." Coyle explained:

> If equalization is to be effective, it has to be done mainly by the Federal Government. Most of the rural States do not contain the cities to which their farm boys and girls migrate. Equalization is a national problem because the economic system is national, and the movements of population usually cross State lines.
>
> If the cities are taxed to help the farm areas, there will be more money in the farm areas and therefore more jobs. Not so many farm boys and girls

will have to move to town. Equalization is therefore self-limiting. The more we do of it the less will need to be done.[19]

Various channels for distribution of income existed, with orthodox economic thinking considering the logical channel to be distribution by business as part of the costs or profits in doing business. Another method was to raise wages by laws, but Coyle found such an approach to be largely counterproductive except to avoid genuine "sweating." Far preferable was a form of distribution that would nourish markets, cause higher employment, and force wages to rise naturally through supply and demand. Another way of improving the distribution of income was through lowering of prices, but some industries had "inelastic" prices and could not do so. The method of distributing purchasing power that Coyle clearly preferred was through taxation. It was preferable, for one reason, because it was "outside the business system, and can therefore be designed to balance whatever unbalances may appear in business," and as "the only independent factor subject to public control it must be regarded as the key to the problem."[20]

The federal budget could be made into an extremely useful instrument for this purpose, Coyle observed. It could be used to pump "money through the arteries of business, speeding up the pump when business circulation is sluggish and slacking off if business shows signs of overstimulation." It could also be used to "pump money out of parts of the economic system that are oversupplied, and into those parts where money is scarce." Coyle explained:

The budget can be arranged, by emphasis on certain items rather than others, so as to distribute income more widely. It may distribute to poor people more than to rich people. It may also distribute to poor states and regions more than to rich ones....if the suction end of the pump is in New York, and the discharge end is in Mississippi, the net effect will be to irrigate Mississippi....

Whether a distribution by the public pump is good or bad depends on the effect. In general, it is common experience that money runs from the poor to the rich, and from Mississippi to New York, like rivers running to the sea....There is no machinery in private business that will automatically send the money in a complete circle....In order to keep up a permanent circulation, the money has to flow round and round with no back pressure. If the balance of trade is in fact unbalanced, no power but the Government can keep the circulation going forever. The Government is therefore responsible, whether it admits the responsibility or not.

There were two ways in which the budget could be used in order to raise the national income: (1) to increase spending, without a corresponding increase in taxes, thereby creating a deficit; this raised income by putting new money into circulation; (2) to increase spending but to balance the budget through increased taxes; this would add no new money to the system, but might be used to pump money "from a slow-moving part of the system to a fast-moving part," and thus raising income by causing money to turn over faster. Looking at recent history, Coyle concluded:

> In 1932, money had been badly deflated; deficit spending was needed to create more money. In 1936, enough money had been created, taxes should have been raised to balance the budget. In a boom, when there is too much money floating about and getting into speculation, the taxes should be high so as to create a surplus and reduce the blood pressure in business. It all depends on the situation. In any case, however, the Federal budget is having its effect, good or bad, planned or accidental, and therefore the Government is responsible for what happens.[21]

Coyle likewise presented his familiar observations on public works and social security. Again he quarreled with both the insistence on "useful" public works, arguing that all public works were more useful than allowing the work of idle men to be wasted, and with the reserve fund established under the social security law. Far better, he continued to argue, that social security be placed on a pay-as-you-go basis from taxes than that it include the cumbersome taxes on employer and employee. The employer's contribution ended up being passed on to the consumer, and also required a "vast amount of record-keeping." "The other principal disadvantage," Coyle wrote of the present system, is that it did "not noticeably change the distribution of income among the population, since the taxes are paid chiefly from the smaller incomes."[22]

Taxation, Coyle wrote, is a "Tool of Democracy," and:

> In a time when democracy is endangered by the competition of tightly organized, fast-moving dictatorships, the democratic countries are obliged to use all the powers that are properly available. The practical meaning of "proper" in a democracy is that a power is proper if it will bring about the required improvement without destroying more freedom than the improvement is worth. When our country must be defended against war or disease, flood or depression, we use many different weapons—laws, organizations, education, tax policies—all of them considered proper in their place. The

special value of taxation is that its power is great compared with its interference with freedom.

Taxation policies should be designed to fulfill three "great purposes:
to keep the economic system in balance, to protect freedom, and to
avoid unnecessary irritation to the taxpayers." The distribution of
the national income was, as Coyle had shown in previous chapters,
seriously out of balance. That imbalance could be corrected through
a system of "national planning," but "taxation and distribution of
money through public works and 'social security" will probably
give better results, with much less loss of freedom."[23] It could be
used not only to redistribute income between classes, but between
geographic regions, and could also be used to promote desired
changes in business and finance.

The unwillingness to face squarely the need for higher income
taxes had led to the proliferation, instead, of a variety of "nuisance"
taxes including sales taxes. The result was "dull business, low incomes and complicated bookkeeping." Federal income taxes were
more closely related to ability to pay than any other taxes, thus
weighing on business less than any others since the larger the income the less that was spent on goods and services. Coyle argued:
"The test of a nation's ability to govern itself by democratic methods is the willingness of the people to pay the price of success."[24]

Tax laws should be simplified. "Complicated tax laws," Coyle
wrote, "are the punishment we suffer for two common sins. The
first is that we carelessly allowed our corporations to set up complex networks intended to avoid taxes," and instead of changing
the laws the government had added new complexities to try to plug
the loopholes. The second was "our simple unwillingness to pay
taxes." Coyle explained:

> If we would set our teeth and boldly throw most of the expenses of govern-
> ment on the personal income tax, the Committee on Ways and Means
> would not have to dig up a hundred little nuisance taxes to piece out the
> revenue.

Government could be simplified, too, by eliminating nearly half of
the 175,000 governments in America, with the elimination of their
taxes.[25]

When Coyle's book, *Roads to a New America*, was published *Time* magazine submitted both author and book to close scrutiny. Describing Coyle as "a widely read economist in the U.S.," the magazine recalled that he had attended the Wirt dinner, after which, through "a series of 25 cents and 50 cents pamphlets (Brass Tacks, Uncommon Sense, Waste), of which he has sold over 1,000,000 copies, he proved himself a persuasive, new fangled economist, but no Red." It noted that Coyle was now with the National Resources Board, and that "Franklin Roosevelt has often espoused Coyle theories, but met their author only once." After his many pamphlets, the appearance of his "first full-length book, a lucid, easy-reading summary of the Coyle philosophy, was news. Certain cobble-stones in Roads to a New America were carefully placed to jolt those who drive too far to the right; others, to jounce left-siders." Coyle, it wrote, "blithely and optimistically charges down the middle of the road to a new U.S." His book was not anti-business, *Time* pointed out, but rather adopted the doctrine that "the common theory of capitalism is not an iron law, but that capitalism is flexible enough to escape and go on."[26]

As outlined in his book *Waste*, conservation of natural and human resources had long been a concern of Coyle's, but he found little enthusiasm for the cause among public opinion or in Washington. A call to "sacrifice" needed to be sounded, he wrote to Morris Cooke, and only the president seemed capable of rousing such a spirit in the American people. It seemed to Coyle that getting "the temperature up and the sacrifice level is what would make the New Deal permanent."[27] Late in February 1938, Cooke sent Roosevelt extracts from the letters he and Coyle had exchanged on the subject of sacrifice, and a few days later the president wrote his secretary that: "I want to have David Cushman Coyle down to dine with me and spend the evening."[28]

Perhaps inspired by that visit, Coyle looked at the "Roosevelt Depression" that struck late in 1937 in an April 1938 article for *Harper's*: "Everyone agrees that what the country needs, in addition to kind words from the White House, is more investment in capital goods. Is there any reason why the government, while patting the backs of worried business men, should not do a little investing in its own business?" One of the tangible assets possessed by the federal government was its ability to collect revenues, including taxes from its citizens. Land did not pay taxes, but land made fertile and productive by soil conservation or reclamation measures would make possible the payment of taxes that would not be paid if the land was desolate, but this "future Federal revenue" was an investment for which the return could not be easily measured. In collecting revenues, however, there was a sharp differentiation made between those that came in taxes and those that were received in fees and charges. In bookkeeping:

> a toll bridge is different from a free bridge in the fact that tolls are thought to be more certain than general tax revenues. The toll bridge is said to be "self-liquidating" because the people pay for it directly as they use it. Inhe same way, municipal bonds bought by the PWA for the Federal Government are held as self-liquidating investments because they are paid by local consumers or taxpayers without calling on Congress to levy taxes.[29]

All of these ambiguities and contradictions resulted from an inconsistency of standards between business and governmental bookkeeping. Coyle insisted that if business and banking practices were followed in balancing the books of the federal government, the budget would be shown to be balanced, thus ending criticism of the Roosevelt administration for its unbalanced budgets. The point Coyle wished to make was: "With proper bookkeeping it should become evident that the Government can afford to do a good job. True economy calls for appropriations that will do away with some of the present loss and inefficiency." Instead of cutting expenditures to try to "balance" an irrationally constructed budget, the government should be investing in America's future. If the American people could only be made to understand this distinction, they would see that "the Federal finances are in a sound condition and that a bold policy of building up the material and human resources of the nation is not beyond our means."[30]

Coyle wrote:

> When the government makes an investment everyone calls it sending. I am one of those who have called it spending, and who have said that spending was what this country needed. The fact is still there, but the name was wrong. It is time to adopt a more accurate vocabulary. When the Federal Government borrows a billion dollars and buys a billion dollars' worth of valuable assets it is no more unbalancing its budget than is a corporation that borrows a million dollars and uses the money to buy a million dollars

worth of property. The bookkeeping methods of the Treasury should make this fact clear. Then we could begin to see what we are about....

This point should be made clear. An intangible investment such as public health is just as sound an investment as the Bonneville Dam, and maybe a good deal sounder....I am suggesting that by removing from the budget all capital items that a bank would admit as assets in examining a private corporation we can make room for the intangible investment items and can put them on an efficient basis....

Once the people understand this distinction, they can be shown that the Federal finances are in a sound condition and that a bold policy of building up the material and human resources of the nation is not beyond our means. Let us hope that this understanding may come soon, for the lack of it is the chief cause of our present confusion, our widespread fear of the future, and our costly delay in putting men to work.[31]

During the winter of 1937-38 a battle raged inside and outside the New Deal over the appropriate response to the continuing "Roosevelt depression" that had begun in late 1937. On the one side were those who charged that federal spending had not produced a recovery, had in fact only resulted in another smash atop the mountain of federal debt created between 1933 and 1937, and that the only way out of the new crisis was to improve business psychology by balancing the budget and freeing business and finance from the New Deal restrictions imposed during those years. For those unwilling to concede that the New Deal was, itself, the cause of the crash, the stimulus, even if only temporary, of renewed spending seemed the only alternative. It was during April 1938, that the issue was resolved. Coyle was by now clearly a member of that small number of lawyers and economists that Corcoran referred to as "the well-integrated group," and according to former brain truster Raymond Moley, it was Coyle who was "the most vociferous evangel" of resuming spending in 1938, using the arguments presented above, that spending was, in fact, an investment in the nation's future. Moley wrote:

Corcoran's susceptibility to this strange and jumbled doctrine seemed to trace back to Brandeis' beliefs, expressed to me in detail in 1933, that private capital investment was virtually at an end because business could no longer find enough attractive opportunities for investment and that government must fill the void this created.

Roosevelt, in Moley's view, embraced the Coyle credo because it furnished him with an excuse to spend.[32] Leading the forces on the other side was Secretary of the Treasury Henry Morgenthau, Jr., who made the mistake of leaving Washington for a one week vacation. During his absence the spending advocates descended on Roosevelt and had, in Morgenthau's words, "stampeded him" into taking their position.[33]

William Castle, who had served as undersecretary of state in the Hoover administration, confided to his diary during this period that Roosevelt "is a blind follower of anyone who happens to be the favorite of the moment and as an adviser David Cushman Coyle seems to be the man of the hour." He continued:

> It frightens me more to think that Roosevelt has got into the hands of this man than in the hands of his young Jews because Coyle has been proved a false adviser long ago and the young Jews are at least experimenters.

Concerned that Roosevelt was imminently going to propose some of Coyle's "crazy ideas," Castle and others had written a short speech for Republican congressman John Taber to deliver on the floor of the House "saying that it was about time for a new white rabbit and that the story had gone around that Coyle's ideas were being listened to, that this at least would prove to be a crazy rabbit from the start."[34]

In July 1938, Coyle entered the den of the enemy, the anti-New Deal *American Mercury*, to publish a short rejoinder, "Why I believe in the New Deal." Coyle began:

> Perhaps the best general definition of a New Dealer can be drawn from the report of President Hoover's Committee on Social Trends: the committee stated that technological changes have created a new set of conditions, and that laws and business practices have lagged behind, causing dangerous strains in the nation. A New Dealer is one who favors changes of law and business methods sufficiently rapid to reduce these strains.

The "automatic self-adjustment mechanism" of business recovery, he argued, had "rusted solid and will never work again. It must look to Government, whether Hoover or Roosevelt is in the White House."

The New Deal, he noted, had "attacked the phony investment racket by means of the SEC," had moved to "improve financial soundness" through the Home Owners Loan Corporation, the banking law, "and the seizure of gold and guarantee of bank deposits." Faced with the reality of the dust storms in the Middle West, which had "suddenly called public attention to conservation," the New Deal had "started several programs for preserving natural and human resources—the PWA, the TVA, the Resettlement Administration, WPA, Federal Housing, CCC, and Social Security." Returning to his attack on "parochial" thinking concerning federal budget balancing, Coyle wrote:

> This country has a large job of maintenance to do, in soil conservation, forestry, education, public health, and several other fields. It should have a bookkeeping system that is in the customary business form, so that business men can look at the figures and not be frightened at the cost....That solution is now embodied in the New Deal spending program, but not as yet in clear outline. Correct bookkeeping, that will convince the taxpayers of the value of paying the bill, is still needed. The delay in general understanding of the budget was the basic cause of slow progress in restoring prosperity, and also of the collapse of 1937.

Coyle then took notice of business concerns over the New Deal, writing: No doubt the first thing that should be done is to dispel

> the paralyzing fear of Government persecution that has settled over the business world. New investment would set us back on the road to recovery. But the hard fact remains in the background that the profitable openings for new private investment will soon be filled, as they were after the recovery from the similar collapse of 1921. From then on, where do we go? We dare not have normalcy again, with every financial racket wide open, leading up to another 1929. Government spending and investment are the only alternative.

Coyle concluded:

> "Through the crude experiments of the New Deal, this country is slowly working its way toward a system of conservation, security, and stability that will avoid the disastrous errors of the 1920's."[35] But Coyle was worried that the New Deal had come to a dead stop by early 1939.[36]

Coyle aired his defense of spending in an April 1939 article for *Forum*, in which he argued that the earlier spending had, in fact, produced a substantial level of recovery, and that it was only its untimely curtailment in 1937 that had led to the new crash:

From 1929 to 1933 the federal government tried hard to economize. Business sank lower and lower; federal revenues withered away; and the budget showed no signs of a balance.From 1934 to 1937, the federal government spent considerable sums for relief and public employment....In spite of a common belief that we could not spend our way into prosperity, business improved; the federal revenue rose; and the budget began to approach a balance.In 1937, under pressure from friends and opponents, the Administration, instead of balancing the budget by heavier income taxes, began to taper off its expenditures....But business had been betting on further public spending; when the policy was changed it promptly went into a tail spin.

Whatever may be the interpretation of these events, they stand as historic facts—two attempts at "economy," with deepening depression; one period of spending, with rising prosperity, Whatever the cause may have been, spending succeeded, and "economy" failed.

Coyle's advocacy of renewed spending was now linked to his heightened concerns about the environment, natural resources, and other such issues that he had begun to articulate in his other writings and in his letters, out of a conviction that taxpayers needed a new motivation that could be linked to the growing concern with national defense.[37]

But Morgenthau was ready for the Brandeisian spenders in 1939. He had already scored a major victory in getting Congress to pass, over Roosevelt's opposition, a tax bill that removed or lessened many of the taxes so dear to Coyle and the other Brandeisians, since Morgenthau regarded them as deterrents to recovery. Now he formulated his own "spending" program, one that would not unbalance the budget and would rely heavily on the financing of the very kinds of self-liquidating projects that were anathema to Coyle. When the plan was presented to Roosevelt, the president liked it "enormously," except that he went beyond Morgenthau is suggesting that it be 100 percent self-liquidating.[38] Morgenthau's spending/lending bill and the tax revision, marked the culmination of Morgenthau's revolt against the anti-business tenets of the New Deal, and the defeat of Coyle and the Brandeisians by July 1939.

In October of 1939, Coyle addressed the problems posed for conservation and reform by the threat of war, sending an outline of his thoughts to Lowell Mellett:

In order to develop the constructive work started by the New Deal, it is necessary to change its reason. If it is to be carried further, the work must be done because the country needs it, not because the unemployed worker is hungry. This country needs to be built up, let the jobs fall where they may.

The taxpayers have run out of pity for healthy but unlucky workers, but in 300 years they have not run out of interest in improving their country. They will pay taxes for measurable improvements as such, which they would refuse to pay for work-relief even though it produced much the same improvements. Note the relative popularity of PWA as against WPA.

The constructive development of the New Deal, therefore, is to be sought in a change of attitude from relief to upbuilding, which will in turn make possible a bold facing of the necessity for heavy direct taxation.[39]

When Coyle published an article, "Social Control of Production," the following month, the New Deal was dead in the water, and there is a note of nostalgia in its pages. While it repeated much of what Coyle had written in earlier articles and books, it was in part retrospective, and in a part a look to the future. Of the past, Coyle wrote:

The pressure toward centralized production grows with the duration of economic paralysis. The pressure comes from both radicals and reactionaries. In 1933 conditions in America favored centralized control. The leftist side of the New Deal was fascinated by Russian national planning, and was therefore ill prepared to resist the advances of Big Business. From the union of these two influences came many features of the N.R.A.

Of the future, he wrote:

American industry, having become adapted to constant subsidy, must have subsidy in some form for a long time to come, but the form need not be either a care-free liquidation of assets or a series of normalcy periods and depressions for taking in and stripping an investor class....The death of capitalism is therefore not inevitable in theory, although the means of establishing capitalism on a viable basis may be difficult in practice. All it needs to provide adequate markets free of paralytic spasms is an adequate tax system and public spending policy to supply constructive subsidy of business. The obstacles to this solution are entirely inside the people's heads, and if time were given, the pressure of events would undoubtedly push these obstacles away.

The chief danger appears to be that the economic solution may be too long blocked by the persistent economy superstition, and that the demand for centralized production control may overcome all resistance in the meantime.

The result, in that case, would be a fascist system, with strict controls over "prices, wages, quality, and quantity of production."

As for democracy, Coyle wrote:

The future prospects of democracy may be defined as dependent on the balance between monopoly or big business, and free capitalism, or competitive business. If the area of admitted monopoly, necessarily socialistic, can be restricted so that the political weight of the capitalistic system is the greater of the two, then this will be a free country. But if the political weight of the monopolistic side overbalances the few remaining tearooms and blacksmith shops, this will be a fascist country, with a fast-vanishing vestigial remnant of free enterprise.

Coyle did not sound very optimistic.[40]

Conclusion

Stuart Chase wandered all over the ideological map during the Great Depression, from technocracy to collectivism, and finally back to something approaching orthodoxy by the end of the 1930s. But even during his collectivist period during the early New Deal years, he was disdainful of the Marxist orientation of many of his fellow collectivists. In Chase's view, Marxism was as obsolete as laissez faire in the machine age. Both had been responses to conditions during the age of production, but the emphasis was no longer on production, it was on consumption. In the age of consumption, the emphasis must shift from increasing the production of goods, to finding buyers for those the economy was already capable of producing.

Thus, Chase grappled with the problem of devising a uniquely American form of collectivism that would focus on gearing output to consumption, what historian Charles Beard called "The Open Door at Home." This would require not only limiting production, but also increasing consumer purchasing power. Under Chase's plan, large industries would be government managed, but not government owned. Management had already been divorced from ownership in large corporations, as Berle and Means had pointed out, so it was no great step to replace private control with public managers who would act in the public interest rather than solely in pursuit of profit. Stockholders would still receive a reasonable return on their investment, and free enterprise would continue to prevail in all but these key industries.

Alas, Chase's proposals did not go far enough to attract the support of many collectivists, who were devoted to purging profits of any kind from American society, while they went too far for the moderates. Thus, Chase ultimately exerted less observable influence on the New Deal than either Coyle or the Committee for the Nation.

The problem with trying to assess David Cushman Coyle's influence is the difficulty involved in separating his influence from that of Brandeisian ideas in general. Coyle's primary value for Roosevelt and the Brandeisian New Dealers lay in his ability to present to the public cogent justifications for a variety of seemingly unrelated actions, even of giving to seemingly punitive policies an economic rationale that went beyond simply a "soak the rich" motivation. This made him of value to Corcoran in the 1936 reelection campaign and after.

For Coyle, the sin of saving and investment must be replaced by the virtue of spending. Thus, high taxes on the wealthy were not simply to redistribute income from the wealthy to the poorer classes, but to move money away from the investments that Coyle regarded as disastrous and into the consumption that he considered indispensable for recovery and a permanent economy of plenty. Social security legislation was similarly not alone to care for the elderly, but to make it possible for all to spend rather than to save for their old age, since the federal government would provide for their retirement years.

Federal control of the monetary system and of investments was not, as in Brandeis' philosophy, simply a war of the federal government against Big Finance, rather it had become a war of business against Big Finance, with the federal government on the side of business. The breaking of the control of the public utility holding companies could be seen as an attack not on the public utilities, themselves, but on their Wall Street manipulators. The Coyle philosophy, like so many others of these years, assumed that productive capacity was already well ahead of capacity to consume, and that the emphasis of governmental policy should be on redistributing income in such a way as to increase consumption and to distribute it more equally.

Aside from his conviction that the collectivist approach was too oppressive to be acceptable in America, the principal difference between Coyle and the collectivists lay in their view of the future of the American economy. The collectivists remained steadfast in their acceptance of America as an industrial society that could be planned and regimented. Coyle was ahead of his time in recognizing that the trend of the economy was in the direction of a growing reliance on services, which required more scope for freedom and innovation, and which were less susceptible to the heavy hand of centralized planning, as the NRA had demonstrated. While acknowledging that some of the larger units in the economy that were not appropriate for decentralization might require government ownership and control, Coyle never envisioned that this share of the economy would be very significant.

Yet Coyle contemplated an active role for the federal government in all of the economy. There is no gainsaying that Coyle was a planner, although of a far different breed from the Tugwells and other collectivists. Coyle described his as a kind of "hormonal" planning, which rather than overseeing every detail of the economy, as the collectivists would be forced to do, would exert its effects in more subtle ways, particularly through the use of the taxing power which was so dear to Brandeis. By appropriate tax legislation businesses and consumers could be encouraged to act in precisely the ways the "planners" sought, without the need for government dictation and control. Like hormones in the blood, these indirect influences would subtly shape the economy according to the desiderata of the time.

The direct influence of the Committee for the Nation is easier to trace, but was of short duration. Its recommendations were specific, and were followed by the Roosevelt administration. For the most part, they yielded the results the Committee promised. It was the misfortune of the Committee that Roosevelt was simultaneously pursuing other programs that affected the economy, some of them in negative ways, while others obscured the contributions from devaluation. When for these and other reasons the gold-buying episode of late 1933 failed instantly to provide the results promised by the Committee, its image suffered and they were never able again to exert the influence of 1933.

Still, the Committee for the Nation did influence New Deal policy during 1933, and its public relations efforts educated not only the public, but business and agricultural leaders, as well, to the benefits that might be achieved from a more innovative monetary policy than the traditional reliance on a rigid gold standard. And in their defensive phase, they served a useful role in opposing the original version of the Eccles banking act and other legislation.

In short, no story of Roosevelt and the New Deal is complete without greater attention being given to Coyle, Chase, and the Com-

mittee for the Nation than has thus far been the case. It is easy to
dismiss them as simply examples of a plethora of "crank" economists who surfaced during the New Deal years, but certainly their
ideas were no more outrageous than those of Louis Brandeis, who
has received the respectful attention of historians, and whose influence on the New Deal has been acknowledged by scholars. Clearly,
Coyle reinforced that influence, and added new dimensions to it,
but his importance goes far beyond Brandeis, or any of his disciples, in the influence he exerted on the public in preparing them
for New Deal policies and in providing them with a rationale through
his voluminous writings in popular magazines, pamphlets and books.
Scholastic magazine observed in late 1936 that Coyle was "credited with influencing more Americans than any other writer on phases
of the New Deal." *Time* magazine wrote of Stuart Chase in 1936:

> Among U.S. economists, Stuart Chase has a reputation for being the best
> story-teller of the lot. Master of the art of leading audiences up the moun-
> tain, he has held out bold and attractive visions of happy economic futures,
> plausible-sounding and easily-attained, in most of the sprightly, bright,
> informal, argumentative volumes he has written in the past eleven years.

He approached, *Time* added, "human problems as an economist,
economic problems as an evangelist, political problems as an engineer, and philosophic problems as an irascible citizen who wants to
know why something is not done." Edmund Wilson called him "the
vividest writer of the liberal camp," with "an unusual knack of
making statistics take shape as things and people." (*New Republic*,
February 10, 1932, p. 345). He was certainly one of the best known
and most widely read "economists" of the 1930s.

Clearly, Chase, Coyle, and the Committee for the Nation cannot
be overlooked in any definitive study of the Roosevelt years.

Notes

Introduction

1. Corcoran mss autobiograpy, ch. 4, p. 1, Corcoran Papers, Library of Congress.
2. Louis Stark, quoted in Leo C. Rosten, *The Washington Correspondents* (New York, 1974), pp. 166-7)

Chapter 1

1. *Farm Journal*, November 1931, pp. 7-8.
2. "The Case for Inflation," *Harper's*, July 1932.
3. Rumely to FDR, November 28, 1932, Rumely Papers, Lilly Library, Indiana U.
4. Ibid., December 19, 1932.
5. Rumely to Vincent Bendix, November 30, 1932, ibid.
6. Rumely to FDR, December 3, 1932, ibid.
7. Tugwell to Rumely, December 6, 1932, ibid.
8. Rumely to Tugwell, December 22, 1932, ibid.
9. Rumely to Coyle, December 9, 1932, ibid.
10. Rumely to Bendix, December 13, 1932, ibid.
11. Ibid., December 20, 1932.
12. Rumely to Buettner, December 20, 1932.
13. Rumely to Coyle, December 21, 1932, ibid.
14. Coyle to Rumely, December 23, 1932, ibid.
15. *New York Times*, December 4, 1932; Rumely to Thomas, December 16, 1932, ibid.
16. Thomas to Rumely, December 22, 1932. ibid.
17. Rumely to Warren, December 16, 1932, ibid.
18. Warren to Rumely, December 18, 1932, ibid.
19. Rumely to Warren, December 22, 1932, ibid.
20. Robert E. Wood to Borah, January 17, 1933, Wood Papers, Hoover Presidential Library.
21. Rumely to Bendix, December 19, 1932, Rumely Papers.

22. Ibid., January 9, 1933.
23. Ibid.
24. Rumely to Tugwell, January 9, 1933, ibid.
25. Rumely to Warren, January 10, 1933, ibid.
26. Rand to Virgil Jordan, January 13, 1933, Rumely Papers.
27. Jordan to Rand, January 16, 1933, ibid.
28. For example, Rumely to Alexander Legge, January 30, 1933, ibid.
29. Rand to Borg, January 30, 1933, ibid.
30. Rumely to "Mary," January 23, 1933, ibid.
31. Rumely to Bendix, February 5, 1933, ibid.
32. Bendix to Rand, undated, ibid.
33. Rumely to Eleanor Roosevelt, January 9, 1933; Eleanor Roosevelt to Rumely,
    February 24, 1933, ibid.
34. Fisher, *The Money Illusion* (New York, 1928), pp. 192-3.
35. Fisher, *Booms and Depressions* (New York, 1932), p. 139.
36. Fisher, *Stable Money* (New York, 1934), pp. 296-7.
37. Fisher to FDR, Fisher Collection, Franklin Delano Roosevelt
    Presidential Library.
38. Fisher to Sprague, June 1, 1933, ibid.
39. Wood to Wallace, February 23, 1933, Wood Papers.
40. Form letter in Rumely Papers.
41. Roper to James Rand, March 20, 1933, Rumely Papers.
42. Wood to LaFollette, March 17, 1933, Wood Papers.
43. LaFollette to Wood, April 5, 1933, ibid.
44. Wood to LaFollette, April 7, 1933, ibid.
45. Wood to Weinberg, March 30, 1933, ibid.
46. Wood to LaFollette, April 13, 1933, ibid.
47. Rumely to Vanderlip, March 22, 1933, Rumely Papers.
48. Rand to Rumely, March 30, 1933, ibid.
49. Rumely to Rand, April 9, 1933, ibid.
50. Rumely to Philip Wrigley, April 10, 1933, ibid.
51. Rumely to FDR, April 15, 1933, ibid.
52. In Rumely Papers.
53. For example, Rumely to Herbert Fox, April 30, 1933, ibid.
54. Rumely to Edmund Stinnes, May 1, 1933, ibid.
55. Jordan to Rumely, March 21, 1933, ibid.
56. Cameron to Rumely, April 20, 1933, ibid.
57. Wood to LaFollette, May 18, 1933, Wood Papers.
58. Wood to Wallace, May 17, 1933, ibid.
59. Rumely to "Mary," May 29, 1933, Rumely Papers.
60. Warren and Pearson, *Prices* (New York, 1933), pp. 61-2.
61. Ibid., p. 2.
62. Ibid., p. 3.
63. Ibid., p. 5.
64. Ibid., p. 90.

65. Ibid., p. 124.
66. Ibid., p. 135.
67. Ibid., p. 141.
68. Ibid., pp. 164-5.
69. Ibid.
70. Ibid., pp. 166-8.
71. Ibid., p. 169.
72. Ibid., p. 173.
73. Ibid., p. 299.
74. Ibid., pp. 302-3.
75. Ibid., p. 384.
76. Ibid., p. 372.
77. Ibid., p. 392.
78. Ibid., p. 393.
79. Ibid., p. 394.

Chapter 2

1. Tugwell, Addendum to Diary for the Hundred Days, Roosevelt Library.
2. Committee to FDR, June 13, 1933, Rumely Papers.
3. Committee to FDR, June 15, 1933, ibid.
4. Committee wire to FDR, June 20, 1933, ibid.
5. Release of July 15, 1933, in Wood Papers.
6. Quoted in *My Father Irving Fisher*, pp. 279-81.
7. Ibid., p. 282.
8. "Calendar of Action Taken by Committee for the Nation, 1933" in Rumely Papers.
9. Quoted in Herbert M. Bratter, "The Committee for the Nation: A Case History in Monetary Propaganda," *Journal of Political Economy* 50 (August 1941), 531-2.
10. Tugwell Diary, January 14, 1933, Roosevelt Library.
11. Addenum to Diary for the Hundred Days, ibid.
12. Tugwell Oral History, p. 8.
13. Release of July 24, 1933, in Rumely Papers.
14. Ibid., July 26, 1933.
15. Mailing of August 9, 1933, ibid.
16. Warren, "The New Dollar," *Forum*, August 1933.
17. Form letter to bank depositors, August 21, 1933, Rumely Papers.
18. Quoted in *My Father Irving Fisher*, p. 183.
19. Ibid., pp. 185-6.
20. Delano form letter of April 2, 1929, Delano Papers, Roosevelt Library.
21. Delano to Kent, February 17, 1931, ibid.
22. Fisher to Delano, September 25, 1933, ibid.
23. Rumely to Wood, September 16, 1933, Wood Papers.

256   Peddling Panaceas

24. Rumely to Rand, Rosenwald and Bendix, September 15, 1933, Rumely Papers.
25. Wood to Rumely, September 20, 1933, Wood Papers.
26. Pinchot to Rumely, September 13, 1933, Rumely Papers.
27. Rumely to "Mary," September 14, 1933, ibid.
28. Rand to FDR, September 21, 1933, ibid.
29. Open letter of October 16, 1933, ibid.
30. Rand form letter, undated, in ibid.
31. "Memorandum on Current Monetary Policy," October 16, 1933, ibid.
32. Committee wire to FDR, September 21, 1933, ibid.
33. Fisher to FDR, October 3, 1933, Fisher Collection, Roosevelt Library.
34. Quoted in PP&P, pp,. 48-9.
35. *Newsweek*, November 25, 1933, pp. 17-8.
36. Vanderlip speech of November 9, 1933, copy in George Warren Papers, Cornell University.
37. Rand to Warren, November 14, 1933, ibid.
38. Rand to Committee, October 23, 1933, Rumely Papers.
39. Wood to Rumely, November 10, 1933, Wood Papers.
40. Rumely to Directing Committee, November 18, 1933, Rumely Papers.
41. Rumely to Howe, November 28, 1933, ibid.
42. Rand to Warren, December 11, 1933, Warren Papers.
43. "Wall Street and the Gold Policy," *Nation*, December 1933.
44. Vanderlip, *Tomorrow's Money* (New York, 1932, 1933), pp. 1-5.
45. Ibid., pp. 26-8.
46. Ibid., pp. 47-8.
47. Ibid., pp. 54-5.
48. Ibid., p. 58.
49. Ibid., p. 69.
50. Ibid., pp. 69-70.
51. Ibid., p. 65.
52. Ibid., pp. 97-8.
53. Ibid., p. 133.
54. Ibid., pp. 147-8.
55. Ibid., pp. 148-9.
56. Ibid., pp. 155-6.
57. *Congressional Digest*, January 1934, p. 19.
58. Ibid., p. 25.
59. Quoted in Don Patinkin, "Irving Fisher and His Compensated Dollar Plan," *Federal Reserve Bank of Richmond Economic Quarterly*, Summer 1993, p. 24.
60. Quoted in *My Father Irving Fisher*, p. 282.
61. Bernhard Ostrolenk, "Battle for an Honest Dollar," *Current History*, 2, 1934, pp. 521-8.

Chapter 3

1. Barnes, *Money Changers vs. The New Deal* (New York, 1934), pp. 10-11.
2. Ibid., p. 47.
3. Ibid., p. 51.
4. Ibid., p. 65.
5. Ibid., p. 75.
6. Ibid., p. 77.
7. Ibid., p. 102.
8. Ibid., pp. 103-4.
9. Ibid., p. 140.
10. Ibid., pp. 144-5.
11. Rand letter of January 19, 1934, in Rumely Papers.
12. Rand wire to Fletcher, January 19, 1934, ibid.
13. Baldwin to Rumely, March 1, 1934, ibid.
14. Rand to Warren, March 1, 1934, ibid.
15. PP&P, p. 62.
16. Westbrook Pegler column of July 24, 1943, Pegler Papers, Hoover Presidential Library.
17. George Soule to Rexford Tugwell, January 14, 1932, Tugwell Papers, Franklin D. Roosevelt Presidential Library.
18. David Seideman, *The New Republic* (New York, 1986), p. 112.
19. "Gold Policy Has Worked," in Rumely Papers.
20. Rand to FDR, May 12, 1934, ibid.
21. Committee wire to Wallace, June 15, 1934, ibid.
22. Committee wire to FDR, June 27, 1934, ibid.
23. Rumely to children, July 16, 1934, ibid.
24. Committee wire to FDR, July 26, 1934, ibid.
25. Press release of July 26, 1934, ibid.
26. Pinchot letter of August 8, 1934, ibid.
27. Rand, "Strikes, Business, and Money," *Scientific American*, October 1934, pp. 178-9, 221.
28. Form letters and pamphlets in Warren Papers.
29. *Chicago Tribune*, April 20, 1934.
30. Fisher to FDR, June 4, 1934, Fisher Collection, Roosevelt Library.
31. Release of August 9, 1934, in Rumely Papers.
32. Fisher to FDR, March 18, 1934, Roosevelt Papers, PPF 431, Roosevelt Library.
33. Fisher to FDR, August 30, 1934, Fisher Collection, ibid.
34. Fisher memorandum, September 6, 1934, in ibid.
35. Fisher to FDR, September 6, 1934, ibid.
36. Fisher to FDR, December 18, 1934, ibid.
37. Warren to Oliphant, December 3, 1934, Warren Papers.
38. Wood to Rumely, February 28, 1935, Rumely Papers.
39. Quoted in Bratter, p. 545.

40. Wife to children, April 14, 1935, Rumely papers.
41. Pinchot to Rumely, April 16, 1935, ibid.
42. Vanderlip to Howe, May 3, 1935, FDR Papers, OF230A, Roosevelt Library.
43. Pinchot to Howe, May 7, 1935, ibid.
44. Bratter, p. 552.
45. Rumely to "Scott," July 2, 1935, Rumely Papers.
46. Rumely to Ford, July 20, 1935, ibid.
47. Rumely to Wood, July 26, 1935, ibid.
48. Rumely to Directing Committee, August 14, 1935, ibid.
49. Committee wire to FDR, August 26, 1935, ibid.
50. Rand to FDR, October 25, 1935, ibid.
51. Rumely to Directing Committee, February 17, 1936, ibid.
52. Rumely to Gannett, March 6, 1936, ibid.
53. Rumely to Wood, June 15, 1936, ibid.
54. Committee telegram to Hull, March 7, 1936, ibid.
55. Wood to Rumely, March 12, 1936, Wood Papers.
56. Rumely to Wood, March 27, 1936, Rumely Papers.
57. Release by Committee, May 31, 1936, ibid.
58. Rumely to Edmund Stinnes, August 6, 1936, ibid.
59. Rumely to Gannett, September 10, 1936, ibid.
60. Wood to Rand, October 21, 1936, Wood Papers.
61. Rumely to Gannett, October 1, 1936, Rumely Papers.
62. Ibid., October 12, 1936.
63. Gannett to Wood, November 4, 1936, ibid.
64. Wood to Gannett, November 5, 1936, ibid.
65. Rumely to Gannett, November 4, 1936, ibid.
66. Ibid., November 18, 1936.
67. Ibid., December 2, 1936.
68. Ibid., February6, 1937.
69. Gary Dean Best, *Pride, Prejudice and Politics* (Westport, CT, 1991), p. 151.
70. Press release of August 3, 1937, in Rumely Papers.
71. Rumely to Borah, August 7, 1937, ibid.
72. *New York Times*, October 10, 1937.
73. Fisher to FDR, December 19, 1937, Fisher Collection, Roosevelt Library.
74. Rumely to wife, March 22, 1938, Rumely Papers.
75. Gannett press release, ibid.
76. Rumely to Ben Ross, June 20, 1938, ibid.
77. Rumely to Hancock and Sherman, memorandum, September 26, 1938, ibid.
78. Gannett form telegram, September 27, 1938, ibid.
79. Rumely to E. F. McDonald, November 3, 1938, ibid.

Chapter 4

1. *New Republic*, February 10, 1932.
2. *Time*, September 21, 1936, p. 5.
3. *Saturday Review of Literature*, August 24, 1940, p. 6.
4. From obituaries in "Vertical File; Chase, Stuart, 1888-1985," Franklin D. Roosevelt Presidential Library.
5. Chase, "A Note on Advertising," *New Republic*, July 8, 1925.
6. "The Tragedy of Waste," ibid., August 19, 1925.
7. "Six Cylinder Ethics," *Forum*, January 28, 1922, p. 34.
8. Chase, "Our Lock-step Culture," *Forum*, April 1929, pp. 238-42.
9. Chase, "Good and Evil of the New Industrialism," *Current History*, 7, 1929, pp. 577-84.
10. Chase, *Men and Machines* (New York, 1929), p. 187.
11. Chase, "Laid Off at Forty," *Harper's*, August 1929, pp. 340-7.
12. Chase, *Prosperity: Fact or Myth?* (New York, 1929), pp. 12-7.
13. Ibid., pp. 124-5.
14. Ibid., pp. 173-6.
15. Ibid., p. 188.
16. Chase, "The Nemesis of American Business," *Harper's*, July 1930, pp. 129-38.
17. Chase, "The Enemy of Prosperity," ibid., November 1930, pp. 641-540.
18. Chase, *Out of the Depression and After—A Prophecy* (New York, 1931), pp. 1-27.
19. Ibid.
20. Chase, "Leisure in a Machine Age," *Library Journal*, August 1931, pp. 629-32)
21. *New Republic*, October 14, 1931.
22. Chase, "Declaration of Independence," *Harper's*, December 1931, pp. 29-36.
23. Chase, *A New Deal* (New York, 1932). p.
24. Ibid., p. 36.
25. Ibid., to p. 59.
26. Ibid., pp. 76-7.
27. Ibid., pp. 82-3.
28. Ibid., p. 87.
29. Ibid., p. 100.
30. Ibid., p. 108.
31. Ibid., p. 137.
32. Ibid., p. 149.
33. Ibid., p. 180.
34. Ibid., p. 241.
35. Ibid., p. 252.

Chapter 5

1. Chase to J. Mildred Schwarz (*Fortune* magazine), March 16, 1939, Chase Papers, Library of Congress.
2. Chase, "A Ten Year Plan for America," *Harper's*, June 1931, pp. 1-10.
3. _____, "Harnessing the Wild Horses of Industry," *Atlantic*, June 1931, pp. 776-87.
4. _____, "If I Were Dictator," *Nation*, November 18, 1931, pp. 536-8.
5. _____, "The Preaching and Practice of Mr. Broadback," *Atlantic*, June 1932, pp. 706-14.
6. _____, "The Case for Inflation," *Harper's*, July 1932, pp. 198-209.
7. *New Republic*, February 10, 1932, pp. 345-9.
8. Ibid.
9. Chase, "Government Economy," *Scribner's*, December 1932, pp. 321-6.
10. _____, "World Without Money," ibid., February 1933, pp. 74-7.
11. *New Republic*, January 25, 1933, pp. 299-301.
12. Means to Chase, January 23, 1933, Chase Papers.
13. Chase, "On the Paradox of Plenty," *New Republic*, January 18, 1933, pp. 258-60.
14. This view of the banking crisis is presented more fully in Gary Dean Best, *Pride, Prejudice and Politics*, pp. 21-4.
15. *The Public Papers and Addresses of Franklin Delano Roosevelt*, 1933 (New York, 1938), pp. 11-12.
16. See, for example, Jerome Frank to Chase, January 19, 1932, Jerome Frank Papers, Yale University.
17. Jerome Frank telegram to Chase, July 20, 1933; Chase telegram to Frank, August 23, 1933. Frank Papers; Chase to Tugwell, October 11, 1933, Chase Papers.
18. Tugwell to Chase, October 23, 1933, Chase Papers.
19. Chase to Tugwell, September 13, 1934, Rexford Tugwell Papers, Franklin Delano Roosevelt Presidential Library.
20. Chase, "Eating Without Working," *Nation*, July 26, 1933, pp. 93-4.
21. _____, "Property in the Power Age," *Scribner's*, March 1934, pp. 161-7.
22. _____, *The Economy of Abundance* (New York, 1934), p. 20.
23. Ibid., p. 23.
24. Ibid., pp. 202-3.
25. Ibid., p. 257.
26. Ibid., p. 279.
27. Ibid., p. 303.
28. Chase, "The Age of Plenty," *Harper's*, March 1934, pp. 377-87.
29. Chase to Frank, April 12, 1934, Frank Papers.
30. _____, "If Roosevelt Fails," *Scribner's*, July 1934, pp. 7-12.
31. The *Nation*, May 16, 1934, pp. 567-8.
32. Strachey, "A Book that Scared its Author," ibid., pp. 537-8.
33. Chase, "The Age of Distribution, ibid., July 25, 1934, pp. 93-5.
34. _____, "Our Capacity to Produce," *Harper's*, February 1935, pp. 343-52.

Chapter 6

1. Chase, *Government in Business* (New York, 1935), p. 5-6.
2. Ibid., p. 21.
3. Ibid., p. 23.
4. Ibid., pp. 59-60.
5. Ibid., p. 62.
6. Ibid., pp. 145-6.
7. Ibid., pp. 199-201.
8. Ibid., p. 239.
9. Ibid., p. 243.
10. Ibid., pp. 278-9.
11. Ibid., pp. 285.
12. Berle, "U.S.A., Incorporated," *Saturday Review of Literature*, September 21, 1935, pp. 3, 14.
13. Chase, "Ode to the Liberty League," *Nation*, November 27, 1935, pp. 613-5.
14. Eccles to Chase, December 4, 1935, Chase Papers.
15. Arnold to Chase, January 30, 1936, ibid.
16. Chase, "Saving and Spending," *Survey Graphic*, December 18, 1935, pp. 533-6.
17. _____, "Recovery," *New Republic*, December 18, 1935, pp. 162-6.
18. _____, "Tugwell Explains The New Deal," *Nation*, January 16, 1935, pp. 78-9.
19. _____, *Rich Land, Poor Land* (New York, 1936), p. 245.
20. Ickes to Chase, April 14, 1936, Chase Papers.
21. *Time*, September 21, 1936, pp. 75-6.
22. Chase, "Elegy for the Elite," *Nation*, November 21, 1936, pp. 598-600.
23. Chase to *New York Times*, February 15, 1937, Chase Papers.
24. *Time*, January 24, 1938, p. 61.
25. Chase, "The Case Against Home Ownership," *Survey Graphic*, May 1938, pp. 261-7.
26. _____, *Idle Money, Idle Men* (New York, 1938), p. 211.
27. Ibid.
28. *Saturday Review of Literature*, August 24, 1940, p. 7.
29. Chase to Frank, December 2, 1938, Jerome Frank Papers.
30. Chase, "How to Stop Dictators," *New Republic*, January 25, 1939, pp. 331-3.
31. _____, "If You Were President," *New Republic*, July 15, 1940, pp. 73-6.
32. _____, "Can We Afford the New Deal," ibid., July 29, 1940, pp. 160-2.
33. _____, "Men First, Money Second," ibid., July 22, 1940, pp. 108-11.

Chapter 7

1. "Writing Engineer," *Scholastic*, October 10, 1936, p. 21.
2. "Does the World Owe Me a Living?" *Scribner's*, May 1934, p. 425
3. The best description of the "new economists" of the 1920s, and of the views of Foster and Catchings, is in William J. Barber, *From New Era to New Deal* (Cambridge, 1985), passim.
4. Coyle, "The Gate of the Promised Land," *Forum*, July 1933, p. 22.
5. Frankfurter to Coyle, May 12-32, Frankfurter Papers, Library of Congress.
6. Coyle to Frankfurter, May 16, 1932 and June 3-32, ibid.
7. Frankfurter to Coyle, June 4, 1932, ibid.
8. Coyle to Frankfurter, June 6, 1932, ibid.
9. Coyle, *The Irrepressible Conflict* (New York, 1932), p. 6.
10. Ibid., pp. 6-7.
11. Ibid, p. 15.
12. Ibid., p. 18.
13. Ibid., p. 19.
14. Ibid., pp 29-30.
15. Ibid., p.34.
16. Ibid., pp. 42-3.
17. "Four Wheel Brakes for Speculation," *New Republic*, February 20, 1929, pp. 4-5.
18. *New York Herald Tribune Books*, September 25, 1932; *Commonweal*, March 8, 1933, p. 530.
19. Coyle, "An Uncyclic Crisis and Capitalism for Culture," *American Scholar*, January 1933, pp. 13-23.
20. *Annals of the Academy of Political and Social Science*, January 1933, pp. 3-24.
21. Rumely to Coyle, December 9, 1932 and December 22, 1932, Rumely Papers.
22. Coyle to Rumely, December 23, 1932, ibid.
23. Coyle, *The Irrepressible Conflict*, 4th edition (New York, 1934), pp. 26-42.
24. Ibid.
25. Ibid.
26. Frankfurter to Coyle, May 18-32, Frankfurter Papers, Library of Congress.
27. Coyle to Frankfurter, June 3-32, ibid.
28. Frankfurter to Coyle, June 4-32, ibid.
29. Coyle to Frankfurter, June 6-32, ibid.
30. "Memorandum for the Sec. of the Treasury, September 25-34," FDR Papers, Roosevelt Presidential Library.
31. Samuel Rosenman, ed., *The Public Papers and Addresses of Franklin D. Roosevelt*, II (New York, 1938), 11-12.

32. Background on Coyle may be found in James S. Olson, ed., *Historical Dictionary of the New Deal* (Westport, CT, 1985), p. 109.
33. "Writing Engineer," *Scholastic*, October 10, 1936, p. 21.
34. Coyle, "Road to Prosperity," *Scribner's*, March 1933, p. 155.
35. Ibid., p. 156
36. Ibid., p. 157
37. Ibid., p. 158
38. Coyle, "Necessary Changes in Public Opinion in the New Social Order," *National Conference of Social Work*, 1933. pp. 29-42.
39. *New York Times*, December 17, 1933.
40. Coyle, "Public Works: A New Industry," *Atlantic Monthly*. December 1933, pp. 756-63.
41. Coyle, "Gates of the Promised Land," *Forum*, July 1933, pp. 22-6.
42. Coyle, "Age of Plenty," *Survey Graphic*, December 1933, pp. 629-31.
43. Coyle, "Wealth and the New Deal," *American Scholar*, 3 (January 1934), 122-3.
44. Arthur Schlesinger, Jr., *The Politics of Upheaval* (Boston, 1960) p. 230.
45. Ibid., p. 194.
46. Coyle, "Illusions Regarding Revolution," *Survey*, July 1934, pp. 211-14.
47. Coyle to Brandeis, February 6-1934, Brandeis Papers, University of Louisville
48. Marriner Eccles, *Economic Balance and a Balanced Budget* (New York, 1940, reprinted 1973), pp. 5-8.
49. Coyle, "Recovery, Reform—or Both?" *Scribner's*, July 1934, pp. 13-5.
50. Coyle, "Recovery and Finance," *Virginia Quarterly Review*, 10 (10-34), 481-501.
51. Ibid.
52. Coyle, "The Capital Goods Fallacy," *Harper's*, December 1934, pp. 1-4.
53. Ibid., pp. 4-5.

Chapter 8

1. Coyle, "What About Public Works?" *Harper's*, January 1935, pp. 146-58.
2. Frankfurter to FDR, May 29, 1935 and May 30, 1935, Frankfurter Papers; Memorandum of meeting on May 27, 1935, ibid.
3. Coyle, "Economic Security and Business Stability," *Scribner's*, March 1935, pp. 129-35.
4. Roy G. Blakey and Gladys C. Blakey, *The Federal Income Tax* (London and New York, 1940), p. 388.
5. *Kiplinger Washington Letter*, January 26, 1935; *Business Week*, 3-2, 1935, p. 44.
6. Quoted in Norman Hapgood to Roosevelt, June 16, 1935, Roosevelt Papers, PPF 278.
7. Quoted in Gary Dean Best, *Pride, Prejudice and Politics*, p. 102.

8. Coyle, "The Fallacy of Mass Production," in Herbert Agar and Allen Tate, *Who Owns America?* (Boston, 1936), pp. 3-17.
9. Coyle, "Decentralize Industry," *Virginia Quarterly Review*, XI (July 1935), 321-38.
10. Copy of Hapgood to Brandeis, in FDR PPF 2278, Roosevelt Presidential Library.
11. Coyle, "The Twilight of National Planning," *Harper's*, October 1935, pp.557-67.
12. Coyle, "If I Were President," *National Education Association Journal*, 10, 1935, pp. 206.
13. Monica Niznik, "Thomas G. Corcoran: The Public Service of Franklin Roosevelt's 'Tommy the Cork.'" PhD. dissertation, Notre Dame, 1981, p. 238.
14. Coyle, "Financing of Public Works," *Annals of the American Academy*, 183 (January 1936) 207-11.
15. Coyle, "Map of the New Deal," *Scribner's*, April 1936, pp. 220-4.
16. Corcoran unpublished autobiography, "Credo," p. 14, Corcoran Papers, Library of Congress.
17. Niznik, p. 238
18. *Time*, September 14, 1936, p. 17; *Scholastic*, October 10, 1936, p. 21.
19. *New York Times*, September 13, 1936; *Nation*, August 12, 1936, p. 314.
20. For example, Corcoran to George Sullivan, July 14-36, Corcoran Papers.
21. Coyle, *Waste* (New York, Indianapolis and New York, 1936), pp. 61-78.
22. Ibid., pp. 93-5
23. Corcoran to Walter Cummings, July 14-36, ibid.
24. Coyle to D. L. Chambers, July 27, 1936, Bobbs-Merrill Papers, Lilly Library, Indiana U.)
25. Paul Aiken to Corcoran, August 28, 1936, Corcoran Papers.
26. Coyle to Chambers, September 13, 1936, Bobbs-Merrill Papers.
27. Corcoran to Paul Aiken, September 9, 1936, Corcoran Papers.
28. *New York Post*, August 28, 1936
29. Corcoran to Coyle, August 25, 1936, Corcoran Papers
30. Corcoran to Frankfurter, September 3-1936, ibid.
31. Memo for Miss LeHand, September 4-1936, in ibid.
32. Chambers to Coyle, February 16, 1937, Bobbs-Merrill Papers.
33. Coyle, "An Uncyclic Crisis and Capitalism for Culture." *American Scholar*, January 1933. pp. 13-23.
34. Best, p. 119.
35. Ibid., pp. 120-1.
36. Brandeis to Frankfurter, March 5, 1936, Frankfurter Papers.
37. Coyle, "Tax for Democracy," *Survey Graphic*, August 1937, pp. 8-37.
38. Moley to Bernard Kilgore, September 17-36, Moley Papers, Hoover Institution
39. Coyle, *Brass Tacks* (Washington, DC, 1936), p. vii, 30-32.
40. Ibid., p. 33
41. Ibid., pp. 38-78.

42. Ibid., pp. 129-31.
43. Ibid., p. 134.
44. Coyle, Uncommon Sense (Washington, DC, 1936), pp. 5, 55.
45. Coyle to Corcoran, undated, but summer, 1937, Corcoran Papers.
46. Delano to Mittell, February 15, 1937; Mittell to Corcoran, May 20, 1937, ibid.
47. Crowley to Houghteling, December 6, 1937, and Houghteling to Corcoran, December 7, 1937, Corcoran to Coyle, December 9, 1937, ibid.
48. Corcoran to Walling, December 15, 1937, ibid.
49. Corcoran to Mcgelever, December 17, 1937, ibid.
50. Corcoran to Voorhees, December 17, 1937, ibid.
51. Coyle, *Why Pay Taxes?* (Washington, DC, 1937), pp. 28, 38, 47.
52. Ibid., pp. 55-6.
53. Ibid., p. 60.
54. Ibid., pp. 90-96.
55. Ibid., p. 122.
56. Ibid., p. 138.
57. Blakey and Blakey, pp. 455-7
58. *Why Pay Taxes?,* p. 141.
59. Ibid., p. 147.
60. Ibid., pp. 148-9, 152, 166.
61. Coyle, "The South's Unbalanced Budget," *Virginia Quarterly Review* XIII (April 1937), 192-208.
62. Coyle to Cooke, September 27, 1937, Cooke Papers.
63. Coyle, "Balance What Budget?" *Harper's*, October 1937, pp. 449-59.
64. Coyle memorandum, "To Stop the Spending Spree," marked "11/23/37," in Cooke Papers.
65. Ibid.

Chapter 9

1. Coyle, *Age Without Fear* (Washington, DC, 1937), pp. 12-3.
2. Ibid., p. 28.
3. Ibid., pp. 36, 44.
4. Ibid., pp. 52-4.
5. Ibid., pp. 58-9.
6. Ibid., pp. pp. 94-6, 98-100, 115
7. Ibid., p. 119.
8. Coyle, *Road to a New America* (Boston, 1938), p. 79.
9. Ibid., p. 81.
10. Ibid., p. 100.
11. Ibid., pp. 147-8.
12. Ibid., pp. 168-9.
13. Ibid, pp. 170-71.
14. Ibid., p. 195.

15. Ibid., pp. 208-10.
16. Ibid., p. 234.
17. Ibid., pp. 260-3.
18. Ibid., p. 264.
19. Ibid., pp. 288-90.
20. Ibid., pp. 297-8.
21. Ibid., p. 305.
22. Ibid., pp. 341-2.
23. Ibid., pp. 346-7.
24. Ibid., pp. 350-2.
25. Ibid., p. 364.
26. *Time*, October 24, 1938, pp. 59-60.
27. Coyle to Cooke, March 18, 1939, Cooke Papers, Roosevelt Presidential Library.
28. Memo re Cooke, Morris L., February 28, 1938, and "MEMORANDUM FOR MAC" from FDR, March 7, 1938, both in Franklin D. Roosevelt Papers, PPF 940, Roosevelt Presidential Library.
29. "Is the Budget Unbalanced?" *Harper's* April 1938, pp. 451-2.
30. Ibid., pp. 453-6.
31. Ibid.
32. Raymond Moley, *After 7 Years* (NY, 1939), pp. 374-5.
33. Henry Morgenthau Diary, July 11, 1939, Franklin Delano Roosevelt Presidential Library
34. Castle Diary, April 14, 1938, Hoover Presidential Library.
35. *American Mercury*, July 1938, pp. 328-32.
36. Coyle to Cooke, April 15, 1939, Cooke Papers, Franklin D. Roosevelt Presidential Library.
37. Coyle, "Government Spending: Success or Failure?" *Forum*, April 1939, pp. 218-20.
38. Morgenthau Diary, July 11, 1939.
39. Coyle to Mellett, October 11, 1939, Lowell Mellett Papers, Franklin D. Roosevelt Presidential Library.
40. Coyle, "Social Control of Production," *Annals of the American Academy*, November 1939, pp. 121-5.

Bibliography

Manuscripts

Bobbs-Merrill Papers, Lilly Library, Indiana University.
Louis Brandeis Papers, University of Louisville.
William Castle Diary, Herbert Hoover Presidential Library.
Stuart Chase Collection, Franklin D. Roosevelt Presidential Library.
Stuart Chase Papers, Library of Congress.
Morris Cooke Papers, Franklin D. Roosevelt Presidential Library.
Thomas Corcoran Papers, Library of Congress.
Frederic Delano Papers, Franklin D. Roosevelt Presidential Library.
Irving Fisher Collection, Franklin D. Roosevelt Presidential Library.
Jerome Frank Papers, Yale University.
Felix Frankfurter Papers, Library of Congress.
Lowell Mellett Papers, Lilly Library, Indiana University.
Raymond Moley Papers, Hoover Institution on War, Revolution and Peace.
Henry Morgenthau Diary, Franklin D. Roosevelt Presidential Library.
Westbrook Pegler Papers, Herbert Hoover Presidential Library.
Franklin Delano Roosevelt Papers, Franklin D. Roosevelt Presidential Library.
Edward A. Rumely Papers, Lilly Library, Indiana University.
Rexford Tugwell Papers and Diary, Franklin D. Roosevelt Presidential Library.
George F. Warren Papers, Cornell University.
Robert E. Wood Papers, Herbert Hoover Presidential Library.

Books and Dissertations

Agar, Herbert, and Tate, Allen. *Who Owns America?* Boston. 1936.
Barnes, Harry Elmer. *Money Changers vs. The New Deal.* New York. 1934.
Barber, William J. *From New Era to New Deal.* Cambridge. 1985.
Best, Gary Dean. *Pride, Prejudice and Politics.* Westport, CT. 1991.
Blakey, Roy G. and Gladys C. *The Federal Income Tax.* London and New York. 1940.

Chase, Stuart. *A New Deal*. New York. 1932.

_____. *The Economy of Abundance*. New York. 1934.

_____. *Government in Business*. New York. 1935.

_____. *Idle Money, Idle Men*. New York. 1938.

_____. *Men and Machines*. New York. 1929.

_____. *Out of the Depression and After—A Prophecy*. New York. 1931.

_____. *Prosperity: Fact or Myth?* New York. 1929.

_____. *Rich Land, Poor Land*. New York. 1936.

Coyle, David Cushman. *The Irrepressible Conflict*. New York. 1932.

_____. *Waste*. Indianapolis and New York. 1936.

_____. *Brass Tacks*. Washington. 1936.

_____. *Uncommon Sense*. Washington. 1936.

_____. *Why Pay Taxes?* Washington. 1937.

_____. *Age Without Fear*. Washington. 1937.

_____. *Road To A New America*. Boston. 1938.

Eccles, Marriner. *Economic Balance and a Balanced Budget*. New York. 1940.

Fisher, Irving. *Booms and Depressions* New York. 1932.

_____. *The Money Illusion*. New York. 1928.

_____. *Stable Money*. New York. 1934.

Fisher, Irving N. *My Father Irving Fisher*. New York. 1956.

Moley, Raymond. *After 7 Years*. New York. 1939.

Niznik, Monica. "Thomas G. Corcoran: The Public Service of Franklin Roosevelt's 'Tommy the Cork.'" PhD. dissertation. Notre Dame. 1981.

Olson, James S. editor. *Historical Dictionary of the New Deal*. Westport, CT. 1985.

Rosenman, Samuel. editor. *The Public Papers and Addresses of Franklin D. Roosevelt*, II. New York. 1938.

Schlesinger, Arthur Jr. The Politics of Upheaval. Boston. 1960.

Seideman, David. *The New Republic*. New York. 1986.

Vanderlip, Frank. *Tomorrow's Money*. New York. 1932.

Warren, George, and Pearson, Frank. *Prices*. New York. 1933.

Periodicals

Adolf Berle, "U.S.A., Incorporated," *Saturday Review of Literature*, 9-21-1935.

Herbert M. Bratter, "The Committee for the Nation: A Case History in Monetary Propaganda," *Journal of Political Economy* 50 (August 1941).

Chase, Stuart. "A Note on Advertising." *New Republic*. 7-8-1925.

_____. "A Ten Year Plan for America." *Harper's*. 6-1931.

_____. "The Age of Distribution." *Nation.* 7-25-1934.

_____. "The Age of Plenty." *Harper's.* 3-1934.

_____. "Can We Afford the New Deal." The *New Republic.* 7-29-1940.

_____. "The Case Against Home Ownership." *Survey Graphic.* 5-1938.

_____. "The Case for Inflation." *Harper's.* 7-1932.

_____. "Declaration of Independence." *Harper's.* 12-1931.

_____. "Eating Without Working." *Nation.* 7-26-1933.

_____. "Elegy for the Elite." *Nation.* 11-21-1936.

_____. "Good and Evil of the New Industrialism." *Current History.* 7-1929.

_____. "Government Economy." *Scribner's.* 12-1932.

_____, "Harnessing the Wild Horses of Industry." *Atlantic.* 6-1931.

_____. "How to Stop Dictators." *New Republic.* 1-25-1939.

_____. "If I Were Dictator." *Nation.* 11-18-1931.

_____. "If Roosevelt Fails." *Scribner's.* 7-1934.

_____. "If You Were President." *New Republic.* 7-15-1940.

_____. "Is the Budget Unbalanced?" *Harper's.* 4-1938.

_____. "Laid Off at Forty." *Harper's.* 8-1929.

_____. "Leisure in a Machine Age." *Library Journal.* 8-1931.

_____. "Men First, Money Second." *New Republic.* 7-22-1940.

_____. "Ode to the Liberty League." *Nation.* 11-27-1935.

_____. "On the Paradox of Plenty." *New Republic.* 1-18-1933.

_____. "Our Capacity to Produce." *Harper's.* 2-1935.

_____. "Our Lock-step Culture." *Forum.* 4-1929.

_____. "The Preaching and Practice of Mr. Broadback." *Atlantic.* 6-1932.

_____. "Property in the Power Age." *Scribner's.* 3-1934.

_____. "Recovery." *New Republic.* 12-18-1935.

_____. "Saving and Spending." *Survey Graphic.* 12-18-1935.

_____. "Six Cylinder Ethics." *Forum.* 1-28-1932.

_____. "Social Control of Production." *Annals of the American Academy.* 11-1939.

_____. "The Tragedy of Waste." *New Republic.* 8-19-1925.

_____. "Tugwell Explains The New Deal." *Nation.* 1-16-1935.

_____. "World Without Money." *Scribner's.* 2-1933.

Commonweal. 3-8-1933.

Coyle, David Cushman. "Age of Plenty." *Survey Graphic.* 12-1933.

_____. "An Uncyclic Crisis and Capitalism for Culture." *American Scholar.* January 1933.

_____. "Balance What Budget?" *Harper's.* 10-1937.

_____. "The Capital Goods Fallacy." *Harper's.* 12-1934.

_____. "Decentralize Industry." *Virginia Quarterly Review.* 7-1935.

_____. "Economic Security and Business Stability." *Scribner's.* 3-1935.

_____. "The Fallacy of Mass Production," in Herbert Agar and Allen Tate, *Who Owns America?* Boston. 1936.

_____. "Financing of Public Works." *Annals of the American Academy.* 1-1936.

_____. "The Gate of the Promised Land." *Forum.* 7-1933.

_____. "Government Spending: Success or Failure?" *Forum.* 4-1939.

_____. "If I Were President." *National Education Association Journal.* 10-1935.

_____. "Illusions Regarding Revolution." *Survey.* 7-1934.

_____. "Necessary Changes in Public Opinion in the New Social Order." National Conference of Social Work. 1933.

_____. "Public Works: A New Industry." *Atlantic.* 12-1933.

_____. "Recovery, Reform—or Both?" *Scribner's.* 7-1934.

_____. "Recovery and Finance." *Virginia Quarterly Review.* 10-1934.

_____. "Road to Prosperity." *Scribner's.* 3-1933.

_____. "The South's Unbalanced Budget." *Virginia Quarterly Review.* 4-1937.

_____. "Tax for Democracy." *Survey Graphic.* 8-1937.

_____. "The Twilight of National Planning." *Harper's.* 10-1935.

_____. "Wealth and the New Deal." *American Scholar.* 1-1934.

_____. "What About Public Works?" *Harper's.* 1-1935.

"Does the World Owe Me a Living?" *Scribner's.* 5-1934.

The Farm Journal. 11-1931.

"Four Wheel Brakes for Speculation." *New Republic.* 2-20-1929.

New Republic. 10-14-1931.

New Republic. 2-10-1932.

Ostrolenk, Bernhard. "Battle for an Honest Dollar." *Current History* . 2-1934.

Patinkin, Don. "Irving Fisher and His Compensated Dollar Plan." *Federal Reserve Bank of Richmond Economic Quarterly.* Summer 1993.

Rand, James. "Strikes, Business, and Money. " *Scientific American.* 10-1934.

"Wall Street and the Gold Policy." *Nation.* 12-1933.

Warren, George. "The New Dollar." *Forum.* 8-1933.

"Writing Engineer." *Scholastic.* 10-10-1936.

Index